WOMAN THE GATHERER

WOMAN THE GATHERER

EDITED BY FRANCES DAHLBERG

New Haven and London
Yale University Press

Designed by Nancy Ovedovitz
and set in Baskerville type.
Printed in the United States of America by
Edwards Brothers, Inc., Ann Arbor, Michigan.

Library of Congress Cataloging in Publication Data
Main entry under title:
Woman the gatherer.

Includes index.
1. Women—Addresses, essays, lectures. 2. Society, Primitive—
Addresses, essays, lectures. 3. Hunting and gathering societies—
Addresses, essays, lectures. 4. Social evolution—Addresses, essays, lec-
tures. I. Dahlberg, Frances.
GN479.7.W64   305.4′2   80-25262
ISBN 0-300-02572-6

10   9   8   7   6   5   4   3   2   1

Lightly she steps across
triangles of jungle glass.
Her young follow. She teaches how to hunt
Country Delight sliced sandwich bread,
how to follow the scent of Flash
lowfat milk. Lounging on nearby cliffs
pale-skinned chiefs display
severed heads.
To her right, sirens bay
of disaster. Darker males
with iron bars escape
in waves. Lightly spring
cockroaches over her feet.
Woman the gatherer embraces
toilet tissue, pale green
sunlight on broad leaves,
forages for jello, for juice
and for cellophane tape
to hold up the jungle sky
one more day.

—*Faith Williams*

CONTENTS

PREFACE

The title of this book, *Woman the Gatherer*, focuses attention on women among the hunting and gathering peoples of the world. The book began at Colorado Women's College in 1974 with a proposal for a course on contemporary hunters and gatherers. The first title of "Man the Hunter" was gently rejected by Dr. Sally Geis, then chairman of the department, with a question: "What did the women do while men hunted?" The new title changed the course.

I found that no book covered the portion of the anthropological universe where women and evolution intersect. The closest scientific attempt is *Man the Hunter*, edited by Richard B. Lee and Irven DeVore, which includes papers from the 1966 conference of the same name. Anthropologists from all over the world, representing all the subdisciplines of the field, gathered together to discuss hunting and gathering as a way of life and as an evolutionary stage, on the basis of data then current. Although the conference did not omit women, it occurred before the woman's movement had revitalized the study of women in anthropology. In the book, editors Lee and DeVore remark that "early woman would not have remained idle during the Pleistocene," but the book concentrates on men and hunting.

Since 1966 much has changed in thought about women, in knowledge of hunters and gatherers, and in the study of evolution. An obvious starting point for understanding woman the gatherer is descriptive data about women in contemporary foraging societies. However, a variety of data and theoretical perspectives are needed to do the topic justice. Systematic coding of the behavior of women from a sample of foraging societies reveals the diversity among societies at this level of complexity and the dangers in generalizations from a few particularly well known groups. Explorations of the meaning of women's status growing from the rich new theoretical work in the anthropology of women demonstrate problems of coverage and reliability in the ethnographic literature on topics relating to women and show the impact of theoretical perspectives on data. The evolutionary framework of anthropology requires data on nonhuman primates, especially man's close relative, the chimpanzee, and data from the fossil record and human biology in addition to data on contemporary foragers.

When the new data and new theoretical concepts from these varied research streams are connected, we can demonstrate the relevance of the study of women to other questions in anthropology and the impact of discoveries in other fields of anthropology on the study of women. Conscious concern with women brings attention to data that have been available but not emphasized. For example, baboons, who are used to illustrate male dominance and organized male defense, have enduring subgroups of mothers and adult, subadult, and infant offspring just as do the chimpanzees. Here is a clue to the origin of the family which is not tied to sex, the pair-bond, or aggression. Similarly, new concepts from other subfields of anthropology and from sociobiology lead us to look at women from a new perspective. For example, Glynn L. Isaac's concept of sharing shifts the focus away from food-collecting activities to the group structure and dynamics that determine who gets the food collected (or hunted). This expands woman's contribution, to include besides food gathering her activities in forming groups and keeping them intact.

Contributors to this book use a variety of disciplines, range geographically over the whole world, and cover a historical depth of over three million years. They have done research on living nonhuman primates, on contemporary hunters and gatherers, or on the application of available data and theories to the study of women in evolution. Taken together, the six contributions add woman the mate chooser, woman the mother, woman the aunt, woman the communicator, woman the power, woman the ritual actor, and woman the hunter to woman the gatherer.

Acknowledgments

I wish to thank the Porter Library of Colorado Women's College, the reference librarians and the Human Relations Area Files of the University of Colorado Libraries, the departments of Sociology and of Human Development at the University of Hawaii at Manoa for support during 1977–78, Duane Quiatt, Walter Taylor, Bob Weeks, and Faith Williams for reading various versions of the introduction and providing support and encouragement, Hal Schofield for his typewriter and general support, and Barbara B. Burnham, Ellen Graham, and anonymous readers for suggestions.

F.D.

INTRODUCTION
Frances Dahlberg

Until the 1960s, reconstructions of the life of ancient hominids started with hunting. A "just-so" story featuring hunting, aggression, and sex eventually reached the public; yet even the more sophisticated versions used by professionals shared the androcentric focus of the popular legend. A brief sample story of ancient hunters illustrates the problems this kind of story provides for scholars or members of the public who are interested in women's roles in evolution.

Imagine a group of people walking beside a lake in East Africa two million years ago: five thin, wiry men who carry spears for throwing at game or enemies walk rapidly away from the group. These hunters will search for bushbuck and may be gone for several days while the women and children stay behind. The women move slowly; they are pregnant, carrying toddlers, and besides they are not going anywhere that day. They will stay close to the edge of the lake, cooking the remnants of the meat the men brought several days before, maybe looking for snails or gathering some squalid roots from the rather sparse vegetation. They will wait patiently until their men return with meat. Each woman was chosen by her husband, so the legend continues, on the basis of her loveliness, especially her prominent breasts and buttocks. Her father or brother gave her to her husband on the basis of his hunting skills and fierceness. Other men will not seduce her because they fear her husband's anger.

In this story, the demands of the hunt shaped the characteristics that make us human: Hunters must be intelligent—to remember

1

where they have gone and successfully return with meat to
their waiting wives and children, to find food and water for
themselves on the hunt, to anticipate their prey's actions, to
make weapons, and to plan with other men for a successful
hunt. Hunters must walk upright for long distances, run
quickly if necessary, and carry weapons and meat. Hunters
must be socially adept to cooperate during the hunt and to
distribute their meat wisely when they return home. Of
course, hunters need language to plan and execute the hunt,
to enjoy their tales of successful chases in the past, and to
reassure their dependent wives of their imminent return.

Research on contemporary hunter-gatherers and on living
nonhuman primates, the archaeological and fossil records,
and contemporary evolutionary theory have made this story
obsolete. The anthropologists who assembled in 1966 for the
conference on "Man the Hunter" modified the story (Lee and
DeVore 1968). Their data showed that gathering was an important part of the foraging way of life. They reported that in
the extant foraging societies of the tropics, women, but also
men, gathered food regularly and this food was the main
source of calories for the whole group. Women's important
contributions as mothers, wives, and daughters were also discussed in papers on marriage arrangements, family forms,
child spacing, and infanticide. But human needs for intelligence and complex social and physical skills were still phrased
in terms of the demands of hunting (Laughlin 1968); no participants addressed themselves exclusively to women.

Then came the woman's movement. Sally Linton (1971)
exposed the male bias in *Man the Hunter:* theories of evolution
that concentrated on the origin of hunting and its impact on
the human body, culture, and society excluded women.
Elaine Morgan's (1972) popular account of evolution fea-
tured women but relied heavily on a long (and undoc-
umented) immersion in water to account for most physiological differences from other primates. Some anthropologists
followed Linton's lead in deploring the absence of data and

theories specific to women. Male archaeologists had not collected, described, and cataloged large numbers of the grinding stones that women use (Kraybill 1977). Male anthropologists and women anthropologists who work in a masculine world investigated issues of interest to men in our society and talked primarily to men in the field. They did not do justice to women's activities or to women's symbolic models of the universe, which may differ from those of men (Ardener 1972; Rohrlich-Leavitt et al. 1975). Anthropologists considering relations between the sexes applied concepts of hierarchy appropriate to our own society (Sachs 1976) and failed to understand women's status when it is qualitatively different from that in our society (Leacock 1978:247). The indigenous beliefs of other societies, having already been transformed by the impact of complex, sexually stratified societies, could not be studied in their pristine condition (Leacock and Nash 1977). Stimulated by the changed consciousness about women reflected here, anthropologists in the 1970s began collecting new information, studying new issues, and asking new questions of existing data.

The study of women is not the only field of anthropology that has changed since 1966. An enormous amount of important data on nonhuman primates in the field has been collected and analyzed. Ideas about the importance of dominance, hierarchy, and aggression in primate societies changed as the field studies of chimpanzees, gorillas, and numerous Old World monkeys such as langurs joined Irven DeVore's well-known studies of baboons. Definitions of man shifted from emphasis on single attributes (e.g., "man the toolmaker") to more complex combinations of social, cultural, and physical qualities as anthropologists became more aware of the multiplex nature of the human adaptation. Research continued to enrich our knowledge of the fossil and archaeological records, and the Leakeys' discoveries of the late 1950s were followed by ever more exciting finds from East Africa that pushed the dates for modern characteristics among hominids further into the past. New archaeological

techniques for analyzing sites forced reevaluation of some of
the evidence for hunting and for aggression. Extending
population biology and evolutionary theory to social organization, sociobiologists showed that the pressures of evolution
operate in the selection of distinctive social organizations as
well as in the more familiar selection of "tooth and nail." To
trace the biological bases for social action as well as the biological consequences of social action became especially exciting when applied to animals with complex social structures,
and these efforts to provide an evolutionary explanation for
human behavior spurred popular and professional interest in
evolution. Studies of contemporary hunters and gatherers
continued. The new emphasis in research on ecology and on
scientifically sampled quantitative data on food, energy expenditure, and behavior provided data on humans comparable to that being gathered by ethologists and ecologists
on other animals. Such data could be used to ask and answer
new questions and fitted well with the renewed interest in
evolution.

The recent data and new theoretical concepts alluded to are
used by the authors of this book to reexamine women's roles
in prehistory and among contemporary foragers. Where con-
crete evidence, as from prehistory, is not available, speculation has seemed justified and, we hope, fruitful.

Sociobiology

The first two chapters look again at the roles of women and
men in prehistory by applying sociobiological concepts to recent data from chimpanzee field studies, from the fossil and
archaeological records, and from contemporary hunters and
gatherers. They are frankly speculative. Although the evidence on bones and stone tools is very solid, it is limited in
quantity and by its very nature limits what can be deduced
about the past. Chimpanzees are definitely not the same as
ancient hominids, nor are contemporary human foragers.
However, by comparing the similarities and differences be-

tween chimpanzees and contemporary humans, we can deduce some features which the putative ancestor of both species exhibited five or six million years ago. When this is done carefully by applying evolutionary concepts to reliable though limited data, the results have validity.

McGrew in "The Female Chimpanzee as a Human Evolutionary Prototype" summarizes current data on chimpanzee ecology, provides details on sex differences in behavior among chimpanzees, and reconstructs a likely path of human evolution. Zihlman in "Women as Shapers of the Human Adaptation" reviews the male bias in much evolutionary thinking about prehistory and then presents a well-documented case for her view that the feeding pattern of gathering and preparing food with tools is the uniquely human innovation. Although both chapters use sociobiological concepts, they arrive at different positions on prehistory. McGrew supports a very ancient sexual division of labor accompanied by male bonding as the basis of living groups while Zihlman believes that the behavioral flexibility of humans precluded a rigid sexual division of labor.

Women join men as shapers of the species when an evolutionary framework focusing on reproductive success is used. The fit survive to reproduce their genes, and their characteristics will be reproduced. Zihlman discusses the large investment that primate mothers make in each child. This investment includes a long gestation period, nursing, carrying, and later assistance with feeding; and it limits the number of offspring a primate female can successfully bear and rear. Meanwhile the male has made the minimal investment of sperm. The number of a human male's offspring may vary widely—for example, the keeper of a harem fathers hundreds of children while the eunuch guard fathers none. The average number of a human female's children today varies by society, and these averages range from four to six children (Dahlberg 1976:165). Among modern Xavante who gather, hunt, and plant in Brazil, the headman, one of thirty-seven men in the village studied, fathered one-fourth (twenty-three) of the surviving children, while most women bore about seven children each (Neel et al. 1964:94–95).

Because of these different parental investments, male and female mating and reproductive strategies will also differ. The male should attempt to father as many children as possible with any available mate; a female should seek mates with genes for desirable characteristics so that her few and costly children will survive (Trivers 1972:137). McGrew reports that chimpanzee females do choose their mates in the consortship form of mating from which half the babies are born, although most sexual acts (73 percent) occur in a promiscuous setting. We would like to know why some females participate in consortships and others do not. But Tutin (1979) provides information on differential involvement of males rather than females in this form of mating. During the ten days or so of the consortship, the female and her offspring will stay quietly at the edge of the chimpanzee group with her mate. Although this form of mating gives the female chimpanzee control over whom she will stay with, it presents risks in safety to herself and her offspring as well as to her mate. Recent long-term field data on pregnancies reveal the importance of female mate choice among chimpanzees, but we still do not know what causes so many offspring to result from these comparatively rare matings.

How did early hominid males demonstrate their fitness to the females who were choosing? Both McGrew and Zihlman believe that early hominid females preferred social males who groomed them and shared food with them and their offspring. These are the males who are chosen today by chimpanzee females in the consortship form of mating. The small canine teeth of early male hominids give further evidence for the importance of sociability rather than aggression among males. The lack of extreme sexual dimorphism in body size among fossil hominids also suggests that aggressive behavior was not selected. Attention to female mate choice shifts our attention from dominance, size, and aggression to grooming and food sharing, which coincides conveniently with the new emphasis on sharing in the study of human evolution.

Sharing

The sociobiological concept of kin selection provides an evolutionary link to sharing which many anthropologists now feel was essential for the emergence of the hominid line (Isaac 1978). When a living-group includes many close kin as it does among chimpanzees, contemporary human foragers, and certainly ancient hominids as well, behavior such as sharing, which promotes the survival of members, will be rewarded by gene representation in following generations. Food sharing contributes to the survival of all the members of a living-group by equalizing differences in daily food production resulting from the uneven distribution of resources and differences in luck or capacity. Sharing in the protection of offspring increases the survival of the young.

Food sharing would have been particularly beneficial to early hominids, as compared to other primates, because of the greater dependence of the infants. Early hominid babies, like human babies today, could not hold onto mother's fur with hands and feet as do other primate babies (Wells and Zelio 1979). Mother had no fur and babies had feet for walking, not for grasping. Zihlman suggests that the burdens of carrying, vividly depicted by Lee (1972) for contemporary !Kung women, sharpened our ancestresses' interest in food-sharing males.

Food sharing need not assume hunting. In the prehistoric past, early humans surely shared plants, nuts, and insects as well as meat. Both Zihlman and McGrew suggest that the sharing of gathered food could have been established before extensive hunting and could have facilitated hunting. Gathered food is abundant, predictable, and requires less energy to find than does hunted food. Without the secure base provided by sharing gathered foods, hunters, both female and male, could never have risked the chase. In the tropics, where there is an abundance of food that can be gathered, regular gathering feeds people when the hunt fails. In the prehistoric past, foragers could gather more easily than they do today, because they lived everywhere. Today, foragers live only in deserts, deep tropical rain forests, hills, and the Arctic, where more technologically advanced peoples have not cared to live. Even so, contemporary foragers enjoy a well-fed and secure life (Lee 1968) and much of their food is still gathered rather than hunted.

Sharing must have begun between a mother and her growing and grown children. Chimpanzee females share with their offspring abundant food such as bananas and hard-to-open fruits. Indeed, McGrew reports that 86 percent of the observed food sharing occurred within the matrifocal unit. Chimpanzees also share meat, which is hunted by males and which provides about 1 percent of their diet as compared to 35 percent of the !Kung diet (Teleki 1975) and 90 percent of the Chipewyan diet (Sharp, chapter 6, this volume). Adult food sharing among chimpanzees does not involve aggression; adults beg for meat, they don't grab it. The successful chimpanzee hunter shares with other males and occasionally with an adult female, especially one who is in estrus. This suggests that when hunting became more important for hominids, those females who were receptive sexually for longer periods, or continuously, or who concealed evidence of sexual cycles received more meat for themselves and their offspring. Possibly this is how human females lost a visible estrus.

Extensive sharing of food other than meat requires containers to accumulate and transport the food. Humans today, particularly women, carry both food and infants and must have carried them in the past; and many scholars have suggested that women must have invented carrying devices. But their containers are perishable, being made generally of flexibles such as bark, grass, folded leaves, and animal skins, which leave no trace in the archaeological record (Oswalt 1976:3).

Analogously, chimpanzee tools are made of perishable leaves and sticks. McGrew and Zihlman remind us that the late appearance of stone tools and their association with hunting does not mean that hominids were not using perishable tools and containers and sharing food much earlier.

Sharing in child care would offer protection to the slow-maturing young hominids while their mothers were absent collecting food. Caring behavior from the father and other relatives would be rewarded by greater gene representation in descendants. Incompatibility between feeding and care of offspring in a variety of species correlates with the presence of a pair-bond (Ember and Ember 1979): one parent seeks food while the other watches offspring. Such a pair-bond does not mean that either male or female is dependent on the other but that both cooperate to feed themselves and their offspring. If kidnapping, incompetence of the nonmaternal caretaker, or rank differences between the mother and the caretaker do not prevent the safe retrieval of the infant (McKenna 1979), sharing the care of infants will not harm them and may be beneficial to them by providing alternative sources of care should they become orphaned. Mothers who share their infants with related young females for practice mothering (aunting) prepare the young females for successful motherhood of their own later on. If the novice is closely supervised, the infant will not be injured (Quiatt 1979:314). Less often discussed, but also important, nurturing behavior toward older children in the living-group will also promote their survival by increasing the safety and security of the children, especially when their mothers are working. Adults in many modern hunting and gathering societies (for examples, see Montague 1978) actively participate in the nurturing of all the children of the group, not just their own.

Both sharing of food and sharing of infant and child care are incompatible with rigid dominance hierarchies or extremely aggressive behavior. If dominant individuals could usurp the food hunted or gathered by a less dominant member of the group, there would be no real sharing. One of De-

Vore's baboon films nicely illustrates the impact of a strong dominance hierarchy on food acquisition when a female baboon relinquishes her bird to an older male. This does not happen among chimpanzees or among contemporary human foragers who share. Female dominance among such species as macaques or baboons prevents child sharing (McKenna 1979:827) since the nondominant mother cannot demand her infant back from a more dominant female.

Sharing requires physical proximity and would be encouraged by stability of group membership. The enduring nature of the primate mother-child tie suggests that groups of mothers and children would be the nucleus of permanent groups among early hominids. Zihlman bases these groups on matrilines of mothers and daughters. McGrew thinks the mother-son tie predominated within the living group while the mother-daughter tie linked groups that exchanged wives. In either case, the mother-child tie is the crucial social link both within and between groups.

Isaac (1978) includes an elaborated communication system as part of the sharing concept. Communication (i.e., speech) might also have first developed between mothers and their babies when the talking baby reinforced its mother's nurturing efforts and received better care than the nontalker (for a review of this idea, see Jonas and Jonas 1975). Surely there is little evidence for the popular notion that hunters need to talk while planning and executing the hunt (Hockett and Ascher 1964) since wolves, chimpanzees, and modern hunters are silent while hunting. Gatherers, as well as hunters, would need to communicate in order to make plans for meeting later, for sharing food, and for enjoying in retrospect the excitement of the day's food quest.

Division of Labor by Sex

Many anthropologists feel that the sharing complex must include the division of labor by sex (Isaac 1978, for example). One suggestion for the origin of division is that the relative immobility of early hominid mothers with severe infant transport problems may have encouraged a specialization in range between the sexes (Wells and Zelio 1979). Unburdened males could travel farther, and when hunting was established it was males who traveled long distances after large game. This fits with popular views about the place of men and women and also fits with the prevalence of males practicing spear and bow and arrow hunting in contemporary foraging societies. But it overlooks the widespread practice of collective hunting, either with nets as by the Mbuti, with fire and beating, or with exploitation of river banks or other natural features. Collective hunting involves both men and women and sometimes children and is unrelated to differences in physical size or geographic range.

Sharing seems more profitable if individuals share different foods and exchange specialized services; such sharing, as well as the important sharing of information, might be facilitated by sexual differentiation in activities and in geographical range. Yet contemporary evidence on differences in range between the sexes is mixed: in the examples in this book, male chimpanzees have wider ranges than females, Chipewyan men travel farther than women, but Agta ranges do not differ by sex. Among contemporary foragers there is also evidence of sharing that does not link the sexes so much as it supports a variety of family and friendship ties. Chipewyan men give to other men, also hunters, shares of meat; Chipewyan women give to other women, also food processors, processed meat. The Agta share whatever food they acquire and may travel long distances to find and give a friend or relative part of their catch of fresh fish or their extra corn. Their only requirement is that each individual work in order to have something to share. In the small groups characteristic of foragers, personal pressure effectively contains deviance and ensures correct behavior, as Turnbull (1965) and Marshall (1961) have eloquently demonstrated for the Mbuti pygmies and the !Kung San bushmen. When nonworkers are systematically expelled and a strong sharing ethic enjoins each individual to share his or her food, a varied and secure diet can be achieved without arbitrary work assignments by sex or reliance on marriage to assure both sexes necessary goods and services. Sharing need not require a sexual division of labor.

Chapter 3 in this book introduces "Woman the Hunter." The Agta do not exhibit a division of labor by sex in food pro-curing and do not assign hunting to men. Yet they share all food. The Agta illustrate that some common generalizations may be misleading, and their case supports Zihlman's argu-ment that early hominids did not exhibit a sharply defined di-vision of labor by sex. Agta women can and do hunt regularly. Hunting is not confined to the oldest daughters in families without sons, young widows, deserted wives, or unusually vigorous personalities like most huntresses in the ethno-graphic literature (for Eskimo examples, see Jenness 1922 and Briggs 1974). Agta women do not hunt only in cooperation with men (as do Mbuti women in net hunting) nor do they hunt only in the absence of men (as do Chipewyan women). As the Griffins suggest, recent emphasis on the importance of gathering may actually obscure the importance and variety of women's activities. The Agta do not restrict any type of food collecting to one sex. Hunters, both female and male, begin hunting when their stamina and ability make it worthwhile and cease when they lose strength. Hunters who enjoy hunt-ing will hunt frequently; those who do not will hunt rarely. Each hunter uses techniques that work for her or for him; hunting techniques are not sex typed.

Modern foragers such as the Agta demonstrate the great flexibility that allows humans to live in a wide variety of envi-ronments and to survive rapid environmental change. Forag-ers' life-styles are based on maximum flexibility of behavior in response to an environment which they manipulate rela-tively little (Peterson 1978:41). Subsistence activities in general, as well as the division of labor by sex, may change with seasonal variations in environment (Halperin 1979). Since a food that is abundant one year and important in the diet may not be available the next, the relative importance of food-procuring activities varies from year to year.

We do not know how or when the division of labor by sex started, or whether it began with sharing. This book's two chapters on prehistory provide two different views, with McGrew supporting an early division of labor, Zihlman rejecting it. The division of labor by sex may have originated in cultural efforts to increase the interdependence of people rather than from differences in food-collecting activities.

Most societies today do divide technological tasks relating to subsistence by sex (Murdock 1937; Brown 1970). The assignment of tasks to females or to males goes beyond anything that might be required by the differential involvement of women and men in reproduction. In fact, many jobs are masculine in one society and feminine in another. Everywhere men hunt large land and water fauna, trap small animals and birds, hunt birds, build boats, and work with wood, stone, bone, horn, and shell (Murdock and Provost 1973:211). Everywhere women gather fuel and food, fetch water, prepare drinks and vegetable foods, and cook. Most of women's activities are performed close to the home and involve monotonous tasks that require no concentration and can easily be interrupted and resumed (Brown 1970:1074). Male activities may require long absences from home and travel over great distances, not possible for women burdened with children. Male tasks may be dangerous, because men do not bear or rear children, and may be more highly valued in order to motivate the expendable male to perform them (Parker and Parker 1979). Men do women's jobs more than women do men's jobs (Murdock and Provost 1972:210). For example, !Kung men often gather food, wood, and water, but !Kung women do not hunt (Draper 1975), and Chipewyan men are more competent in women's tasks than women are in men's tasks. Is this a sign of the Zihlman and Tanner (1978) theory that gathering preceded hunting, or simply the result of boys learning their mothers' work while under their care? As for tools, in most societies, the sex using the tools makes them;

indeed, usually the individual makes his or her own tools. Since the first tools were probably containers and wooden digging sticks, our hominid ancestress might have been the tool inventor, as McGrew suggests.

Women's contribution to subsistence varies. Australian aboriginal women provide much food by gathering and hunting small animals and, for coastal groups, shellfish; but Chipewyan women provide no food and Agta women prefer hunting, fishing, and trading to gathering. Everywhere women's work is crucial among foragers, but it need not produce food directly. Chipewyan women process food; Eskimo women sew; women everywhere, like men, contribute indirectly by collecting and sharing information.

Most assessments of contribution to subsistence use data from the Ethnographic Atlas, which by its very nature stresses patterns and neglects individual differences, assigning hunting to men and gathering to women. When we rely on these data to calculate the relative contributions of women and men to subsistence, we find that in most places, regardless of level of societal complexity, women contribute about 30–40 percent to subsistence (Sanday 1973:1690; Heath 1958:78; Whyte 1978*a*:60). Sanday found variation from a low of 24 percent in the Mediterranean region to a high of 43 percent in Africa. These figures measure the share of the food supply provided, not the hours spent or the physical strain. They do not include many time-consuming female tasks like the preparation and preservation of foodstuffs and the associated wood gathering and water carrying. Nobody has measured the amount of work required by childbearing and child care, although Richard Lee has calculated the energy requirements of child transport (Lee 1972).

Using the same data from the Ethnographic Atlas, published in the journal *Ethnology* (Murdock 1967), different anthropologists find different work patterns among foragers. Lee (1968:42), who uses data on fifty-eight foraging societies, finds that foragers depend on hunting for about 35 percent of their food supply; hence, gathering, usually considered to be woman's job, provides two-thirds of the food supply.

Hunting becomes the dominant mode of subsistence only in the higher latitudes (sixty degrees or above). Martin and Voorhies (1975:181), using ninety foraging societies, find that gathering is more important in 58 percent of the societies. Ember (1978:441), who uses all the foraging societies in the *Atlas*, rather than a sample, finds that men contribute substantially more to primary subsistence than do women. Men predominate in 83 percent of the cases, whereas in only 8 percent do women predominate. Using the odd-numbered foragers of the standard sample,[1] Whyte (1978b) finds that women contribute 44 percent to subsistence and that in two-thirds of the societies men contribute more to subsistence than women do. Some foragers rely on gathering (30 percent), some on hunting (25 percent), and some on fishing (38 percent) (Ember 1978:442).

All of these terms present practical and theoretical problems to those measuring contribution to subsistence. Lee (1968) classifies shell collecting as gathering, yet Meehan (1977) speaks of hunters of shellfish. Or should shellfish collection be termed fishing? Does hunting imply spears or bows and arrows? Does the catching of large sea mammals such as seals count as hunting or fishing? Is trapping hunting? And what of the collective hunting practiced today and represented in the archaeological record? Not all people have access to seas, lakes, or streams today, and it is unclear what role, if any, fish played in the evolutionary past. Since fishbones and gathered foods do not preserve well, fishing and gathering are more difficult to document in the past than hunting. All three activities may be done alone or in same- or mixed-sex groups, and hence they are difficult to categorize accurately by sex.

Status of Women

Women's work in food production has become an important issue in discussions about the status of women. Without an assignment of tasks by sex, the differential societal evaluations of women and men and their activities would lack a material basis (Schlegal 1977:25). Some anthropologists base the status of women directly on their economic contribution, including how this contribution is structured and who controls the conditions of work and the dispensation as well as the amount of goods produced. For example, Sanday (1973) finds that in twelve societies food production by women is a necessary but not sufficient condition for high female status. Where women contribute very much or very little to subsistence, they lose status. Friedl (1975:61) argues that rights of distribution of goods and services rather than rights and control over production determine status. Whyte's comprehensive cross-cultural study of the status of women in all types of preindustrial societies includes two scales—the value of labor and the control over property—which tap the economic dimension. He finds no grounds for assuming that the relative contribution to subsistence has any general status implications whatsoever (Whyte 1978*a*:169).

The Marxist approach to the study of inequality, which Eleanor Leacock espouses, believes that inequality arose with the advent of private property and the alienation of the worker from the ownership and control of the means of production. As Leacock (1978) eloquently argues, in most foraging societies private property is minimal and all people have access to the means of production; hence women in such societies cannot have low status. Leacock envisions an egalitarian society among hunters and gatherers where issues of status are irrelevant because both women and men produce goods and services for their own use, make decisions about their activities, and hence control their own lives directly.

In this book, we find that among the Agta, the Australian Aborigines (chapter 4), and the Mbuti pygmies (chapter 5), women as well as men contribute substantially to the food supply. Do women in these societies make decisions about their own lives, as Leacock expects?

The Griffins rest their case for the equality of Agta women on decision making as well as on women's contribution to the food supply. Agta women make decisions about the disposal of their own bodies in marriage, divorce, and childbearing, about their daily activities, and about the distribution of the food they hunt, fish, trade for, and collect. They participate in decisions made by the whole group and are in no way subordinate to men. Do Australian Aboriginal and pygmy women also make decisions? Berndt reminds us that although Aboriginal women do not pick their first mates, neither do the men. The importance of age for establishing authority in this culture means that older women and older men make the decisions for the young bride. Older brides, those in second or later marriages, make their own arrangements. Traditionally, Australian men aspired to more than one wife, and in this they resemble the men in about half of foraging societies and about half of societies relying on other means of subsistence.[2] The Australian Aboriginal wife will live with her husband's group, as do wives in about half of the foraging societies of the standard sample.[3] Residence with the husband's relatives may give men a temporary advantage as compared to newly married women, but women soon become established in the group. In any event, Aboriginal women are always in control of their daily activities and own their own property (Kaberry 1970:141). Residence in the husband's band does put a woman at a disadvantage in participation in the political, jural, or religious activities of her own group (Kaberry 1970:180). Unlike young Australian Aboriginal women, Mbuti women do choose their own mates. Indeed, the female mate choice which sociobiologists discuss is quite evident at the girls' coming of age ceremony, when the *elima* girls pick the young men who are allowed to enter the *elima* hut. This is not marriage but is definitely considered to be the first step in the process. The Mbuti women determine their own day's activities, which are not limited by their sex. Female elders have both power and authority that male elders cannot match, according to Turnbull. Female elders make explicit criticisms from the center of the group, while male elders confine themselves to grumbles.

In their small living groups the Agta, Mbuti, Australian Aborigines, and Chipewyan resemble other foragers, among whom two-thirds live in groups of fewer than one hundred persons.[4] Decisions are usually made within the immediate living group since few foragers (11 percent)[5] have a political structure beyond the local group. In such small groups, particular personalities, female as well as male, influence events. Not only are living groups small, but their size and membership change throughout the year in response to changing seasons, to ceremonial demands, and to personal preferences. This flux regulates social relationships in the absence of a formal political structure (Turnbull 1968). In addition, the few men in the group will be of different ages. The combination of changing membership and varied ages precludes the formation of solidary male peer groups, which are crucial in making women as a category subordinate to men (Draper, personal communication).

The mobility of foragers, including the four groups in this book, may be important for women, and lack of mobility may increase their dependence. The women dependent on man the hunter stayed home while the men moved about. Draper's provocative comparisons of foraging and sedentary !Kung women (Draper 1975) show that they enjoy more equality in the foraging life-style. Is this a special case or does permanent residence always undermine the high status women enjoy among many mobile foragers? Boulding (1976:331) notes that the view from the road is a liberating one for women. Few goods are carried, hence women's housekeeping burdens are light. Roles remain fluid, and male and female worlds intersect. Mobility reinforces the interdependence among all the members of the group that the sharing of work by adults has already established.

The chapters on the Agta, Mbuti, and Australian Aborigines demonstrate a variety of ways in which both women's and men's roles are broader and less rigid than stereotypes based on complex Western societies. Such contemporary flexibility supports Zihlman's theories about women and men in prehistory. These cultures are, as Leacock (1978) observes, qualitatively different from our own. Two of them—the Agta and Mbuti—are clearly egalitarian and are proof that, unlike matriarchies, which many feminists believe to have existed but which have never been found (Fleur-Lobban 1979), egalitarian hunting and gathering societies in which women are not (or not very) subordinate to men exist. Foragers represent for some feminists a trace of a golden androgynous past. These societies are the basis for generalizations about sexual egalitarianism (Schlegal 1977:26) and the "separate but equal" status of women at this level of societal development (Martin and Voorheis 1975:190) that are part of the growing literature on the anthropology of women. Yet the status of women in foraging societies is not always unambiguously high. Along with the joyous pygmies, we find the wife-beating Australian Aborigines.

The flexibility of foragers leads to ambiguous results when systematic scaling is used to measure women's status. Low scores on measures of status do not predominate among foragers, but neither do high scores (Dahlberg 1980:406–07). The range in scores contradicts Leacock's assertion that the status of women among foragers today will "affirm the virtual universality of the Western ideal for women's status" (Leacock 1978:247), resulting as it does from inadequate data on women, a failure to appreciate societies qualitatively different from our own, or a Western bias in the observer and his or her informants.

Berndt's chapter on "Interpretation and 'Facts' in Aboriginal Australia" discusses the problems with data that have led to misunderstandings about the status of women in band societies. Berndt reminds us that Australian Aboriginal culture is the product of a long evolution of its own, during which many changes have occurred, especially, but not solely, in the past two hundred years of European contact. Studies of the many distinct groups date from times of varying degrees of contact with Western culture, and each observer has explored topics of special interest to him or her but chiefly

with focus on male activities. Only Kaberry's classic study
(Kaberry 1970) devoted itself wholly to women. Data on Australian Aborigines in cities, on reservations, and in settlements and data from Aborigines of mixed blood have been
linked with data from more traditional people. Despite this
uneven coverage, Berndt finds agreement everywhere that
Aboriginal women are the breadwinners. In addition, the social reality of sex and age as organizing principles of culture
emerges from all sources. Yet it is not clear how these culturally elaborated differences between old and young, men and
women, affect the status of women, the meaning of their
many activities, or their symbolic value. Berndt does not find
the egalitarian autonomy among Australian Aborigines that
Leacock hypothesizes should exist there. Cooperation is of
more concern than autonomy: both women and men have essential tasks to perform in religious work as well as in food
collecting and reproduction.

Motherhood

If women contribute to the food supply and have the authority to make decisions affecting their own lives, why would they
be less highly valued than men? Many contemporary theorists
base the frequently lower status of women squarely on
motherhood. It is not surprising that Western scholars tend to
dismiss maternity as a source of self-esteem and honor, since
motherhood has often been the excuse in the West for
confining women to the home and excluding them from more
varied—and rewarded—activities. In individualistic Euro-
American culture, successful adulthood does not require
family membership and the perpetuation of the family as it
does in many other cultures (MacFarlane 1979). Hence
childbearing and childrearing can be perceived by Western
theorists as exclusively a handicap to participation in the
wider society. Sex differences based on reproductive tasks are
projected back into prehistory when a sexual division of labor
developed because women were burdened by children and

had to remain near home base. Theorists believe that the negative effects of maternity extend beyond the task of physical reproduction into childrearing, an activity that cannot be escaped by women, because of the essential, biologically based, intense relationship between the mother and her infant (Rossi 1977:24). Women writing today uniformly assume low status for maternity, which they see as constraining activities, hindering personality development, and reducing women's symbolic value. They project the values of our culture onto other cultures. Even Rosaldo's fruitful idea (Rosaldo 1974:23) that the opposition between domestic and public spheres underlies asymmetries in the evaluation of the sexes associates women's lower status with maternity. The domestic realm includes institutions and activities organized around mothers and their children. When public and private domains separate, women who stay in the domestic sphere lose power and value. Where there is no distinct public sphere and men act in the domestic sphere, women gain status.

Why should maternal duties exclude women from desired activities or restrict them? Brown (1970) suggests that women's subsistence activities must be compatible with simultaneous child-care responsibilities—maternity first, then work. This will exclude all women, not just those with children, from dangerous or distant tasks. Yet there is considerable evidence (DuBois 1944; Levine 1966; Nerlove 1974) that many women put their work first and adjust child care to work needs. A mother faced with a heavy work load may also use older children, especially girls, to care for smaller children, thus freeing herself to work. Contemporary foragers provide little evidence of maternal constraints in activity; for example, Agta and Mbuti women restrict their activities for only a few days after childbirth. Shell hunting does drop off for several months among Anbara (Australian Aborigines) mothers, however.

Why do childbearing and child care seem to restrict these foragers so little? Possibly because they have abundant leisure time (Sahlins 1968); adult !Kung involvement with children declines dramatically when work load zooms in the sedentary situation (Draper and Cashden 1974). Berndt notes that modern Aboriginal women, who are more isolated than their grandmothers, are hard-pressed to handle their more numerous offspring. Compared to more technologically advanced peoples, foragers generally have few children to care for. They may use techniques such as infanticide (Birdsell 1968 on Australian Aboriginals) or medicines to prevent conception or cause early abortions in order to restrict the numbers of their children, or they may rely on involuntary physiological factors such as inadequate fat layers for ovulation (Lee 1972), the interruption of ovulation during prolonged nursing (Masnick 1979), or even genetic tendencies to low fecundity.

Many observers believe that problems of infant transport and feeding provide the chief motivation for wide child spacing among foragers. A pregnant woman will have trouble carrying a small child; two children cannot thrive on one limited milk supply. Hence the older child must be at least four or five years old before baby sister or brother arrives. But it is not on economic grounds only that foraging culture discourages rapid childbearing (Dumond 1975). Foraging women, like women in contemporary industrial society, are responsible for their own children. The adult relatives available in peasant extended families are not on hand to share responsibility in child care, although other adults do participate. The weaned child cannot be entrusted to its own peer group or a slightly older child nurse, as in many horticultural societies, because most foragers live in such small groups that child peer groups do not form. The lack of inheritable property among foragers, the impermanence of social groups, and the close ties between a variety of kin, not just parents and children, discourage the emphasis on group continuity through offspring found in many horticultural and agricultural societies and hold in check the total reliance on children for security in old age. Hence gatherers may consider the direct impact of each child on the mother's life when deciding to bear a child or to keep one after it is born.

Besides accentuating the constraints of maternity, some Western theorists also project its low status onto the symbolic plane. Ortner (1974) equates women's involvement with physical reproduction and the transformation of untamed children into civilized members of society with nature, which, she claims, is universally valued less than culture. Hence women, by their biological nature, will be valued less than men. This neat but too simple formula has already attracted criticism. The chapters in this book fail to support it. The last three—Berndt's, Turnbull's, and Sharp's—discuss the differential evaluation of the "nature" of each sex, and Berndt and Turnbull deal explicitly with the contributions of motherhood in providing recognition and honor for women.

Writing on "Mbuti Womanhood," Turnbull directly addresses the issue of the impact of motherhood on the evaluation of women. His data contradict the idea that maternity lessens the value of women or that women are valued less than men. But his data do support the unpopular idea that "anatomy is destiny." Usually this kind of biological determinism is associated with female inferiority, but Turnbull provides a glorious female destiny. Rosaldo and Atkinson (1975) have warned us, however, that biologically based glory is a trap for women which keeps them bound forever to nature.

Among the Mbuti, prestige and respect for women characterize only one phase of the life cycle, that of adulthood, the only time of life when sex is acknowledged in terms of address or reference. Women then are seen as possessing the ultimate power of all—that of life—which brings them closer to the forest than men can be. Men approach the forest in the *molimo* ceremonies, but women during their childbearing years are already close. The esteem of childbearing is to some extent shared with men, who as "male mothers" enjoy some of the experience of mothering once the child is about two years old.

Maternity or the possibility of maternity changes the sexual experience for both sexes. Turnbull describes marital sex, from which children are expected, as ecstasy compared to the mere joy of premarital sex from which no children are born. The Mbuti appear to be seeking a balance between the sexes by compensating men for the fundamental biological inadequacy of being unable to give birth.

Symbolic and Ritual Representations

The Mbuti, like many other peoples, including contemporary Americans, use sex and age as structural means of dividing labor and authority. But the fact that male and female are different kinds of creatures does not mean to the Mbuti that one is subordinate or that the other is superordinate. In the ritualized conflict between the sexes at the girls' initiation of *elima,* neither side wins. Male youths have the special ceremony in the forest, *molimo madé,* while the girls have their *elima.* In the *ekokomea,* each sex dresses as its opposite and ridicules a physiological feature of its opposite—the penis or menstruation. The older men conduct the supreme ceremony, the *molimo mangbo,* but women can ritually "kill" their song. A balanced interdependence of the sexes in the ritual realm parallels that experienced in everyday life.

Do the relationships between the sexes in the Agta's symbolic world reflect their lack of sexual differentiation in the economic and social world? Regrettably, we do not have data to answer this. However, we can look at this question among the Australian Aborigines and the Chipewyan, who, like the Mbuti, use sex as a differentiating principle but who have a much more clearly defined sexual division of labor in food production than the Mbuti exhibit. They also have a ritual division of labor by sex, with Australian Aboriginal women providing a larger share of food and with men predominating in ceremonial activities. As men hunt meat to supplement the bulk of the food, which is gathered by women, so also women as well as men contribute to the religious life. They do not do the same things, but what women do is as essential as what men do. The Aboriginal mother introduces her children, boys as well as girls, to their religion. Berndt notes that the conception site, which will be critical in her son's later spiritual life, is decided by his mother. There may be an attempt to balance differential contribution to food supply by differential contributions in symbolic life, rather as the Mbuti balance men's forest rituals against women's contribution of children.

The Chipewyan women do not gather, and they contribute little to the food supply; Sharp has therefore titled his chapter "The Null Hypothesis." The men among the Chipewyan provide most (90 percent) of the food, primarily through trapping and trading today as compared to hunting in the past. Looking at these people against the norm of flexibility, diversity, and interdependence among foragers, Sharp asks how the Chipewyan can balance such disparate economic contributions. An answer may lie in their concept of power. Chipewyan men need, and must seek, power/knowledge in order to be successful hunters. Women simply by being female *are* power. The case is similar to that of the Mbuti, who view women as by nature closer to the forest.

The Chipewyan artificially create a division of labor by sex by dividing food production into two parts—procuring and processing. This is a social division. The Chipewyan man knows perfectly well how to dry fish or meat, but he must give his catch to his wife or mother for her to dry and to dispose of as she wishes. Such culturally prescribed differences between the sexes increase the interdependence of people and create distinct public groups. The teasing (or nagging) between groups and the esprit de corps within groups provide important incentives to work. Chipewyan women urge men to work at hunting; men assert their superiority (or at least their difference) by relying on spirits and power rather than regular work. The differences between men and women are paralleled by divisions between bush and camp. In the bush, men own the game that they butcher and divide and then transport back to camp. In camp, the women own the meat they dry, cook, and share with other people. This private system of sharing, based on ownership of the dried meat, provides the flexibility which the Chipewyan, like all foragers, need to even out differences in food supply. Even today, when the Chipewyan are heavily involved in trapping and trading, unevenness in food supply creates difficulties. Private borrowing to redress shortfalls experienced by individual households does not impinge on the public image of the man as a competent provider full of knowledge/power; if a man were to fail publicly, he and others might question this public image. For women, the control of borrowing balances the disadvantages that accompany patrilocal residence. Theories that base women's status on primary food production alone will not be helpful for the Chipewyan, whose women possess "power" despite their dependence on man the hunter.

Symbolic, ritual, and mythic material as it affects women may be particularly difficult for theorists who come from cultures where gods and priests are always male and where equal means the same. The stress on interdependence, which we have found in the economics and social relationships of foraging groups in this book and which McGrew and Zihlman postulate for early hominids, is found in women's active presence in ritual as described in the ethnographic literature on hunters and gatherers as well. Women among foragers participate in religious ceremonies and rituals; and the gods, mythical founders, and shamans are both male and female.[6] Witches may be of either sex; they are not predominantly male, as is common in pastoral or agricultural societies. This means that among foragers women as well as men have access to this type of supernatural power. The Mbuti's *elima* ceremony to dramatize the coming of age of girls is not unusual for foragers, who more commonly perform such ceremonies for girls than do other peoples (69 percent to 40 percent, Schlegal and Barry 1979) and who may omit them for boys. Data on the symbolic value of women are much harder to evaluate or compare than data regarding economics. The literature is uneven, and interpretations are questionable.

Women whose very nature is feared are interpreted as having less status than those who are not feared (Whyte 1978*a*). Yet this fear could be a way of recognizing the special quality of women.

The chapters in this book do not support the idea that women are valued less than men because of the restrictions of maternity or because of differential economic contributions. In the realms of ritual activity and symbolic values as well, the evidence shows flexibility and diversity that produce balance and interdependent cooperation between the sexes. Might not a similar balance have prevailed between the sexes in prehistory? Yet a new "just-so" story cannot be written: it would contradict the very heterogeneity that the new research emphasizes.

Research that starts with the majority—women and children—does not support a legend of man the hunter or woman the gatherer but leads to a more complicated story. An accurate reconstruction of early hominid life is still being fashioned, minus the high drama of man the hunter. Heroic qualities seldom come into play in securing protein from catfish, termites, snails, gerbils, and baby baboons. But what is lost in drama is gained in diversity and complexity.

Notes

1. The standard cross-cultural sample (Murdock and White 1972) contains 35 foraging societies out of 186 societies. This sample or the odd or even half of it has been used for many systematic comparative studies. These societies are included in the Ethnographic Atlas, and a majority of them are part of the Human Relations Area Files. The reliability and extent of available data vary widely. Often when scholars, especially those employing this comparative style of research, refer to "most foragers," it is these particular foragers whom they actually mean. The foragers in the sample are arranged in numerical order by geographical region as follows:

Africa: !Kung, Hadza, Mbuti

Eurasia: Semang, Andamanese, Vedda, Gilyak, Yukaghir

Pacific: Tiwi, Aranda (both Australian Aboriginal groups)

North America: Ingalik, Aleut, Copper Eskimo, Montagnais, Micmac, Northern Saulteaux, Slave, Kaska, Eyak, Haida, Bellacoola, Twana, Yurok, Pomo, Yokuts, Paiute, Klamath, Kutenai, Gros Ventre, Comanche, Chiricahua

South America: Botocudo, Aweikoma, Tehuelche, Yahghan

Notice the preponderance of North American Indians in the sample, while the recent, high-quality data on the !Kung, Mbuti, Australian Aborigines, and Eskimos provide the majority of the examples and theoretical insights into this way of life.

2. This figure was calculated from data on the odd half of the standard sample coded in Whyte (1978*b*) on the variable Preferred Marriage Form, column 31.

3. This figure was calculated from data on the foraging portion of the standard sample as recorded in column 9, Marital Residence, in Murdock and Wilson (1972).

4. This figure was calculated from data published on the foraging portion of the standard sample published in column 3, Settlement Size, in Tuden and Marshall (1972).

5. This figure was calculated from data on the foraging portion of the standard sample published in column 3, Levels of Sovereignty, in Tuden and Marshall (1972).

6. This was calculated from data published on the foraging portion of the odd half of the standard sample coded in Whyte 1978*b*.

References

Ardener, E. 1972. Belief and the problem of women. In *Interpretation of ritual,* ed. J. S. LaFontaine, pp. 35–58. London: Tavistock.

Birdsell, Joseph B. 1968. Population control factors: Infanticide, disease, nutrition and food supplies. In *Man the hunter,* ed. Richard B. Lee and Irven DeVore, pp. 229–40. Chicago: Aldine.

Boulding, Elise. 1976. *The underside of history: a view of women through time.* Boulder, Colo.: Westview Press.

Briggs, Jean. 1974. Eskimo women: makers of men. In *Many sisters: women in cross-cultural perspective,* ed. Carolyn J. Matthiason, pp. 261–304. New York: Free Press.

Brown, Judith K. 1970. A note on the division of labor by sex. *American Anthropologist* 72:1073–78.

Dahlberg, Frances. 1976. More on mechanisms of population growth. *Current Anthropology* 17:164–66.

———. 1980. Further comments on women's status in egalitarian society. *Current Anthropology* 21:406–08.

Draper, Patricia. 1975. !Kung women: contrasts in sexual egalitarianism in foraging and sedentary contexts. In *Toward an anthropology of women,* ed. Rayna R. Reiter, pp. 77–109. New York: Monthly Review Press.

Draper, Patrica, and Elizabeth Cashden. 1974. The impact of sedentism on !Kung socialization. Paper given at the American Anthropological Association meeting, Mexico City, November 1974.

DuBois, Cora. 1944. *People of Alor.* Minneapolis, Minn.: University of Minnesota.

Dumond, Don R. 1975. Limitation of human population: a natural history. *Science* 187:713–21.

Ember, Carol R. 1978. Myths about hunter-gatherers. *Ethnology* 18:439–48.

Ember, Carol R., and Melvin Ember. 1979. Male-female bonding: a cross-species study of mammals and birds. *Behavior Science Research* 14:37–56.

Fleur-Lobban, Carolyn. 1979. A Marxist reappraisal of the matriarchate. *Current Anthropology* 20:341–60.

Friedl, Ernestine. 1975. *Women and men: an anthropologist's view.* New York: Holt, Rinehart and Winston.

Halperin, Rhoda. 1979. Ecology and mode of production: seasonal variation and the division of labor by sex among hunter-gatherers. Department of Anthropology, University of Cincinnati. Manuscript.

Heath, Dwight B. 1958. Sexual division of labor and cross-cultural research. *Social Forces* 37:77–79.

Hockett, Charles F., and Robert Ascher. 1964. The human revolution. *Current Anthropology* 5:135–68.

Isaac, Glynn L. 1978. Food sharing and human evolution: archaeological evidence from Paleo-Pleistocene of East Africa. *Journal of Anthropological Research* 34:311–26.

Jenness, Diamond. 1922. *The life of the Copper Eskimos. Report of the Canadian Arctic Expedition 1913–1918,* vol XII, part 9. Ottawa: Acland.

Jonas, Doris F., and A. David Jonas. 1975. Gender differences in mental function: a clue to the origin of language. *Current Anthropology* 16:626–30.

Kaberry, Phyliss M. 1970 (1939). *Aboriginal woman: sacred and profane.* London: Routledge & Kegan Paul.

Kraybill, Nancy. 1977. Pre-agricultural tools for the preparation of foods in the Old World. In *Origins of agriculture,* ed. Charles A. Reed, pp. 485–521. Chicago: Aldine.

Laughlin, William S. 1968. Hunting: an integrating biobehavior system and its evolutionary importance. In *Man the hunter,* ed. Richard B. Lee and Irven DeVore, pp. 304–20. Chicago: Aldine.

Leacock, Eleanor, and June Nash. 1977. Ideologies of sex. *Annals of the New York Academy of Sciences* 285:616–46.

Leacock, Eleanor. 1978. Women's status in egalitarian society: implications for social evolution. *Current Anthropology* 19:247–75.

Lee, Richard B. 1968. What hunters do for a living or how to make out on scarce resources. In *Man the hunter,* ed. Richard B. Lee and Irven DeVore, pp. 30–48. Chicago: Aldine.

———. 1972. Population growth and the beginning of sedentary life among the !Kung. In *Population growth: anthropological implications,* ed. Brian Spooner, pp. 329–42. Cambridge, Mass.: MIT Press.

Levine, Robert. 1966. Sex roles and economic change in Africa. *Ethnology* 5:186–93.

Linton, Sally. 1971. Woman the gatherer: male bias in anthropology. In *Women in cross-cultural perspective,* ed. Sue Ellen Jacobs. Champaign, Ill.: University of Illinois Press. Reprinted under S. Slocum, in *Toward an anthropology of women,* ed. Rayna R. Reiter, pp. 36–50. New York: Monthly Review Press.

MacFarlane, Alan. 1979. *The origins of English individualism.* New York: Cambridge University Press.

McKenna, James J. 1979. The evolution of allomothering behavior among Colobine monkeys: function and opportunism in evolution. *American Anthropologist* 81:818–40.

Marshall, Lorna. 1961. Sharing, talking and giving: relief of social tensions among !Kung bushmen. *Africa* 31:231–49.

Martin, M. Kay, and Barbara Voorhies. 1975. *Female of the species.* New York: Columbia University Press.

Masnick, George. 1979. The demographic impact of breastfeeding: a critical review. *Human Biology* 51:109–26.

Meehan, Betty. 1977. Hunters by the seashore. *Journal of Human Evolution* 6:363–70.

Montague, Ashley. 1978. *Learning non-aggression*. New York: Oxford University Press.

Morgan, Elaine. 1972. *The descent of woman*. New York: Bantam.

Murdock, George Peter. 1937. Comparative data on the division of labor by sex. *Social Forces* 15:551–53.

———. 1967. Ethnographic Atlas: a summary. *Ethnology* 6:109–236. Additional entries published in later issues; also published separately as a book by the University of Pittsburgh Press in 1967.

Murdock, George Peter, and Caterine Provost. 1973. Factors in the division of labor by sex: a cross-cultural analysis. *Ethnology* 12:203–35.

Murdock, George Peter, and Suzanne F. Wilson. 1972. Settlement patterns and community organization: cross cultural codes 3. *Ethnology* 11:259–95.

Neel, J. V., F. M. Salzano, P. C. Junqueira, F. Keiter, and D. Maybury-Lewis. 1964. Studies in the Xavante Indians of the Brazilian Mato Grosso. *American Journal of Human Genetics* 16:52–140.

Nerlove, Sara B. 1974. Women's workload and infant feeding practices: a relationship with demographic implications. *Ethnology* 13:297–314.

Ortner, Sherry B. 1974. Is female to male as nature is to culture? In *Women, culture and society*, ed. M. Z. Rosaldo and L. Lamphere, pp. 67–88. Stanford, Calif.: Stanford University Press.

Oswalt, Wendell H. 1976. *An anthropological analysis of food getting technology*. New York: Wiley.

Parker, Seymour, and Hilda Parker. 1979. The myth of male superiority: rise and demise. *American Anthropologist* 81:289–309.

Peterson, Jean. 1978. *The ecology of social boundaries: Agta foragers of the Philippines*. Champaign, Ill.: University of Illinois Press.

Quiatt, Duane. 1979. Aunts and mothers: adaptive implications of allomaternal behavior of nonhuman primates. *American Anthropologist* 81:310–19.

Rohrlich-Leavitt, Ruby, Barbara Sykes, and Elizabeth Weatherford. 1975. Aboriginal woman: male and female. In *Toward an anthropology of women*, ed. Rayna R. Reiter, pp. 110–26. New York: Monthly Review Press.

Rosaldo, Michelle. 1974. Women, culture and society: a theoretical overview. In *Women, culture and society*, ed. Michelle Z. Rosaldo and

Louise Lamphere, pp. 17–42. Stanford, Calif.: Stanford University Press.

Rosaldo, Michelle, and Jane Monnig Atkinson. 1975. Man the hunter and woman: metaphors for the sexes in Ilonget magical spells. In *The interpretation of symbolism,* ed. Roy Willis, pp. 43–76. London: Malaby Press.

Rossi, Alice S. 1977. A biosocial perspective on parenting. *Daedalus* 196:1–32.

Sachs, Karen. 1976. State bias and women's status. *American Anthropologist* 78:565–69.

Sahlins, Marshall. 1968. Notes on the original affluent society. In *Man the hunter,* ed. Richard B. Lee and Irven DeVore, pp. 85–88. Chicago: Aldine.

Sanday, Peggy. 1973. Toward a theory of the status of women. *American Anthropologist* 75:1682–1700.

Schlegal, Alice. 1977. Toward a theory of sexual stratification. In *Sexual stratification: a cross-cultural view,* ed. Alice Schlegal, pp. 1–40. New York: Columbia University Press.

Schlegal, Alice, and Herbert Barry III. 1979. Adolescent initiation ceremonies: a cross-cultural code. *Ethnology* 19:199–210.

Teleki, Geza. 1975. Primate subsistence patterns: collector predator and gatherer-hunter. *Journal of Human Evolution* 4:125–84.

Trivers, Robert L. 1972. Parental investment and sexual selection. In *Sexual selection and the descent of man 1871–1971,* ed. Bernard Campbell, pp. 136–79. Chicago: Aldine.

Tuden, Arthur, and Catherine Marshall. 1972. Political organization: cross-cultural codes 4. *Ethnology* 11:434–64.

Turnbull, Colin M. 1965. *Wayward servants.* New York: Natural History Press.

————. 1968. The importance of flux in two hunting societies. In *Man the hunter*, ed. Richard B. Lee and Irven DeVore, pp. 132–37. Chicago: Aldine.

Tutin, Caroline E. G. 1979. Mating patterns and reproductive strategies in a community of wild chimpanzees. *Behavioral Ecology and Sociobiology* 6:29–38.

Wells, Pat, and Judy Zelio. 1979. The role of infant care in hominid labor division. Department of Anthropology, University of Colorado, Denver. Manuscript.

Whyte, Martin King. 1978a. *The status of women in preindustrial societies.* Princeton, N.J.: Princeton University Press.

————. 1978*b*. Cross-cultural codes dealing with the relative status of women. *Ethnology* 17:211–37.

Zihlman, Adrienne L., and Nancy Tanner. 1978. Gathering and the hominid adaptation. In *Female hierarchies*, ed. Lionel Tiger and Heather Fowler, pp. 163–94. Chicago: Beresford Book Service.

1 THE FEMALE CHIMPANZEE AS A HUMAN EVOLUTIONARY PROTOTYPE
W. C. McGrew

This chapter critically examines recent findings on sex differences in the ecology and ethology of the chimpanzee (*Pan troglodytes*) in nature. It seeks a new, synthetic perspective, since many accepted generalizations about chimpanzees no longer hold in the light of recent knowledge; and it seeks in the behavior of living chimpanzees clues to the most likely path of early hominid evolution. Others have presented the chimpanzee as a model for hominid evolution (e.g., Goodall and Hamburg 1974; Goodall 1975, 1976; Reynolds 1976; Tanner and Zihlman 1976; Isaac 1978; Zihlman 1978; Zihlman and Tanner 1978), but the rapid advance of field studies of chimpanzees has dated these efforts.

It is important to state what the chapter does *not* include. In concentrating on the chimpanzee, it excludes other species of nonhuman primates, seeking to gain in depth what is lost in breadth. For the whole primate order, several other excellent and recent syntheses already exist (e.g., Clutton-Brock and Harvey 1976; Lancaster 1976, 1978). Some primatologists have advanced an evolutionary model based on baboons (e.g., Washburn and DeVore 1963; Jolly 1970; Dunbar 1976), which are savanna dwellers, as early hominids are believed to have been. Baboons, however, although superbly adapted to life on the savanna, do not show evidence of the complex cognitive capacities that such an environment is thought to have elicited in early hominids. Moreover, baboons are not

the only primate savanna dwellers. Although many populations of chimpanzees live in forests or mosaic habitats of
forest, woodland, and grassland, some of the populations at
the limits of the species' range subsist in hot, dry, and open
savanna environments where the amount of forest available
is minimal (McGrew et al. 1980).

No attempt is made in this chapter to draw comparisons
between the natural history of chimpanzees and the cultural
ecology of living human societies of gatherers and hunters.
Such comparisons might be stimulating and fruitful, but they
would require much more space than is available here.
Readers interested in such comparisons are invited to bear in
mind points raised in this chapter as they read succeeding
chapters which deal with various human societies. No use is
made here of studies of chimpanzees in captivity. However
fascinating and provocative the implications of laboratory
studies, they tell us nothing *directly* about adaptive responses
by chimpanzees or early humans to natural selection.

Why choose the chimpanzee as a model for early humans?
The great apes (Pongidae), especially the African forms
(chimpanzee and gorilla), are the nearest living relations of
the human species. The close affinity on morphological
grounds is well established and was reinforced more recently
by detailed comparisons of proteins (King and Wilson 1975)
and chromosomes (Miller 1977). It remains unclear which of
the two species of African apes is more closely related to the
human species, but King and Wilson (1975) showed that the
genetic distance between humans and chimpanzees, as determined by electrophoretic comparison of proteins, falls well
within the range of sibling species. They are as closely related
as the domestic dog (*Canis familiaris*) and the wolf (*Canis
lupus*). Comparisons on behavioral and intellectual criteria are
standardized less easily, but several lines of evidence suggest
that chimpanzees possess cognitive capacities which are only
quantitatively different from those of humans. Chimpanzees
show capacities for symbolic communication (Linden 1974)
and self-recognition and therefore possess a rudimentary

concept of self (Gallup 1977). They make tools as opposed to simply using tools in a variety of activities (Beck 1975).

It is necessary to sound a cautionary note, however. The chimpanzee is not now and never has been a forebear of early or modern *Homo sapiens*. We are neither descended nor ascended from apes in the form that we know them today. The African apes are the other living primates with which we last shared common ancestry, and the two families, Pongidae and Hominidae, have been separated for millions of years. Just how many millions of years were involved remains a matter of controversy, but whether it has been five or thirty million years, the differences are acute. Our hominid predecessors are, however, extinct and chimpanzees are (just) extant. The best that we can do to reconstruct our prehistoric heritage is to infer the capacities and characteristics of the long-lost ancestral hominoid from the accessible apes.

The Chimpanzee in Nature

Before assessing recent knowledge of chimpanzees, one must consider two key points about the research itself: a given study's duration and the use of provisioning.

A brief study in the field may produce misleading and unrepresentative findings, because of the seasonal habitats in which most wild chimpanzees live. A study lasting only a few months in the depths of the rainy season may produce a very different picture compared with another study at the same site during the dry season. In this chapter, field studies of more than twelve consecutive months (i.e., one annual cycle) are classed as long term and will receive most attention.

Provisioning is a technique by which desirable food is provided artificially to tempt wild chimpanzees. It is used to overcome the shyness of the apes, which otherwise avoid humans and are difficult to observe. Presenting the food, usually a domesticated species of plant such as bananas or sugar cane, in conjunction with innocuous observers, leads gradually to habituation to humans at closer and closer distances.

Provisioning also occurs unintentionally; for instance, when chimpanzees become crop raiders. This intrusion into the natural life of a wild animal may lead to distortions of natural behaviors, especially those involved in feeding and ranging (e.g., Wrangham 1974; Reynolds 1975). However, the only field studies so far to have yielded systematic data on the individual behaviors of wild chimpanzees are those in which habituation was achieved by provisioning (e.g., Goodall 1968; Nishida 1979). In this chapter, findings from unprovisioned populations will be preferred whenever possible, but most cases come from studies using provisioning. Table 1 lists field studies on which the chapter is based.

The common chimpanzee occurs across equatorial Africa from Uganda and Tanzania in the east and south to Guinea and Senegal in the west and north. The species is divided into three geographical races (subspecies?).

Chimpanzees are classified as diurnal, terrestrial, and frugivorous because they spend much of the day on the ground and the bulk of their diet is fruit (Milton and May 1976; Gaulin and Konner 1977). They also collect and feed upon other parts of plants: leaves, seeds, shoots, stems, flowers, buds, bark, pith, and resins. Moreover, they capture and consume animals: invertebrates, eggs and nestlings of birds, immature ungulates, monkeys, and other chimpanzees (Hladik 1977; Wrangham 1977). Thus they should be classified as omnivores (Teleki 1973). Although they travel on the ground, most of their daily activities, especially feeding, take place higher up, in vegetation (Wrangham 1977), so they are at most only relatively terrestrial. Finally, although they are active by day, chimpanzees sleep in trees at night. They build fresh sleeping platforms every evening by interlacing branches and twigs (Goodall 1968).

The social organization of wild chimpanzees is not easily defined; compared to that of most other nonhuman primates, it is loosely structured and variable. This has led to several terms being used to describe the basic social unit: *community, unit group, troop, regional population*. In seeking to generalize, it

Table 1. List of long-term studies of wild chimpanzees cited in this chapter.

Site	Country	Habitat	Provisioned?	Authors
Budongo	Uganda	Forest	No	Reynolds and Reynolds 1965; Suzuki 1971; Sugiyama 1972
Gombe	Tanzania	Mixed woodland	Yes	Teleki 1973; Wrangham 1974, 1977; McGrew and Tutin 1978; Goodall et al. 1979; Pusey 1979
Kasoge	Tanzania	Woodland/ forest	Yes	Nishida 1979
Ipassa	Gabon	Forest	Yes	Hladik 1977
Mt. Assirik	Senegal	Savanna	No	McGrew et al. 1980
Okorobiko	Rio Muni	Forest	No	Jones and Sabater Pi 1971

is best to start with the particular. The only invariant association between individuals is that of a mother and her unweaned offspring (Goodall 1968); all other patterns of association are differentially probabilistic. Parties of variable composition form and disperse; they may merge with other parties or split into fragments. These parties may last for minutes, hours, or days. Moreover, during adolescence and adulthood, individuals may spend much of their time alone. Some types of parties are more common than others: adult and subadult males on their own or in association with females in estrus; nursery parties of unrelated mothers and their young offspring; matrifocal parties even after older offspring have reached maturity; a consorting, reclusive party of an adult female and an adult male. Finally, all or most of the individuals known to reside in a given area occasionally come together. This happens only rarely but forms the basis for classification of chimpanzees as a species living in multimale troops (Eisenberg et al. 1972).

Chimpanzees do not form enduring heterosexual bonds, so that offspring are half-siblings through their mother. The average birth interval approaches six years, and weaning coincides with the mother's resumption of sexual cycling after lactational amenorrhea (Clark 1977). Puberty occurs at nine or ten years of age, but offspring continue to associate preferentially with their mothers into adolescence (Pusey 1979). By that stage males spend more time in parties of adult males, and females begin mating with adult males in their natal or adjacent social units. After a period of adolescent infertility, the female first conceives at thirteen or fourteen years of age. Gestation lasts about eight months. Once reproduction begins, a female chimpanzee will spend most of the rest of her life either pregnant or encumbered with dependent offspring (Tutin 1980). There is no evidence of menopause. Males only attain full adult size at the age of about fifteen years. In adulthood, the degree of sexual dimorphism is moderate by comparison with the other primates; males are about 120 percent of the weight of females (Leutenegger 1978). A chimpanzee that survives infancy has a life expectancy of forty to forty-five years.

The preceding summary of the natural history of the chimpanzee is admittedly sketchy and superficial but should serve as a general background for my more detailed treatment of particular topics in which sex differences exist and which are reckoned to be important aspects of human evolution. In the final section, I attempt to interrelate these topics and discuss their implications for the role played by the ancestral female hominid.

Feeding

Chimpanzees are primarily vegetarians, and a population may feed upon as many as 285 species of plants (Hladik 1977). Only a fraction of these are staple foods, however, and an individual eats only fifteen to twenty types of food in an average day (Hladik 1977; Wrangham 1977). All chimpanzees forage independently for plant foods, and no cooperation is necessary at any stage of feeding. No sex differences in the collecting and processing of plant foods have been reported.

Two instances at Gombe of sex difference in activities related to feeding exemplify the importance of the environment and of social relations. The former is reflected in ranging behavior. Females show more limited ranging than males, whether this is measured by mean distance traveled per day or area covered in a year (Wrangham 1979). Moreover, females concentrate their daily activities in individual core areas which are distributed over the males' collective range. The greatest source of variation in females' patterns of ranging is reproductive state: estrous females range more widely than anestrous females. The influence of social relations is reflected in "food-calling": males but not females sometimes broadcast long-range vocalizations to attract other chimpanzees to the food source. Such behavior can be explained in nonaltruistic terms (Wrangham 1977); briefly, males' calling

Figure 1.1. An adult male at Mt. Assirik feeds on figs.

may enhance their attractiveness to females or serve to en-
large or create parties of chimpanzees more likely to prevail
in agonistic encounters between social units (see below).

Chimpanzees also prey upon animals for food, and indica-
tive sex differences exist (see fig. 1.2). Males specialize in
hunting for mammals, and females specialize in gathering social insects (McGrew 1979). Hunting involves the detection,
stalking, pursuit, capture, killing, and eating of mobile prey.
Chimpanzees do all of these, but the technique employed
varies with the species of prey; Teleki (1973) gives detailed
accounts of predatory behaviors. The most commonly eaten
prey are other species of primates, usually arboreal monkeys,

Figure 1.2. An adult male at Gombe feeds on the skull of a red colobus monkey.

which move skillfully through the canopy (Teleki 1975). Successful hunting of these requires speed, agility, and strength, and male chimpanzees make virtually all kills of monkeys. The other general category of prey is the young of ungulates, such as bushpig and bushbuck, which are cached on the ground by the adults and depend on concealment for protection. Female chimpanzees are somewhat more successful in feeding on ungulates than on monkeys, but here also males predominate. Meat is a significant part of the male chimpanzee's diet. At Gombe, two neighboring units of chimpanzees each make about thirty kills per year, so that each individual has an average annual consumption of about ten kilograms of meat (Wrangham 1977). On average, the male chimpanzees studied ate meat about once every two weeks.

Three further aspects of the carnivorous propensities of chimpanzees deserve attention: cooperation in hunting, scavenging, and the effects of provisioning. Teleki (1973) reports that groups of chimpanzees may cooperate actively to bring down prey. The prototypical example is that of chimpanzees dispersing to block the escape routes of a cornered prey, thus increasing the chances of the group capturing the animal when it breaks into flight. The same behavior could be explained as individual chimpanzees seeking to maximize their own chances, however. Busse (1978) recently compared the rates of hunting success of Gombe chimpanzees alone and in groups. Groups show greater success overall, but from the point of view of participating individuals they obtain more meat by hunting alone.

Many predators are also scavengers; that is, they eat the flesh of animals they have not killed. Chimpanzees fall at the minimal extreme, appropriating only fresh-killed prey (i.e., prey that they have seen or heard being killed) in limited numbers from baboons (Morris and Goodall 1977). This forms only a fraction of their intake of meat; they have not been observed to usurp prey from any other species of predator; they ignore carrion and even newly dead prey when the cause of death is unknown to them (Teleki 1973).

Almost all published cases of meat eating by chimpanzees come from populations that have been provisioned (Teleki 1975). Consequently, some critics characterize meat eating as an unnatural distortion of feeding resulting from the behavioral, biochemical, or bioenergetic effects of provisioning (Reynolds 1975; Gaulin and Kurland 1976; de Pelham and Burton 1976). Recent data from the undisturbed and unprovisioned population of wild chimpanzees at Mt. Assirik, however, show levels of meat eating comparable to those of provisioned populations (McGrew et al. 1979*b*).

Both sexes of chimpanzees eat insects, but only two types of social insects make substantial contributions to the diet: termites and ants. All long-term studies of wild chimpanzees that have recorded individual behavior or analyzed the contents of feces have revealed social insects to be a regular component of diet, although the species of prey eaten varies from one population of chimpanzees to another (e.g., McGrew 1974; Nishida 1973). At Ipassa, insects make up about 4 percent of the chimpanzees' food intake throughout the year, although they spend a greater proportional time than this in seeking insects (Hladik 1977). At Gombe, individuals average 3 percent of their waking hours feeding on one species of termite (McGrew 1979). In this case, however, the availability of the termites is highly seasonal, so that in the dry season they eat almost none, while at the onset of the wet season, they eat termites daily. For all cases in which a sex difference in insect eating by chimpanzees has been mentioned, it is females that predominate (McGrew 1979). Fecal analysis at Gombe revealed that 56 percent of samples from female chimpanzees contained at least one type of insect remains, while only 27 percent of male samples did so.

Whereas most mammalian prey are encountered opportunistically while chimpanzees travel through their range many social insect prey occur at fixed points. The chimpanzees periodically monitor these sources, often by set routes from one to the next, whether these be trees containing ants' nests (Nishida 1973) or the mounds of termites (Teleki 1974). Several techniques for obtaining insects involve the use of tools (see below). Feeding on insects involves collecting or gathering: sedentary prey are obtained with a minimal expenditure of energy, as no stalking, chasing, or subduing of prey is necessary. Insect eating is self-paced and can be interrupted; for example, once a chimpanzee has plucked a weaver ants' nest from a tree and rolled it between its palms to crush the inhabitants, it may peel off the leaves and eat the ants inside at its leisure. Competition over insect foods is negligible compared with that over meat (Wrangham 1977).

Food Sharing

Chimpanzees are the only nonhuman primates that regularly share both plant and animal foods, especially among adults. Here, *sharing* is used in its broadest functional sense, that is, the amicable distribution of food among individuals. This ranges from the recipient being allowed to take scraps, to unsolicited donation of food by its possessor. Early reports concentrated on the sharing of meat by chimpanzees after a successful hunt (Goodall 1968; Suzuki 1971; Teleki 1973). The latter two authors diagrammatically detailed the distribution of meat through the group. Typically the possessors of meat were adult males and those seeking to share in it were other adult males and adult females (Teleki 1973). Immature individuals usually receive meat after begging for it from their mothers (see fig. 1.3). Recipients of more than expected amounts of meat are old ("past prime") males, females in estrus, and close kin.

Few natural plant foods are as prized as meat, but

Figure 1.3. An infant male at Kasoge is allowed to take sugar cane from his mother's hand.

provisioning may create conditions that encourage the kind of food sharing seen with meat (Nishida 1970). McGrew (1975) analyzed the extent and direction of the sharing of bananas in the artificial feeding area at Gombe. Sharing within the matrifocal family accounted for 86 percent of the observed cases, although such kin represented only 5 percent of the potential dyadic combinations of donors and recipients. Mothers providing food to offspring accounted for almost all cases. Among nonrelated chimpanzees, the most common pattern of sharing was from adult males to adult females (see fig. 1.4).

Adult chimpanzees rarely share plant foods among themselves (Wrangham 1977). The vast majority of plant food sharing is from mothers to unweaned infants. Silk (1978) showed that the foods most often solicited and shared are

Figure 1.4. An adult male at Gombe gives a banana to an adult female with an infant.

those difficult to procure or prepare. For example, infants cannot open the hard-shelled fruits of *Strychnos* and depend upon cadging pieces from their mothers (McGrew 1975). As infants mature, foods they can process independently cease to be shared, and at the same time, maternal resistance to begging increases (Silk 1978). Such developmental changes in food sharing between mothers and progeny are explicable in terms of a model of parent-offspring conflict over parental investment (Trivers 1974).

Use of Tools

Chimpanzees are the only nonhuman primates which in nature regularly use tools for a variety of purposes (Beck 1975). All wild populations that have been subject to long-term studies show tool use, regardless of the type of habitat in which they live, whether forest (Sabater Pi 1974), woodland (Goodall 1973), or savanna (McGrew et al. 1979*a*). Most tool use by chimpanzees is preceded by toolmaking, that is, the modification of an inanimate object so that it is used more efficiently as a tool (Goodall 1970). This is limited to tools made from plants; lithic tools are used without modification (Rahm 1971; Struhsaker and Hunkeler 1971). Tools that chimpanzees use regularly fall into three functional categories: accessories for feeding and drinking, weapons in agonistic interaction, and aids in bodily hygiene.

The most common type of tool use by wild chimpanzees involves tools that facilitate the acquisition or processing of water or food. Common examples (see figs. 1.5 and 1.6) are probes for obtaining termites, ants, or honey (Goodall 1973; Nishida 1973; McGrew 1974), stones as hammers to smash open tough-skinned fruits (Rahm 1971; Struhsaker and Hunkeler 1971; Boesch 1978), and leaf "sponges" to soak up water in tree holes (Goodall 1968). In some cases, chimpanzees depend on tools to be able to utilize certain resources; for instance, water in narrow tree holes is virtually inaccessible without the use of sponges. Tool use may occupy a significant

Figure 1.5. An adult female at Gombe uses a tool to dip for driver ants.

proportion of feeding time; at the peak of the season, chimpanzees average 10–15 percent of their waking hours in this activity (McGrew 1979). Finally, one further example of tool use in connection with feeding deserves mention, although it has been seen only once. Plooij (1978*b*) saw an old male chimpanzee hurl a large rock during a predatory interaction with bushpigs. It hit an adult pig, and two minutes later the chimpanzees captured a piglet, which they ate.

Figure 1.6. An adult female and her two offspring at Gombe use tools to fish for termites.

In all cases that allow sex differences to be examined, it is females that use tools more commonly in feeding (McGrew 1979). These activities are usually performed quietly at a fixed location. Fishing for termites is the best-documented example. Female chimpanzees fish for termites over three times as frequently as males, whether this is measured in terms of frequency or cumulative duration of bouts of fishing. Furthermore, females feed on termites in all months of the year, whereas males do not; and in all months of the year, females' totals exceed males'.

In contrast, male chimpanzees predominate in the use of weapons. This takes several forms: boughs dropped from trees, logs dragged or stones rolled during charging displays, sticks and rocks brandished toward adversaries, sticks drummed against buttresses of trees or clubbed against other chimpanzees during high excitement, attached branches or saplings whipped against others, objects thrown with and without aiming at living targets (Goodall 1970). These activities are usually performed vigorously, often while moving bipedally. Goodall (1968) presented quantitative data on aimed throwing at targets. Male chimpanzees performed all forty-four cases of this behavior, which was directed at other chimpanzees, baboons, humans, and a monitor lizard. Of the objects thrown, 66 percent were stones.

Wild chimpanzees use parts of plants, especially leaves, to wipe clean their bodies of foreign substances such as blood, feces, urine, sap, and semen (Goodall 1970). Such tool use is almost always directed to the self rather than to others. No data on sex differences in this type of tool use have been presented.

Sex

Early reports from field studies indicated that chimpanzees mated promiscuously; that is, that males did not compete with one another for access to receptive females, nor did females exercise choice over which males they accepted (see the review in Tutin 1980). Such a system of random mating would be exceptional among primates, and later results from longer-term studies altered this picture (Tutin 1980). Before going on to discuss the mating systems of wild chimpanzees, the physiological and demographic factors that underlie sexual behavior require mention.

In all mammalian species, the female sex places limitations on reproduction. Mammals have invested heavily, in evolutionary terms, in a system that entails prolonged gestation leading to altricial young which are dependent on a sole food, milk, produced only by the mammary glands of females that have been primed suitably by hormones. Higher primates added even more restrictive features to this: they produce

only one offspring at a time, which must be carried constantly. In chimpanzees, the trend is taken even further: reproductive maturity is delayed, postpubertal infertility is
prolonged, as are the lengths of gestation and lactation (and
therefore the interval between births). Following birth,
females are solely responsible for childrearing, with no direct
help from adult males. The combined effect of all these factors is a limited reproductive potential: the typical chimpanzee female bears no more than five living offspring (Tutin
1980). Given such restrictions, it would be surprising if sexual
selection had not produced a mating system in which female
choice of mates played an important part (Trivers 1972; Short
1979).

In contrast, male chimpanzees are little constrained by
physiology: the production of spermatozoa continues from
puberty until death. Their only direct contribution to reproduction is fertilization. From the males' point of view, the
limiting factor is availability of impregnable females. Given
the small size of the social unit of chimpanzees, the average
male in his lifespan would be expected to achieve only a few
impregnations (Tutin 1980). Any actual gain on this could
only be achieved at the expense of other males, that is,
through male-male competition, which is the other fact of
sexual selection (Tutin 1979).

Only two long-term studies of reproduction have been
done, on the provisioned populations of Gombe and Kasoge
(Goodall 1975; Nishida 1979). However, one can draw certain
generalizations about mating patterns. Most copulations
occur in *opportunistic* mating, with males rarely competing
overtly for access to sexually cycling females. Such sexual
free-for-alls in which several males may mate in close succession with the same female are conspicuous, and it is not surprising that earlier observers accepted them as the norm.
Fewer copulations occur when a male shows *possessive* behavior toward a female in estrus. Such a male seeks to
monopolize mating with her by excluding other males. He
does this by remaining close to her and interrupting the

courtship of other males. Since male chimpanzees in a social unit show a hierarchy of dominance (Bygott 1979), this pattern of mating is only useful to the highest-ranking male (Nishida 1979). Even fewer copulations occur in the third pattern of mating, *consortships*. An adult male and an adult female (plus her dependent offspring) seclude themselves from other chimpanzees of the social unit. They travel to the edge of the unit's range and actively avoid others, remaining away for as long as twenty-eight days. Tutin (1979) provided details on the three mating patterns and outlined the costs and benefits to both sexes of engaging in them.

The reasons for these differing patterns of mating may be sought in data on conceptions, for evolution acts through genes successfully passed on, not through attempts to do so. Tutin (1979) found that 50 percent of the impregnations leading to live births occurred during consortships, although these accounted for only 2 percent of the observed copulations. In consorting, the female has the greatest choice of which male is to father her progeny, since consorting is a collaborative enterprise. That is, no estrous female can be forced to leave a party of males. In contrast, if she remains in such a party, she is subject to coercion by the dominant male, who can discourage other suitors by acting possessively. In the absence of consorting or possessiveness, even opportunistic mating is of use to the female, since associating with many males provides information on their fitness during periods when she is unlikely or unable to be impregnated, for example, during adolescent sterility or postconception mating.

From the male's point of view, the choice of mating pattern seems to be a function of stages of his life history (Tutin 1980). The benefits of possessiveness to the dominant male are obvious: he can maintain nearly exclusive copulatory rights to a female while remaining in the center of social interaction within the unit. For subdominant males in their prime, consorting seems the best tactic, although it is likely to succeed only infrequently. For adolescent and old males, opportunistic mating seems to be the only choice, since females tend to refrain from consorting with them. The frequency of all patterns is probabilistic; it depends on the number of females in estrus at once.

Such may be the ultimate, evolutionary explanations for sexual behavior in chimpanzees, but causal features of day-to-day sexual interaction are also discernible. Individuals show preferences or aversions toward sexual partners (Tutin 1979). Females prefer males who associate with them in parties, who groom them, and who share food with them (see fig. 1.7). Both sexes avoid mating with close kin (Pusey 1980). Matings between mothers and their mature sons are rare, only one case being known. Sisters avoid being mated by their brothers. Paternity apparently is unknown, but daughters usually are not available to their fathers at times when impregnations could occur (see below). Finally, differences exist in rates of copulation which probably reflect long-standing relationships between individuals (Hinde 1975). Such differences can exist because males vary in motivation to mate with particular females—for example, preferring older ones—but most result from differences in compliance by females with certain males. Tutin (1979) showed that 86 percent of incomplete copulatory sequences resulted from female avoidance or lack of responsiveness.

Social Structure

Does a social organization as apparently amorphous as that of chimpanzees have any enduring integrity? Answers to this question come from recent long-term data on ranging behavior and patterns of association between identifiable individuals. Wrangham (1979) showed that a group of adult males, who are probably genetically interrelated, cooperate to control an area which constitutes their collective range. The males show a linear hierarchy of dominance which is strongly affected by kinship ties (Riss and Goodall 1977; Bygott 1979). The males' range overlaps a number of individual ranges of adult females and their offspring. The females, who may be

Figure 1.7. An adult female and an adult male at Kasoge engage in mutual grooming. The grooming-handclasp pattern is a social custom found only in this population.

unrelated to each other, do not maintain exclusive ranges, and competition rather than cooperation exists between matrilines. The coincidence in space of the two sexes results in a social unit, which may be stable over time. However, as the range of the group of adult males expands or contracts, so will the number of female core areas encompassed. From the males' point of view, a successful social unit is one in which the ratio of postpubertal females to males increases. From the females' point of view, the composition of the social unit is less important than other social factors such as population density and its effect on food resources.

At Kasoge, regular seasonal oscillations in ranging patterns occur (Kawanaka and Nishida 1975). This means greater integrity for the males, which migrate together, but lesser integrity for the females, which do not always migrate with them. If a female's range lies in the seasonal overlap zone between neighboring units, she may be part of different social units at different times of year (Nishida 1979). At Budongo, chimpanzees exist in large "regional populations" which apparently never congregate at a single place at once (Reynolds and Reynolds 1965; Sugiyama 1972, 1973). In what sense this regional population represents a social unit is unclear, as no systematic data on patterns of individual associations have been presented.

In relations between social units the pattern seems to be that the more integrated the unit, the more antagonistic the interactions between units. At Gombe, parties of males patrol the boundaries of the collective range (Wrangham 1979). They give loud calls, which increase in frequency with the size of the party and which may serve to repel outsiders (Bygott 1979). If strangers intrude, they may be attacked, killed, and, in the case of infants, eaten (Suzuki 1971; Bygott 1972). Such territorial defense may spill over into incursions into neighboring ranges which result in fatalities (Goodall et al. 1979). Eventually, the larger unit of males at Gombe exterminated the neighboring males and extended their range to include that of the defunct unit (Goodall 1977).

At Kasoge, annual shifts in range occur when the bigger unit displaces the smaller and gains access to seasonal food sources (Kawanaka and Nishida 1975). Separation of the units is achieved by exchanges of loud calls, but when contact occurs, fighting may ensue. At Budongo, interunit relationships are unclear, but antagonism seems to be absent. Members of different populations may travel and feed together temporarily, although such meetings are characterized by higher than normal levels of excitement and tension (Sugiyama 1972, 1973).

Whatever the extent of xenophobia present in different populations of chimpanzees, exchanges of individuals (and genes) occur. Unlike almost all other species of higher primates, however, it is the female chimpanzees that migrate, not the males (Nishida 1979; Pusey 1979). Female chimpanzees begin to emigrate at adolescence and may continue into adulthood, when they are accompanied by offspring. Such migration may be temporary or permanent. The genetic advantages of outbreeding are assumed here, especially for units of the small size of chimpanzees, but a further advantage results from female as opposed to male emigration. In a species in which paternity is unknown, incest avoidance is more efficient if the female migrates, thereby precluding inadvertent father-daughter matings. Mother-son and brother-sister kinship are established through familiarity in the enduring relationships of a matriline.

Finally, sex differences exist within the social unit of chimpanzees in response to immigrants (Pusey 1979). Males usually behave solicitously toward female newcomers and may protect them from the hostility of resident females. The latter are less accommodating and initially resist the entry of the newcomers with threats and even attacks. This resistance may continue in the form of direct and indirect competition between matrilines. At Gombe, one female and her adolescent daughter seem to have taken this to its logical extreme. They kidnap and sometimes eat the young infants of other females (Goodall 1977). As might be expected, persecuted females sometimes seek and receive protection from the unit's males.

Possible Implications for Human Evolution

Evolution as a continuum is difficult to conceptualize. There is a tendency to pick out obvious points and to erect a complex of features about them, thus creating stages and thresholds.

I shall try to avoid this here. Instead, I shall discuss possible changes in particular aspects of the overall system described above for the chimpanzee as representative of an ancestral Pliocene hominid. Most of the ideas are not new (see especially Tanner and Zihlman 1976 and Zihlman and Tanner 1978) but most have been tempered or refined in the light of recent findings on the natural history of chimpanzees. *Although the arguments are speculative, I shall present them definitively, for the sake of convenience.*

The chimpanzee data suggest paths by which the uniquely human pattern of food gathering, transporting, and sharing might have developed from individual feeding. Precursors of the sexual division of labor, which is marked among humans, can be found in the differential involvement of male and female chimpanzees in hunting and termiting and in their different geographical ranges. Likewise, the minimal tool use and limited sharing of chimpanzees suggests how the extensive tool using, carrying, and sharing of humans began. Distinctive features of human families, which include sexual bonding and the assistance of males in childrearing, were made possible by changes in human female physiology, particularly continuous sexual receptivity and the elimination of estrus. The generally antagonistic relations between bands, which present-day chimpanzees exhibit, were supplanted by the sometimes sociable relationships between bands of humans.

The trend toward a sexual division of labor in feeding started from sexual dimorphism and continued to develop in the early hominids. Sexual dimorphism represents a preadaptation if it originally arose as a response to sexual selection or to natural selection on the basis of predator pressure (Dobzhansky et al. 1977). If it arose as a means of allowing the sexes to exploit different ecological niches, then the sexual division of labor, with males hunting and females gathering, represents a continuation of this trend.

Hominid males transferred cooperation already used to patrol and defend a collective home range to the context of hunting. This was of little use for small game, as the small size of shares in a monkey or piglet do not justify the effort of individuals. However, by increasing the size of prey only marginally, that is, from piglets to half-grown pigs or from infant baboons to juvenile baboons, the trend toward big-game hunting was under way. The dental armament of the chimpanzee-like early hominid was sufficient for this. True big-game hunting (i.e., when the body size of the prey exceeds that of a single predator) depends on other factors to be discussed below: food sharing and transport to a semipermanent home base. However, males retained an important advantage over females: in times of poor hunting, they fell back on gathering, while the converse was not the case.

Advances in feeding efficiency among hominid females were intellectual and technological rather than social. Gathering is an essentially individual activity. Intellectual advances were made in the increasing ability to predict, detect, and remember the locations of food sources. Such cognitive maps are especially important in a savanna habitat where seasonality is great and resources are quiescent or absent for most of the year. As ability to generalize about the cycles of prey species grew, so did ability to travel purposefully to feeding sites (rather than to forage opportunistically). For example, tubers are noticeably absent from the chimpanzee's diet, yet the ability to recognize a few shriveled leaves in the dry season as an indication of a hidden tuber below the ground constituted a useful advance. Long-term memory based on topographic cues permitted more efficient use of limited resources such as surface water in the dry season. Such knowledge increasingly became the province of the female hominid. Communication of such knowledge, which is absent in chimpanzees (Plooij 1978a), had obvious advantages, starting with the basic gesture of pointing to indicate direction.

Technological advances were of two types: increased use of tools (see below) and more efficient food acquisition and processing. Examples of the latter are washing foods, such as soil-encrusted rhizomes, or digging and cleaning out seepage scrapes in dry watercourses for drinking. Another opportunity came from the annual fires that swept savanna areas. These fortuitously roast both plants and animals and may render them more accessible or edible. Fire *making* came later, but chimpanzees comprehend adequately the *use* of fire (Brink 1957).

Sex differences in ranging increased, as all-male parties roamed wider in hunting, and females and offspring concentrated on efficient extraction of resources from a limited, well-known area. Such separation of the sexes is only feasible if they can find each other again. Rendezvous need not require symbolic communication, for in savanna environments few suitable sites exist for home bases. In open habitats, chimpanzees have little choice of nesting sites in the dry season; they return again and again to the few areas of evergreen forest. Limited supplies of drinking water similarly influence ranging; in the dry season, early hominids drank only at the beginning and end of the day at the same sources near safe sleeping sites. Such comings and goings of parties led to increasingly more predictable reunions, until day ranging and return to a temporarily favored site led to overnight forays and return to a fixed seasonal site.

Scavenging was not of evolutionary importance for hominids. It is too risky for a basically vegetarian form. An obvious hazard came from competition with large carnivores, which is successful only with relatively sophisticated weapons. Early hominids might have occasionally attempted to pilfer the kills of predators such as canids and hyenids which could not pursue them into the trees. Such interest provided opportunities for imitation of successful adaptations in social carnivores (Kühme 1965). Another form of scavenging was parasitization of the accumulated labors of other animals. The best example is the raiding of bees' nests for honey, but fungus-growing termites or seed-storing ants were also exploited.

Significant advances in subsistence occurred when the activity of feeding became mediated by social relationships and tool use (Zihlman and Tanner 1978). The difference is crucial: when an individual gathers and eats food only for herself, social interactions influence the behavior. When individuals collect foods which they transport and exchange later with others, social relationships become paramount (Isaac 1978). Males can afford to invest time and energy beyond a certain point only if they can count on collected food from females being available when they return empty-handed. In this sense, females were the facultative sex, and in the tropics male big-game hunting relied on female gathering, rather than vice versa. An important advance occurred when mothers continued to share food with offspring after weaning. This led to sharing among matrilines and eventually enabled food to be distributed in the reverse direction, from offspring to parent. Such reciprocity allowed younger individuals to profit from the accumulated knowledge of elders who otherwise would not have survived. A key development in familial food sharing was when adult sons exchanged food with their mothers. This generalized to unrelated females, that is, potential reproductive partners. Food sharing between siblings, especially brothers, also extended from the matriline to cement male-male solidarity as the basis for the band. Female gathering, not male hunting, which later developed from it, provided the evolutionary basis for exchange of food (Zihlman and Tanner 1978).

Accumulation of food on a short-term or long-term basis requires containers (Tanner and Zihlman 1976). The first step was to make use of natural containers, such as the dry pods produced by many trees of the savanna which contain seeds with concentrated protein stores (Janzen 1975). These tough-shelled pods (e.g., of *Adansonia digitata*, the baobab) discourage consumption by animals. (This contrasts with the brightly colored fleshy fruits of the forest, which are meant to be eaten by animals for dispersion of the seeds.) Such dry savanna fruits remain intact and resist microbial invasion and so may remain edible for weeks (Janzen 1977). Containers were one problem; transport was another. Initially, branches bearing fruits were slung over shoulders and carried tripedally. Eventual bipedalism doubled the possible load. A bigger advance was the invention of containers in which only seeds (and not the bulkier fruits and branches) could be hoarded. Chimpanzees normally discard the skins of mammalian prey, but early hominids used these skins for the first bags or slings. The female hominid probably invented such containers. Most of the foods she gathered could not be easily slung over poles or shoulders as could the male's game. She also had the problem of child carrying, and a sling answered two purposes: it could help carry the baby or it could hold gathered foods. Containers for transport eventually led to containers for storage, and then for processing or cooking. Because animal foods spoil so quickly in the tropics (i.e., cannot be stored without curing), hunting males did not need to store their contribution.

Chimpanzee females make and use tools for food gathering more than males do. Among contemporary hunters and gatherers the most basic tool is the woman's simple one-part digging stick. In the Pliocene the first tools used by hominids were likely to have been invented by gathering females. While males were still hunting small game successfully without tools, females were using a tool kit to obtain (as in fishing for termites) and to prepare (as in smashing hard-shelled fruits) gathered foods (Zihlman 1978). Most tools were of perishable raw materials such as parts of plants; other, nonperishable tools, such as stones, were unmodified natural objects (cf. "naturefacts," Oswalt 1973). Such early tools left no archaeological record, but flaked lithic technology was built on this earlier, simpler form. Interpretations that align the origins of tool use with hunting are one-sided; for example, hammer stones function just as well in the breaking open of fruits as in the smashing of bones (McGrew 1979).

Tool use advanced as part of adaptation to more open savanna habitats. An example of this was the digging stick, which allows subterranean access to roots, egg caches of rep-

"Hey! Come back here with my lazy Susan!"

Figure 1.8. Sex differences in early hominid technology.
Drawing by Handelsman; © 1974 The New Yorker
Magazine, Inc.

tiles, social insects, small burrowing mammals, and so on.
Having nails instead of claws, living nonhuman primates are
otherwise ill-adapted for digging. Further advances required
no quantum leaps in intellectual capacity. Use of a tool to
make another tool is only a step beyond detaching twigs which
are then used to construct a sleeping platform, which chimpanzees do regularly (Goodall 1968). The trend accelerated
as reductions in dentition and craniofacial musculature pro-
ceeded in parallel. Reuse of tools at suitable sites—for example, natural anvils near food sources (e.g., Struhsaker and
Hunkeler 1971)—led to tools being retained rather than
abandoned after the first use. Two factors encouraged this:

scarcity of appropriate tool materials and increased investment of time and energy in tool manufacture. The development of more than a transitory set of possessions was dependent upon the rise of bipedalism and the invention of
containers, which together enable tools to be carried while
foraging. Finally, the use and manufacture of *implements* led
to *facilities*. According to Oswalt (1973) the critical distinction
between the two is that of the direct versus indirect application of energy by the user. Implements physically impinge
upon objects; facilities attract, restrain, and redirect living
masses. Wild chimpanzees occasionally use facilities (Nishida
1973; McGrew 1974) but rely upon implements. Many early
hominid facilities, such as pitfalls, lures, hides, barriers, and
windbreaks, are direct extensions of fortuitous natural features such as overlooks, salt licks, water holes, and rock
fissures. All of these advances in tool use seem more likely to
have evolved from female gathering than from male hunting,
because the former is a deliberate, predictable activity which
occurs daily. It provides the grounds for slight trial-and-error
modifications which accumulate to form cultural innovation.

Sexual dimorphism is another way of saying that "might
makes right" in the battle of the sexes. A positive correlation
exists between polygyny and degree of sexual dimorphism in
body size in living primates (Leutenegger 1978). This has
been extrapolated to australopithecines (Leutenegger 1977).
Little alteration was necessary in chimpanzee-like mating
systems to produce a system of sexual bonding in which some
males had more than one female, others had only one, and
others had none. To explain this in terms of male dominance,
however, would be misleading. The essential element was
female choice. The early hominid female in the tropics was
economically independent and free to move in or out of association with groups of males.

Why did females sexually bond themselves to males at all?
This occurred only when males were willing to assist selectively in childrearing. Male assistance took the form of pref-
erential sharing of meat as the hunting of larger prey de-

veloped, or of providing specific protection to a female's offspring. These forms of assistance developed from haphazard sharing and general protection of all young. In the early stages, exceptional males attracted several mates and others none. As the genetical and cultural attributes spread among successive generations of males, the variation between individuals in degrees of paternal contribution leveled out, and monogamy increased in frequency. Menopause was an adaptation to the greater advantage served by older females' transferring caretaking to grandchildren rather than continuing to risk orphaning infants born after their middle age. Later, it enabled females to continue into old age bonds with males who could no longer provide meat and protection. The selective shaping process also acted upon immature males, as females became more discriminating. For the males, adolescence became even more a matter of proving fitness, not just to the older collective of males but to females as prospective mates. Such testing was a precursor to the eventual ritualization of initiation rites. Finally, with the advent of sexual bonding, the avoidance of inbreeding focused on the nuclear family and led eventually to increasingly stringent aversion to incest.

Of the proximal mechanisms that enabled these evolutionary elaborations, many of the neuroendocrine bases of female reproduction remained basically the same; for example, adolescent infertility or lactational amenorrhea. Two linked developments occurred, however, which had considerable repercussions: continuous female sexual receptivity and elimination of morphological signals of ovulation. Chimpanzee males can ignore females except at the stage of maximal perineal tumescence and receptiveness which predictably accompanies ovulation. Hominid females evolutionarily divested themselves of cyclical estrus and perineal swelling and color change, and thus coerced constant attention from their mates. (The sole remaining dependable signal of reproductive cyclicity, menstrual bleeding, assumed disproportionate significance to both sexes.) The evolutionary origins of the

feminine mystique lie in the burden of uncertainty (i.e., potential cuckoldry) foisted onto hominid males by the females.

Of all the living species of nonhuman primates, only chimpanzees show a social structure based on enduring male-male
relationships. In all other species with multimale/multifemale
basic social units, males emigrate from their natal troops,
which are based on matrilines. In early hominids, these
male-male relationships strengthened to bonds (Tiger 1969).
Correspondingly, female-female relationships were limited
by the practice of female emigration, which eventually led to
ritualized exchange of females between neighboring male
bands. This female migration prevents long-term matrilines
of mothers, aunts, daughters, granddaughters, and so on,
from forming but puts a premium on relationships between a
mother and her sons. An adult female who early in her reproductive life produced consecutive sons that survived to
adulthood could be expected to exercise considerable
influence in the band. (At Gombe, each of the five dominant
[alpha] chimpanzee males was known or strongly suspected to
have had an immediately older brother who assisted his
younger sib in the rise to dominance.)

As in chimpanzees, relations between bands of early
hominids were mutually antagonistic, but like chimpanzees
the degree of hostility varied tremendously according to environmental circumstances. Where resources were highly seasonal and variable from year to year, neighboring bands were
forced periodically to share them, whether these were water
holes or fruiting groves. These enforced, transitory contacts
between bands were mediated by residual kinship ties, the
foundations of which were laid in the long period of matrifocal childhood and adolescence. If local population densi-
ties rose and threatened to exceed the carrying capacities of
the habitat, hostility between bands increased, usually in the
form of mutual avoidance. Exceptionally, in extreme conditions, bands warred, and weaker ones perished or were incorporated into stronger ones. With such small units, however, warfare was only a last resort, since only one or two
fatalities or serious injuries could alter drastically the viability

and integrity of the unit. In any case, some basis for exchange of females was maintained, as no band could cut itself from others and endure. Normally, the ties of female kinship between neighboring bands, whether between mother and daughter or brother and sister, served to maintain sociable if uneasy relations.

The arguments in the preceding speculative exercise may stimulate as many disagreements as there are readers to consider them. I can only hope that readers will agree, however, on the usefulness of recent findings on the chimpanzee in nature. Field studies of chimpanzees have much yet to reveal, but it is a race against time. The rate of destruction of wild populations of chimpanzees and the habitats in which they live is accelerating, and they have virtually disappeared from many regions in Africa. If the chimpanzee represents a valuable source of knowledge applicable to the unanswered questions of human evolution, it is up to the anthropologist to join in efforts to preserve it.

Acknowledgments

The author thanks P. J. Baldwin for critical comments on the manuscript and C. E. G. Tutin for stimulating discussions and photographs. The New Yorker Magazine, Inc., granted permission for the cartoon.

For financial support of field research in Africa on chimpanzees, grateful acknowledgment is made to the American Philosophical Society, Carnegie Trust for the Universities of Scotland, Grant Foundation, L. S. B. Leakey Foundation, Royal Zoological Society of Scotland, Science Research Council, and Wenner-Gren Foundation for Anthropological Research.

References

Beck, B. B. 1975. Primate tool behavior. In *Socioecology and psychology of primates*, ed. Russell H. Tuttle, pp. 413–47. The Hague: Mouton.

Boesch, C. 1978. Nouvelles observations sur les chimpanzés de la forêt de Tai (Côte d'Ivoire). *Terre et Vie* 32:195–201.

Brink, A. S. 1957. The spontaneous fire-controlling reactions of two chimpanzee smoking addicts. *South African Journal of Science* 53:241–47.

Busse, Curt D. 1978. Do chimpanzees hunt cooperatively? *American Naturalist* 112:767–70.

Bygott, J. D. 1972. Cannibalism among wild chimpanzees. *Nature* 238:410–11.

————. 1979. Agonistic behavior, dominance and social structure in wild chimpanzees of the Gombe National Park. In *The great apes*, ed. David A. Hamburg and Elizabeth R. McCown. Menlo Park, Calif.: Benjamin/Cummings.

Clark, Cathleen B. 1977. A preliminary report on weaning among chimpanzees of the Gombe National Park, Tanzania. In *Primate bio-social development*, ed. Suzanne Chevalier-Skolnikoff and Frank E. Poirier, pp. 235–60. New York: Garland.

Clutton-Brock, T. H., and P. H. Harvey. 1976. Evolutionary rules and primate societies. In *Growing points in ethology*, ed. P. P. G. Bateson and Robert A. Hinde, pp. 195–237. Cambridge: Cambridge University Press.

Dobzhansky, Theodosius, Francisco J. Ayala, G. Ledyard Stebbins, and James W. Valentine. 1977. *Evolution*. San Francisco: W. H. Freeman.

Dunbar, R. I. M. 1976. Australopithecine diet based on a baboon analogy. *Journal of Human Evolution* 5:161–67.

Eisenberg, J. F., N. A. Muckenhirn, and R. Rudran. 1972. The relation between ecology and social structure in primates. *Science* 176:863–74.

Gallup, Gordon G., Jr. 1977. Self-recognition in primates. A comparative approach to the bidirectional properties of consciousness. *American Psychologist* 32:329–38.

Gaulin, Steven J. C., and M. Konner. 1977. On the natural diet of primates, including humans. In *Nutrition and the brain*, vol. 1, ed. Richard J. Wurtman and Judith J. Wurtman, pp. 1–86. New York: Raven Press.

Gaulin, Steven J. C., and Jeffrey A. Kurland. 1976. Primate predation and bioenergetics. *Science* 191:314–15.

Goodall, Jane van Lawick-. 1968. The behavior of free-ranging chimpanzees in the Gombe Stream Reserve. *Animal Behavior Monographs* 1:161–311.

————. 1970. Tool-using in primates and other vertebrates. *Advanced Studies of Behavior* 3:195–249.

————.1973. Cultural elements in a chimpanzee community. In *Precultural primate behavior*, ed. E. W. Menzel, pp. 144–84. Basel: Karger.

————. 1975. The chimpanzee. In *The quest for man.*, ed. V. Goodall, pp. 130–69. London: Phaidon.

————. 1976. Continuities between chimpanzee and human behavior. In *Human origins,* ed. Glynn Isaac and E. R. McCown, pp. 80–95. Menlo Park, Calif.: W. A. Benjamin.

————. 1977. Infant killing and cannibalism in free-living chimpanzees. *Folio Primatologica* 28:259–82.

Goodall, Jane, and David A. Hamburg. 1974. Chimpanzee behavior as a model for the behavior of early man. New evidence on possible origins of human behavior. *American Handbook of Psychiatry* 6:14–43.

Goodall, Jane, A. Bandora, E. Bergmann, C. Busse, H. Matama, E. Mpongo, A. Pierce, and D. Riss. 1979. Inter-community interactions of the chimpanzee population of the Gombe National Park. In *The great apes,* ed. David A. Hamburg and Elizabeth R. McCown, pp. 13–53. Menlo Park, Calif.: Benjamin/Cummings.

Hinde, Robert A. 1975. Interactions, relationships and social structure in non-human primates. Symposium 5th Congress of the International Primatology Society, pp. 13–24.

Hladik, C. M. 1977. Chimpanzees of Gabon and chimpanzees of Gombe: some comparative data on the diet. In *Primate ecology,* ed. T. H. Clutton-Brock, pp. 481–501. London: Academic Press.

Isaac, Glynn L. 1978. The food-sharing behavior of protohuman hominids. *Scientific American* 238(4):90–108.

Janzen, Daniel H. 1975. *Ecology of plants in the tropics.* London: Edward Arnold.

————. 1977. Why fruits rot, seeds mold, and meat spoils. *American Naturalist* 111:691–713.

Jolly, Clifford H. 1970. The seed-eaters: a new model of hominid differentiation based on a baboon ecology. *Man* 5:5–26.

Jones, C., and Jorge Sabater Pi. 1971. Comparative ecology—*Gorilla gorilla* (Savage and Wyman) and *Pan troglodytes* (Blumenbach) in Rio Muni, West Africa. *Bibliography Primatology* 13:1–96.

Kawanaka, K., and T. Nishida. 1975. Recent advances in the study of inter-unit-group relationships and social structure of wild chimpanzees of the Mahali Mountains. Symposium 5th Congress of the International Primatology Society, pp. 173–86.

King, Mary-Claire, and A. C. Wilson. 1975. Evolution at two levels in humans and chimpanzees. *Science* 188:107–16.

Kühme, Wolfdietrich. 1965. Communal food distribution and division of labour in African hunting dogs. *Nature* 205:443–44.

Lancaster, Jane B. 1976. Sex roles in primate societies. In *Sex differences*, ed. Michael S. Teitelbaum, pp. 22–61. Garden City, N.Y.: Anchor Press.

———. 1978. Sex and gender in evolutionary perspective. In *Human sexuality*, ed. Herant Katchadourian, pp. 51–80. Berkeley, Calif.: University of California Press.

Leutenegger, Walter. 1977. Sociobiological correlates of sexual dimorphism in body weight in South African australopiths. *South African Journal of Science* 73:143–44.

———. 1978. Scaling of sexual dimorphism in body size and breeding system in primates. *Nature* 272:610–11.

Linden, Eugene. 1974. *Apes, men and language.* New York: Penguin.

McGrew, W. C. 1974. Tool use by child chimpanzees in feeding upon driver ants. *Journal of Human Evolution* 3:501–08.

———. 1975. Patterns of plant food sharing by wild chimpanzees. In *Contemporary primatology*, ed. S. Kondo, M. Kawai, and A. Ehara, pp. 304–09. Basel: Karger.

———. 1979. Evolutionary implications of sex differences in chimpanzee predation and tool use. In *The great apes*, ed. David A. Hamburg and Elizabeth R. McCown, pp. 440–63. Menlo Park, Calif.: Benjamin/Cummings.

McGrew, W. C., and C. E. G. Tutin. 1978. Evidence for a social custom in wild chimpanzees? *Man* 13:234–51.

McGrew, W. C., C. E. G. Tutin, and P. J. Baldwin, 1979*a*. Chimpanzees, tools, and termites: cross-cultural comparisons of Senegal, Tanzania, and Rio Muni. *Man* 14:185–214.

McGrew, W. C., C. E. G. Tutin, and P. J. Baldwin. 1979*b*. New data on meat-eating by wild chimpanzees. *Current Anthropology* 20:238–39.

McGrew, W. C., P. J. Baldwin, and C. E. G. Tutin. 1980. Chimpanzees in a hot, dry, and open habitat: Mt. Assirik, Senegal, West Africa. *Journal of Human Evolution* 9.

Miller, Dorothy. 1977. Evolution of primate chromosomes. *Science* 198:1116–24.

Milton, Katherine, and Michael L. May. 1976. Body weight, diet and home range area in primates. *Nature* 259:459–62.

Morris, Kathryn, and Jane Goodall. 1977. Competition for meat between chimpanzees and baboons of the Gombe National Park. *Folia Primatologica* 28:102–21.

Nishida, Toshida. 1970. Social behavior and relationships among wild chimpanzees of the Mahali Mountains. *Primates* 11:47–87.

———. 1973. The ant gathering behavior by the use of tools among wild chimpanzees of the Mahali Mountains. *Journal of Human Evolution* 2:357–70.

———. 1979. The social structure of chimpanzees of the Mahali Mountains. In *The great apes*, ed. David A. Hamburg and Elizabeth R. McCown, pp. 72–121. Menlo Park, Calif.: Benjamin/Cummings.

Oswalt,Wendell H. 1973. *Habitat and technology*. New York: Holt, Rinehart and Winston.

De Pelham, Alison, and Frances D. Burton. 1976. More on predatory behavior in nonhuman primates. *Current Anthropology* 17: 512–13.

Plooij, F. X. 1978a. Some basic traits of language in wild chimpanzees? In *Action, gesture and symbol: the emergence of language*, ed. A. Lock. pp. 111–31. London: Academic Press.

———. 1978b. Tool-use during chimpanzees' bushpig hunt. *Carnivore* 1:103–06.

Pusey, Anne E. 1979. Intercommunity transfer of chimpanzees in Gombe National Park. In *The great apes*, ed. David A. Hamburg and Elizabeth R. McCown, pp. 464–79. Menlo Park, Calif.: Benjamin/Cummings.

———. 1980. Inbreeding avoidance in chimpanzees. *Animal Behavior* 28:543-52.

Rahm, U. 1971. L'emploi d'outils par les chimpanzés de l'ouest de la Côte d'Ivoire. *Terre et Vie* 25:506–09.

Reynolds, Vernon. 1975. How wild are the Gombe chimpanzees? *Man* 10:123–25.

———. 1976. *The biology of human action*. San Francisco: W. H. Freeman.

Reynolds, Vernon, and Frances Reynolds. 1965. Chimpanzees of the Budongo Forest. In *Primate behavior*, ed. Irven DeVore, pp. 363–424. New York: Holt, Rinehart and Winston.

Riss, David C., and Jane Goodall. 1977. The recent rise to the alpha-rank in a population of free-living chimpanzees. *Folia Primatologica* 27:134–51.

Sabater Pi, Jorge. 1974. An elementary industry of the chimpanzee in the Okorobiko Mountains, Rio Muni (Republic of Equatorial Guinea), West Africa. *Primates* 15:351–64.

Short, R. V. 1979. Sexual selection and its component parts, somatic and genital selection, as illustrated by man and the great apes. *Advanced Studies in Behavior* 9:131–58.

Silk, Joan B. 1978. Patterns of food sharing among mother and infant chimpanzees at Gombe National Park, Tanzania. *Folia Primatologica* 29:129–41.

Struhsaker, T. T., and P. Hunkeler. 1971. Evidence of tool-using by chimpanzees in the Ivory Coast. *Folia Primatologica* 15:212–19.

Sugiyama, Yukimara. 1972. Social characteristics and socialization of wild chimpanzees. In *Primate socialization,* ed. Frank E. Poirier, pp. 145–63. New York: Random House.

———. 1973. The social structure of wild chimpanzees: a review of field studies. In *Comparative ecology and behavior of primates,* ed. Richard P. Michael and John H. Crook, pp. 375–410. New York: Random House.

Suzuki, A. 1971. Carnivority and cannibalism observed among forest living chimpanzees. *Journal Anthropological Society of Nippon* 70:30–48.

Tanner, Nancy, and Adrienne Zihlman. 1976. Women in evolution. Part I: Innovation and selection in human origins. *Signs: Journal of Women in Culture and Society* 1:585–608.

Teleki, Geza. 1973. *The predatory behavior of wild chimpanzees.* Lewisburg, Pa.: Bucknell University Press.

———. 1974. Chimpanzee subsistence technology: materials and skills. *Journal of Human Evolution* 3:575–94.

———. 1975. Primate subsistence patterns: collector-predators and gatherer-hunters. *Journal of Human Evolution* 4:125–84.

Tiger, Lionel. 1969. *Men in groups.* New York: Vintage Books.

Trivers, Robert L. 1972. Parental investment and sexual selection. In *Sexual selection and the descent of man 1871–1971,* ed. Bernard Campbell, pp. 136–79. Chicago: Aldine.

———. 1974. Parent-offspring conflict. *American Zoologist* 14: 249–64.

Tutin, Caroline E. G. 1979. Mating patterns and reproductive strategies in a community of wild chimpanzees (*Pan troglodytes schweinfurthii*). *Behavioral Ecology and Sociobiology* 6:29–38.

————. 1980. Reproductive behavior of wild chimpanzees in the Gombe National Park, Tanzania. *Journal of Reproductive Fertility,* Supplement 28. In press.

Washburn, Sherwood, and Irven DeVore. 1963. Social behavior of baboons and early man. In *Social life of early man,* ed. S. L. Washburn, pp. 91–105. Chicago: Aldine.

Wrangham, Richard W. 1974. Artificial feeding of chimpanzees and baboons in their natural habitat. *Animal Behavior* 22:83–93.

————. 1977. Feeding behavior of chimpanzees in Gombe National Park, Tanzania. In *Primate ecology,* ed. T. H. Clutton-Brock, pp. 503–38. London: Academic Press.

————. 1979. On the evolution of ape social systems. *Social Science Information* 18:335–68.

Zihlman, Adrienne L. 1978. Women and evolution. Part II: Subsistence and social organization among early hominids. *Signs: Journal of Women in Culture and Society* 4:4–20.

Zihlman, Adrienne L., and Nancy Tanner. 1978. Gathering and the hominid adaptation. In *Female hierarchies,* ed. Lionel Tiger and Heather Fowler, pp. 163–94. Chicago: Beresford Book Service.

2 WOMEN AS SHAPERS OF THE HUMAN ADAPTATION
Adrienne L. Zihlman

Fossil discoveries in Africa provide evidence that the earliest
hominids lived on the savannas as long as 3.5 million years
ago, that they were about the size of chimpanzees with somewhat larger brains, that they walked upright, and that they
began making stone tools about two million years ago. What
was their social organization like? From bones and teeth we
can deduce much about locomotion and diet, but it is more
difficult to reconstruct sharing habits, reproductive behavior
and mating patterns, how the young were socialized, and the
roles of males and females in all these activities.

The most popular reconstruction of early human social behavior is summarized in the phrase "man the hunter." In this
hypothesis, meat eating initiated man's separation from the
apes. Males provided the meat, presumed to be the main item
in early hominid diet, by inventing stone tools and weapons
for hunting. Thus males played the major economic role,
were protectors of females and young, and controlled the
mating process. In this view of things, females fade into a
strictly reproductive and passive role—a pattern of behavior
inconsistent with that of other primates or of modern
gathering and hunting peoples. In fact, the obsession with
hunting has long prevented anthropologists from taking a
good look at the probable role of women in shaping the
human adaptation.

Evolutionary success is reproductive success, which of

course makes women's contribution both critical and central. In this chapter, I take a close look at women's and men's roles in influencing early human evolution, using an interpretive framework constructed with detailed knowledge of primate behavior, especially that of our closest living relatives, the chimpanzees, and of the behavior of gathering and hunting peoples. Their life-styles are much nearer to the ancestral one than are the urban hierarchies used by so many anthropologists to "explain" human evolution and behavior. Much of my argument will be based on anatomy, in particular the examination of "sexual dimorphism." Specific female-male differences, detectable in the fossil record, offer clues to the behavior and sex roles of our ancestors who lived millions of years ago and left no other historical record than their own bones and teeth and footprints.

Historical Background: Darwin to E. O. Wilson

Our notions of women's and men's roles in prehistory derive in part from currently perceived differences in status of the sexes. Popular pictures drawn of the past are too often little more than backward projections of cultural sex stereotypes onto humans who lived more than a million years ago. Themes of male aggression, dominance, and hunting have long pervaded reconstructions of early human social life; and this has led to a belief that present-day inequality of the sexes has its roots in an ancient life-style and in inherent biological differences between the sexes.

These views, which this chapter questions, may be better appreciated by noting their historical development. Male concern with male dominance in studies of humans and animals has been integral to past theories of human origins, human nature, and human evolution (Haraway 1978*a,b*). Beginning with Darwin's discussion of human evolution, the theme of male dominance and female passivity and the use of tools as weapons has run through thinking about evolution. The emphasis on hunting, as with male dominance, is an outcome of male bias, however unconscious it may be, and this bias pervades even studies of primate behavior. In Darwin's case, given the values of Western society, especially Victorian England, and the nature of available evidence, his emphasis on males is not surprising. Even so, facts or concepts without the proper theoretical framework are useless, as is well illustrated by E. O. Wilson (1975). His "new synthesis" in *Sociobiology* presents some concepts that are intrinsically pro female (e.g., his ideas on kin and sexual selection). Yet he concludes with a century-old view of human evolution and sex roles that is more like an "old synthetic."

Darwin and Sexual Selection
Darwin and Huxley, over one hundred years ago, first brought human evolution into the scientific realm (Washburn 1968*a*). Darwin provided the mechanism of natural selection to explain evolutionary change. Though he did not comment on human origins in *The Origin of Species* (1859), his closing paragraph indicates that he believed natural selection could "throw light" on the subject. Huxley picked up on the theme soon after and, in his essays on *Evidence as to Man's Place in Nature* (1863), showed how man is, anatomically, closely related to the African apes. Darwin later (1871) built upon Huxley's thesis and offered a behavioral model for human origins; he maintained that evolution occurred in Africa with the human line emerging as the "third ape," differing from gorillas and chimpanzees, and being characterized by bipedalism and tool using, and small canine ("fighting") teeth.

Progressive on the one hand, Darwin split from the scientific orthodoxy of his time in holding that species were not immutable but changed with time through natural selection. But on the other hand, the traditional constraints of Victorian England are apparent in *The Descent of Man and Selection in Relation to Sex*, published in 1871. In this work, Darwin pointed out that sexual selection, as an aspect of natural selection, could explain human secondary sexual characteristics (sexual dimorphism). But there is a curious discrepancy in his argument. When describing the process of sexual selection among all animals save the human species, he not only describes competition among males for females but also stresses the importance of female choice. The secondary sexual characteristics of the males, such as bright coloration, fine plumage, or special vocal qualities, are seen as important to the extent that they are attractive to females:

> The females are most excited by, or prefer pairing with, the more ornamented males, or those which are the best songsters, or play the best antics. . . . Thus the more vigorous females, which are the first to breed, will have the choice of many males. [1871:573]

However, when Darwin approaches the discussion of sexual selection among humans, male choice is now assumed, and it is female beauty which is seen as attracting the male. In accounting for this presumed reversal, he writes:

> Man is more powerful in body and mind than woman, and in the savage state he keeps her in a far more abject stage of bondage than does the male of any other animal; therefore it is not surprising that he should have gained the power of selection. [1871:901]

Darwin was aware of the inconsistency and it worried him. He therefore went on to consider the possibility that female selectivity in choosing mates occurred among our progenitors. Without direct evidence of the sexual practices of the past, he looked to travelers' anecdotes concerning non-Western peoples for evidence as to whether "primitive" women might not exercise somewhat more sexual initiative than the Victorian ladies of his day. He concludes with a cautious affirmative: ". . . for in utterly barbarous tribes the women have more power in choosing, rejecting, and tempting their lovers, or of afterwards changing their husbands, than might have been expected" (1871:901).

One Hundred Years Later
The framework of human evolution Darwin set forth is still utilized, and his approach to female choice is very much in

evidence one hundred years later. A centennial volume, *Descent of Man and Selection in Relation to Sex 1871–1971,* edited by Bernard Campbell (1972), commemorates Darwin's work and contains eleven articles on sexual selection and human evolution. Interpretations range from the articles by Trivers and Selander, which discuss the role of female choice, to those of Fox and Crook, which neglect it. Most of the subject matter of Trivers's and Selander's articles is birds and insects; Crook and Fox deal with primates and humans—as if the closer we approach the human condition, the less is female choice confronted and dealt with directly.

Both Crook and Fox carry on the theme that men have gained the power of selection. Crook, for example, in his discussion of human behavior, notes the role of the secondary sexual characteristics of young women that make them attractive to young men: "Hairlessness, voice tone, complexion and girlish behavior all have a childlike character that . . . appear to lower the probability of a male aggressive response or to appease if one is present" (1972:372). This approach is similar to the part of Darwin's argument that stresses female beauty as a lure to males. Thus male choice is assumed, in the face of all the evidence of female choice in other species, so that it follows "logically" that females had only a passive role in forming uniquely human cultural practices.

Fox develops this view in approaching human kinship systems. Following the structural male-behavior anthropological approach developed by Lévi-Strauss (1949), Fox views human intelligence as an outgrowth of male behavior and male-male interaction, whereas females are merely objects of exchange between men. Hence, females have had little role in the development of human kinship systems. Fox goes so far as to say that "it is the role of women as labor and as objects of exchange that is important. This control of women by the older, dominant males is probably the clue to all human kinship systems" (1972:313).

Campbell's book perpetuates and compounds Darwin's difficulty with male versus female choice (Zihlman 1974). The relatively insignificant role historically given to human females in mating might help explain why neither Darwin nor Campbell (nor E. O. Wilson) could fully integrate sexual selection and the descent of "man" and why the view that males control females still pervades reconstructions of human evolution.

Primate Behavior and the Dominant Male
From the earliest studies of primate behavior, selectivity in observation and bias in sampling and interpretation are apparent. For instance, Zuckerman (1932) concluded from a limited study of hamadryas baboons in the London zoo that the sexual bond is the cohesive mechanism of primate societies (see Haraway 1978*b* for an extensive discussion). In short-term field studies later, human observers considered the dominance hierarchies and aggression of male baboons, twice the size of the smaller females, as prominent features of primate societies (DeVore 1963). The centrality of savanna baboon adult males in mating (DeVore 1965), controlling group movement, maintaining social order, forming hierarchies, and acting as protectors becomes a basis for extrapolating to human societies, even though Rowell (1966, 1967) reported that baboons in forest environments behaved quite differently. Drawing from the baboon example, Kummer writes in *Primate Societies*:

> Man's latent or overt inclinations for dominance hierarchies, closed groups and discrimination against outsiders, suggest that he approached the baboon type of society, at least at one stage of his evolution. In many respects the hamadryas baboon's society of closely coordinated family units is a better model of human social structure than that of the chimps. [1971:152]

Dominance behavior—and its function and transmission in monkey and ape groups—has entailed a number of assumptions: that it is a major determinant in structuring social relationships within multimale/multifemale primate societies; that it equates with successful aggressive encounters; that it is a determinant of reproductive success; and that it is passed on genetically (implying a link to the Y chromosome) from one generation of males to the next.

However, dominance behavior is insufficient to describe the complexity and variability of nonhuman primate social behavior (Gartlan 1968). There may be little correlation between high rank and reproductive success of males, and dominance behavior may have little adaptive significance (Rowell 1974). "Dominance" is more correlated with length of tenure in a social group than with winning fights, and reproductive success correlates with living to maturity (Lancaster 1978).

Furthermore, a different picture of dominance acquisition emerges from data collected on monkeys and apes during long-term studies that considered the entire life cycle of individuals of both sexes of all ages. Such studies have shown the centrality of the mother rather than of males in determining the dominance status of offspring (Sade 1972). Kin relations, including physical closeness and intense social interaction, are an important factor in social organization, and for monkeys and apes "kin" consists of a mother and her offspring, as well as the siblings of a common mother.

Paternity is unknown among nonhuman primates, nor can human observers "know" paternity from watching social interaction, especially in multimale/multifemale social groups. Since "adoption" is relatively rare among primate groups, kin relations are also genetic relations. Dominance rank of both male and female offspring is influenced by the status of the mother (Koyama 1967; Sade 1967; Eaton 1976). Further, in many primate societies, this female core provides the principal social continuity of the group. It is noteworthy that these important facts about primate societies and female centrality have been minimized.

The Ubiquitous Hunting Model
The theme of male dominance and male centrality extends into interpretations of the economic and social life of early human society through the emphasis on hunting. The inven-

tion of hunting as the major economic and technological pursuit is credited with the consequent human departure from the ape forebears and with producing the essential "human" traits—intelligence, manual skill, toolmaking, tool using, sociability. Hunting is assumed to have been in practice for 99 percent of human history, thus providing "the master behavior pattern of the human species" (Laughlin 1968:304).

Robert Ardrey's *African Genesis* is an early, popular version of the hunting hypothesis (1961). (A later book, in 1976, was titled *The Hunting Hypothesis.*) According to Ardrey, our forebears were killer apes who wiped out their peaceful vegetarian brothers (he uses the Cain and Abel analogy) and so passed on to us all those nasty but successful human traits that we know so well today from genocidal wars and nuclear weapons. In fact, Ardrey's ideas are rooted in those of Raymond Dart (1955, 1957), the discoverer of *Australopithecus*. Dart, who was trained in England, was no doubt influenced by Darwin and Huxley, and the thread runs through from the founder to the present.

Tiger (1969) and Tiger and Fox (1971), in their popularizations of hunting, emphasize "male bonding" (the buddy system) as the focal point of human evolution. In their view, predatory aggression is genetically wired into our (male) nature (Zihlman 1973). Desmond Morris (1967), on the other hand, stresses the sexual bonds between males and females but still accepts the central role of males in hunting.

These popularizations and innumerable other versions tend to dismiss the facts: women and children constitute at least 75 percent of human society; women are the primary socializers; the human diet is omnivorous, not carnivorous; and meat and other protein can be obtained in numerous ways besides hunting. If one ignores these considerations, it becomes "logical" to draw analogies between early human groups and the social carnivores like lions and wolves (Schaller and Lowther 1969; Peters and Mech 1975; Thompson 1975; King 1976). Hominids and carnivores seem to have in common cooperative hunting for food, sharing of meat, division of labor, large home range, and long dependency of the young. But in all these features, carnivores and humans are also fundamentally different.

Carnivores have specialized for millions of years in preying upon a few species. Unlike carnivores, humans prey on almost any species, of any size, and rely not on canine teeth, less on strength and speed, and more on technology and planning. Sharing among carnivores has been greatly overrated. Lion cubs often eat last and do die of starvation (Schaller 1972). Wolves and hunting dogs regurgitate part of their meal for the young. Adult hyenas do not share but merely tolerate others eating alongside (Kruuk 1972). The orderly distribution of foods, both plant and animal, among human societies is a complex social mechanism, totally different from "sharing" among carnivores (Washburn and DeVore 1961).

Similarly, "cooperation" among carnivores merely means that several individuals hunt at the same time—a far cry from human cooperation involving language and self-identification as a group member. Female lions do all the killing for sharing with young. Some carnivores, such as lions, do have a long period of dependency (two to three years) before they master the skills of predation, but mothers cache rather than carry their young and have multiple rather than single births. Critically, unlike carnivores, human mothers continue to feed their dependent young for years after they are weaned, even when nursing and carrying other offspring, and maintain close emotional ties throughout life. Overall, the comparison of early hominids with carnivores is superficial, misleading, and essentially an extension of the "hunting hypothesis."

Sociobiology: "New Synthesis," Old Biases
Whether or not E. O. Wilson's *Sociobiology* (1975) is, as he claims, "the new synthesis," his view of human behavior is male-oriented all the way. Sociobiology attempts to explain the evolution of social systems, from insects to humans. The concept of natural selection is expanded to encompass the notions of "inclusive fitness" and "kin selection," as mecha-

nisms to explain mating strategies and relative reproductive success. But at the same time, Wilson's *Sociobiology* uncritically emphasizes male dominance, male fitness, and male reproductive success (Kleiman 1977). To Wilson, dominance is the essence of reproductive success:

> In the language of sociobiology, to dominate is to possess priority of access to the necessities of life and reproduction. . . . With rare exceptions, the aggressively superior animal displaces the subordinate from food, from mates, and from nest sites. It only remains to be established that this power actually raises the genetic fitness of the animals possessing it. On this point the evidence is completely clear. [1975:287]

Expanding this concept to primate societies, Wilson says that "the reproductive advantages conferred by dominance are preserved even in the most complex societies" (p. 288). And the leitmotif is sounded again fourteen chapters later: "What we can conclude with some degree of confidence is that primitive man lived in small territorial groups within which males were dominant over females" (p. 567). Finally, all the "objective" considerations and "new syntheses" lead, like a Sherlock Holmes solution, to the good old hunting hypothesis, in sociobiological garb: "By the time *Australopithecus* . . . had begun to feed on large mammals, group hunting almost certainly had become advantageous and even necessary" (1975:567).

The concepts of parental investment and mate choice, pillars on which sociobiology is founded, are never in this book applied to female mammals or primates. Though Wilson mentions that maternal care is prolonged in higher primates and humans, and that social relationships are to some extent matrilineal, these facts play no essential role in his theoretical formulation of human societies today or yesterday. The intellectual tradition of Wilson's emphasis on male reproductive success appears as a barrier to his employing sociobiological concepts of maternal investment, female choice, and mechanisms of sexual and kin selection, which he applies so impressively to ant and wasp societies, for incorporating women into human evolution.

Thus male-oriented reconstructions wherein males play the main economic (hunting) and reproductive (mate choice) roles have dominated the last one hundred years of discussions on human evolution. The "old model" built around weapons, hunting by males, and meat eating, in which women play no economic role, may be viewed as an extension of Darwin's ideas which emphasize the loss of large canine teeth for fighting and their replacement by weapons for protection: the dominating males thereby gain control of mate selection.

The Interpretation of Evidence

Any serious reconstruction of the past must "fit" within a growing body of data on living apes and gathering-hunting peoples, the hominid fossil record, genetic relationships of living species, as well as concepts in evolutionary biology. The human species has only one evolutionary history, and reconstructing that pathway must integrate this wide range of information from the genetic to the behavioral level, from millions of years ago to the present.

Evidence of the Past
The fossils, as well as associated tools and animal bones, and the ancient environmental setting, provide information from which we can directly deduce something about body size, motor capabilities, habitat, available food, potential predators, and circumstances of death of our earliest ancestors. To go beyond this evidence, to formulate the social aspects of life, requires supporting studies of closely related species, particularly the apes and gathering-hunting peoples (see Goodall 1968; Gale 1970; Bicchieri 1972; Teleki 1974; Lee and DeVore 1976; see also chapters 1 and 3, this volume).

Studies of anatomy, behavior, and especially protein structure and DNA indicate that chimpanzees, gorillas, and humans apparently diverged from a common ancestor as recently as five or six million years ago (King and Wilson 1975; Sarich and Cronin 1976). The oldest well-documented fossils come from Laetoli, Tanzania, and are about 3.5 million years old (M. D. Leakey et al. 1976; M. D. Leakey and Hay 1979). Other material, particularly pelvic and limb bones, comes from two sites—Hadar, Ethiopia, and Sterkfontein Cave, South Africa—which are over 2.5 million years old (Howell 1978). These sites in the savannas of eastern and southern Africa have yielded an abundance of fossil hominids, mostly jaws and teeth, though a dozen or so skulls have been found, and almost all parts of the skeleton.

The fossil evidence indicates that the earliest hominids were small, about the size of pygmy chimpanzees (thirty-two to thirty-five kilograms) (Zihlman 1979). Their pelvises and feet were constructed for walking in an upright position; the legs were not much longer than those of chimpanzees, and the arms were much shorter. Overall their body build was distinct from chimpanzees in spite of similar body weight. Their teeth were also distinct: small canines and large cheek teeth, with thick enamel and extensive wear. Cranial capacity ranged from 430 to 530 cubic centimeters, larger than the chimpanzee average of 390 cubic centimeters.

Fossil footprints indicate that the hominids of 3.5 million years ago could no longer use the great toe for grasping, as monkeys and apes can. Their tree-climbing ability was thereby reduced, and, more importantly, infant hominids could not effectively cling to their mother's hair. Though the pelvis was redesigned to orient the muscles for bipedal locomotion, brain size was still small and birth would not have been difficult (Leutenegger 1974).

Stone tools and "campsites" are not found in an archaeological context dated older than two million years—over one million years *after* the appearance of the hominids. By this time the tools are found in association with hominids, or with animal bones, or with both, particularly on the "living floors" at Olduvai Gorge (M. D. Leakey 1971). At such sites, sealed by subsequent deposits and undisturbed by water action, stones and bones remained as they were left, until un-earthed by archaeologists. Plant remains and organic tools, on the other hand, preserve less readily, and we must therefore recognize that the paleontological and archaeological records are biased in the evidence they preserve. The importance of plants and organic tools cannot be dismissed in our recon-struction.

The Evolutionary Framework

In a court of law, some evidence is thought to be so clear that "it speaks for itself" (*res ipsa loquitur*), but in anthropology an analytical framework is needed for the interpretation of data. That framework is evolution. Evolution is and has been a continuous process, whether or not the record of the past re-flects this precisely. It is in the recombination of existing be-havioral elements that a new way of life is initiated; this demonstrates that evolution is also change. Often the fossil evidence appears discontinuous, but there must have been *be-havioral* continuity during all phases of human evolution. For example, stone tools were not invented "out of the blue" without a prior tradition of perhaps several million years of tool using, whether of organic materials that do not leave traces, or of stone so little modified that the ensuing "tools" are not recognizable by archaeologists. The regular use of or-ganic, and later stone, tools was a key aspect of the early hominids' adaptation.

Furthermore, continuity in evolution assumes an inte-grated way of life, and to appreciate that fully it is necessary to explore interrelated patterns, which include social, tech-nological, economic, and ultimately ideological features. So, in reconstructing dietary patterns, for instance, it is not sufficient to know the kind of food eaten and with which tools it was obtained. Equally important would be the group mem-bers who obtained the food, how they learned its location, what motor patterns had to be mastered, and through what social networks the food was shared. And determining how all of this contributes to reproductive success is essential.

An evolutionary approach requires a consideration of the mechanism of natural selection, which in its broader application includes kin and sexual selection. In formulating natural selection, Darwin observed that a species is composed of individuals with varying abilities to survive and reproduce in a particular environment. Thus a population's "gene pool" represents those individuals producing the most surviving offspring; natural selection, then, measures this differential reproduction and survival. The "fitness" of individuals can be defined by their comparative success in contributing genes to succeeding generations. "Inclusive fitness," a term particularly applicable to social species like primates, takes into account not only reproductive strategies but also social behavior that contributes to the survival of the young: parental investment and kin investment (Hamilton 1964; Alexander 1974).

In primates, each sex contributes the same number of genes to a new individual, but the sexes do *not* contribute *equally* to its prenatal or postnatal survival. The more time and energy a mother invests in each of her offspring, the fewer offspring she can produce in a lifetime. Trivers (1972) proposes that the sex investing the most energy in its offspring is the sex that chooses its mates and thus influences the gene flow into the next generation: this is the principle of sexual selection.

Kin investment includes parental investment as well as time and energy devoted toward the survival of related individuals. In primate societies, "kin" engage in a great deal of social interaction, and, because adoption is infrequent, kin are also genetically related. Therefore, by contributing to the survival of kin with whom genes are shared, both females and males may influence evolution through kin selection, whether or not they mate and produce their own offspring.

Reproduction: A Female View
Although two sexes are essential for mammalian reproduction, the degree of involvement in rearing the offspring varies widely among species. Most discussions of primate reproduc-

tion have been male-oriented, considering only the sex act, in which the male makes his contribution; but for females this is only the beginning. Reproductive success involves the female in a greater investment of time and energy—ovulating, gestating, nursing, feeding, carrying, and establishing lifelong social ties.

The evolutionary roots of women's role in reproduction lie in mammalian and primate patterns. Primate mothers are a special kind of mammal: there is a long gestation, relative to body size, and a long period during which the infant nurses and develops physically and socially. Rather than make nests or have dens, as is the case for almost all other mammals, primate mothers carry their babies on their bodies until the young are weaned; the infants cling to their mother's hair with well-developed grasping hands and feet. Thus monkey and ape mothers with dependent young retain their ability to move around the environment at will, but at the price of increased physical stress and strain and energy output. The prolonged physical closeness between mother and offspring results in enduring social and emotional attachments; these are essential for observational learning by the young from their mothers and hence for the transmission of behaviors and information vital to individual survival and to perpetuation of the group and the species.

This mobility of primate mothers, the prolonged physical contacts, and the lasting emotional ties continued and were elaborated among early hominids. Contrary to many reconstructions of early human social life that picture women burdened with young, sitting back at camp waiting for the hunter's return, hominid mothers must have been moving actively around the environment, getting food and carrying infants while doing so. To postulate that early human females were sedentary denies their primate heritage as well as evolutionary continuity, and implies that their behavior has no counterpart among all female monkeys and apes and women in gathering societies today. In fact, there are no such sedentary females in gathering and hunting societies.

From the beginning of human evolution, because young hominids had lost their grasping feet and could not cling, the burden of holding on shifted to the mothers. Hence, females took a more *active* role in the generation of mother-infant attachments: mothers acted as initiators of attachment as well as perpetuators of it.\With upright posture and hands no longer needed for locomotion, the mother developed a new way of carrying her infant, a way that ensured her own mobility without jeopardizing the mother-infant contact and relationship. The first tools, as many have suggested, may have been invented by mothers to carry their offspring who could not cling or walk. Such a "tool" is a unique development among primates, and to the mother it meant that physical mobility was not impaired and that she could search for, obtain, and carry food while carrying a dependent infant. This flexibility of being able to engage in a wide range of activities depended upon the initial invention of a sling/container.

Parental investment is an integral part of reproductive success. Maternal investment of early hominid mothers increased in terms of both time and energy from that exhibited in our female ape ancestors. Hominid young were born helpless and matured slowly. In close physical contact to their mothers, they learned about the physical environment, how to make tools, and developed social bonds that endured for life. The time and energy spent in carrying and caring for long-dependent offspring were even more extensive than among the ape forebears because mothers were usually caring for weaned, but still dependent, offspring while continuing to nurse younger infants. In a hominid mother's lifetime she may have had five or six children, a maximum estimated from the !Kung San average (about five) (Howell 1979) and chimpanzee populations. Unlike men, who invest less in each offspring, and hence can have more, women are confined to these few.

According to sociobiological theory, this heavy maternal investment should mean that females were choosing their mates. And precisely because of the burden of long-dependent offspring, females must have selected sociable males, willing to share food and protect them and their off-spring. This turns around the traditional picture of human reproduction, where the dominant males pick suitable females, who do their best to remain attractive and thereby be assured of having a mate, food, protection, and offspring.

Women's Role in Subsistence

In the early 1960s, studies among the !Kung San of the Kalahari gatherer-hunters in southern Africa revealed women's major economic role in obtaining and sharing food through gathering activities.

Richard Lee documented in some detail the economics of hunting and gathering (1965, 1968a) to show that in some cultures at least females are not as dependent as it might seem from the perspective of Western industrialized society. In 1966, Lee, with Irven DeVore, organized the conference on hunting/gathering societies referred to earlier in this book, to present new data and to relate them to reconstructing human evolution. The subsequent volume was titled *Man the Hunter* (1968a) in spite of the statement in the editors' introduction that "it was generally agreed to use the term hunters as a convenient shorthand, despite the fact that the majority of peoples considered subsisted primarily on resources *other than meat*—mainly wild plants and fish" (1968b:4; emphasis in the original). The information presented in this misnamed volume, as well as in related studies appearing later, provided the basis for questioning the hunting model and for expanding our understanding of women's roles and for proposing alternative views of sex roles in human evolution (Linton 1971; Gale 1970; Martin and Voorhies 1975; Tanner and Zihlman 1976).

Lee and DeVore, commenting on the applicability of the findings on women's gathering activities to human evolution, noted:

> Vegetable foods . . . were always available to early man and . . . easily exploited by even the simplest of technologies. . . . Early

Figure 2.1. A !Kung woman living in the Kalahai in southern Africa today illustrates the role of women in reproduction and production. She carries her three-year-old child and is also seven months pregnant. As she returns from a day in the bush, she brings along her digging stick and the food she has gathered to be shared with her kin. Photograph courtesy of Richard B. Lee.

women would not have remained idle during the Pleistocene and
. . . plant foods . . . so important in the diet of inland hunter-
gatherers today would have played a similar role in the diet of
early peoples. [1968*b*:7]

But concerning the actual recovery of such information,
Lee astutely says: "The !Kung have a very substantial subsistence base largely made up of vegetable foods and small animals, but . . . there would be *almost a total loss* of this evidence
to the archaeologists" (Lee 1968*b*:344; emphasis in original).
This phenomenon would hold equally for all gatherer-hunter
groups. These studies show the importance of women in
these groups as an economic force, as they must have been in
the past, though the evidence for this role would leave little or
no trace in a record of the past.

Gathering and Reproductive Success:
The Alternative Model

I argue here, as I have elsewhere, that gathering and not
hunting was the initial food-getting behavior that distin-
guished ape from human. This was an innovation whereby
human females used tools to obtain food for themselves, as
well as to sustain their young through the long period of dependency, walked long distances, and carried food bipedally
on the African savannas (Tanner and Zihlman 1976; Zihlman and Tanner 1978). From the beginning of the human
adaptation, a woman's role encompassed reproductive, economic, and social components. Furthermore, rather than a
leading force, hunting must have emerged late in human
evolutionary history from a technological and social base in
gathering (Zihlman 1978*a*).

Gathering as a subsistence technique, not hunting, com-
bines behavioral elements that existed in the prehuman ape
ancestor (chapter 1, this volume). At first the tools would have
been modified only slightly, a simple digging tool or a crude
container, but through evolutionary time, the manufacture of

these tools and the skill for using them became refined. (Among peoples today, digging tools appear simply made, but are often fire-hardened and regularly sharpened with stone tools.) Implements for collecting termites by chimpanzees, and presumably by the hominid ancestors, may have been the basis for developing digging sticks. Containers must also have been an early invention making it possible to transport food to a safe spot for leisurely consumption and sharing. A modified container could act as a baby sling, or vice versa, as the kaross does among Kalahari San women. With the use of tools, sufficient food could be collected and transported to permit sharing with offspring and perhaps others. A nomadic way of life, in which female mobility was critical, was facilitated by bipedal locomotion, permitting long-distance walking even while carrying infants, food, and tools.

Children raised in the gathering way of life remained dependent on adults until they could walk long distances, master the skills of collecting and processing food with the use of tools, and acquire sufficient knowledge of the social and physical environments. Presumably, a young hominid with a more prolonged developmental period needed at least five years to master the art of chimpanzee "termiting" or "ant dipping" with tools (McGrew 1977), and this in part accounted for delayed maturation already expressed among early hominids (Mann 1975). Further, the ability to walk long distances bipedally does not develop until children acquire the body build of adults, thereby decreasing oxygen consumption and increasing stamina. A hominid child's survival depended upon its mother's ability to carry it great distances for several years, her skill in finding and gathering food, using tools, her ability to space infants, to feed her weaned offspring, and to maintain social ties with the group (Zihlman 1978*b*).

The importance of the gathering technique is that it involves tools for collecting a quantity of food that can be carried elsewhere for consumption and sharing. This technique is a departure from the ape's way of plucking and eating food "on the spot" with each weaned animal foraging for itself. The food obtained requires manipulation by tools for extraction, carrying, or preparation. The type of foods may have been mostly plants, which require less energy or risk of failure than predation or hunting. However, the gathering technique can also be applied to protein sources in "small packages," such as insects, other small invertebrates, reptiles, small animals, and shellfish (Marshall 1976; Tanaka 1976; Meehan 1977*a,b*).

Continuous with the ancestral ape pattern, though adding a new dimension through recombining existing elements, the hominid diet was omnivorous and included predation on small animals, as among chimpanzees. The frequency of chimpanzee meat-eating varies by habitat (McGrew et al. 1979; Nishida 1979), and the technique of capture or utilization does not require tools. The savanna environment into which the early hominids moved has now, as it did then, considerable biomass of large ungulates (Bourlière 1963). Due to this greater availability of potential prey, meat consumption of early hominids is likely to have increased compared to the forest-living ape ancestors. Particularly, newborn and young ungulates hiding in the grass while their mothers grazed would have been easily captured. Early hominid women could have obtained small or young animals by capturing them with only bare hands, as has been reported among women in gathering societies today (Shostak 1976). However, because meat may require a high output of energy for an unpredictable return, it seems unlikely that hominid mothers and infants living two to four million years ago depended for their survival on meat, whether obtained from their own efforts, or the efforts of others.

Role of Males in Reproduction and Subsistence
Males in human evolution are traditionally depicted as the primary food getters, protectors of females and young, dominant to females, and in control of the mating process through choosing females as their lifelong partners. Such a

picture fits with twentieth-century Western society but less well with the information on sexual behavior and mate choice, food sharing, and social behavior among chimpanzees. The view presented here suggests that a departure from the behavioral pattern of the ancestral male ape is the incorporation of early hominid males into social groups of their own "kin." Males, unburdened by young and so even wider ranging than many females, may have obtained the unpredictable meat by pursuing small animals more frequently than females with young were able to do, and they may have assumed an important role in protecting the group, although group protection included means other than male fortitude (Tanner and Zihlman 1976).

Males also gathered food, although probably in early evolution little more than for themselves. After all, a male infant was carried by his mother as she gathered and would learn this way of life while growing up. Through his efforts in sharing food with his mother and siblings, aiding in group protection, and carrying and playing with young, a male increased the likelihood that his kin would reach adulthood. Males contributed to the survival of the species through kin selection.

Because maternal investment was high, females were choosing precisely those males who were friendly, nurturing, tool-using, and willing to share food. Chosen males then contributed to the gene pool by investing in their kin, usually but not necessarily in their own offspring, and were integrated into the food-sharing and social network. These male behaviors would have been advantageous in a system where the males probably could not know who their offspring were. In a "pair bond" situation, there is greater confidence in identifying paternity and hence in direct paternal investment in a particular offspring. Widespread social nurturing by males would appear more likely in contexts of polygamous matings and would be a significant factor in the survival of the young.

This view of male, as well as female, roles recognizes the contribution of male nurturing of young, as well as the critical role of a female's economic behavior as integral to her reproductive success. The supposed specialization of sex roles—females as nurturers and males as economic providers—ignores the potential flexibility of behavior of both sexes and sets up a social system too rigid for utilizing opportunistically the range of food sources on the savanna. *Both* sexes must have been able to care for young, protect themselves from predators, make and use tools, and freely move about the environment in order to exploit available resources widely distributed through space and time. It is this range of behaviors—the overall behavioral flexibility of both sexes—that may have been the *primary* ingredient of the early hominids' success in the savanna environment.

Sexual Dimorphism and the Division of Labor
The basis for arguing that there were very different economic and reproductive roles for each sex has been tied to the physical differences between women and men. Among nonhuman primates and humans, males are usually larger in body size; and size is often equated with dominance and, by extension, with strength and "power of selection" of mates. Very different behaviors are thus assumed to have existed between the sexes. Among nonhuman primates, sex differences in body and canine size were thought to be correlated primarily with ground living and with the ability of males to protect the social group (DeVore 1963; Crook and Gartlan 1966; Leibowitz 1978). DeVore maintained that an increase in dominance behavior is accompanied by increased development of features equipping males for fighting (e.g., body and canine size), resulting in extreme sexual dimorphism in some species.

Linking male dominance behavior and larger body size to their role in predator defense and terrestrial living was assumed valid for human evolution (Tiger 1969). Sexual dimorphism conjures up the image of big, strong, dominant men as hunters of large beasts and protectors of small, fragile women and helpless children from the dangers of the savanna environment. So the evolution of sexual dimorphism has been assumed to account for the enhancement of men's hunting activities and, by extension, for a division of labor; or, the reverse has also been assumed—that the evolution of hunting would select for sexual dimorphism. Mating strategies whereby a male chooses a dependent female as a pair-bonded mate followed as part of the hunting premise (Washburn and Lancaster 1968; Tiger 1969; Tiger and Fox 1971).

Discussions of sexual dimorphism and the division of labor in reconstructions of human evolution must be grounded in the actual expression of sexual dimorphism in living apes and humans and its behavioral correlates, if any. With this basis one can then turn to the fossil record. This section attempts to clarify how sexual dimorphism is expressed in apes and modern humans and what can be pieced together from the early hominids' bones and teeth. Behavioral correlates to sexual dimorphism where they can be demonstrated will be discussed. Sexual dimorphism as it relates to an early division of labor and to the hominids' mating system can then be assessed in this light.

Sexual dimorphism is the phenotypic expression of *morphological* variation in male and female types of the same species (di = two, morph = form). (Sexual dimorphism does *not* apply to the behavioral correlates that may be associated with it.) Besides reproductive anatomy, male and female nonhuman primates vary in nonsexual characters such as body weight and muscular development, overall size expressed in head, body, and tail dimensions, coat and hair color and markings, and canine tooth length, as well as in maturational, seasonal, or periodic morphological changes associated with reproduction, such as sexual skin changes (Crook 1972). The pelvis and related birth canal in females, body size and weight, and canine tooth size are the most consistent characters, though not the only ones, in which sexual dimorphism is expressed among primates. Size of canine teeth is the best single indicator of sex for most species (Garn et al. 1966). For fossil species, bones and teeth are the only preserved indicators of sexual dimorphism. Body size must be reconstructed only from these pieces, and in turn the size differences, if bimodal, are assumed to represent two sexes. Finally, hypotheses are made about behaviors that may correlate with the supposed degree of sexual dimorphism.

Studies of living humans and of nonhuman primate species show that sexual dimorphism in canine and body size, head proportions, body weight and proportions involves a mosaic of characters and constitutes a distinct pattern in all species of apes and some species of monkeys (Zihlman 1976; Grand 1978; Janszen and Zihlman 1979). Sexually dimorphic features such as body size and weight, canine tooth size, or pelvic proportions do not all correlate with the same behaviors across species. For example, confusion about the behavioral correlates of sexual dimorphism has derived from attempts to infer mating patterns from a particular morphological feature such as body length (e.g., Alexander et al. 1979). In this way, researchers are making hit-and-miss attempts to draw causal generalizations out of the many diverse and complex variables which are involved in each species' way of life (Janszen 1978). Not only is sexual dimorphism inappropriately reduced to a single trait, but this approach also fails to view sex differences as expressions of *different* strategies adopted by *each sex* in accordance with its particular life history.

I focus here on body size and weight and canine size among living humans and apes because these are the forms of sexual dimorphism we can derive from the fossil record. Body weight in two species of chimpanzees and humans, for example, may be moderately different between the sexes, yet degree of sex difference in social behavior and in other morphological features of each species varies. In humans, women have about 84 percent of male body weight among a rain forest horticultural group and in savanna hunter-gatherers (Truswell and Hansen 1976; Chagnon and Hames 1979). A similar percentage is found in pygmy chimpanzees (*Pan paniscus*) (80 percent) and common chimpanzees (84 percent)

(Zihlman 1976; Cramer and Zihlman 1978). Moderate body weight sex differences may or may not correlate with size differences in other anatomical features such as cranial capacity, long bone lengths, or robusticity or joint size. In humans and in common chimpanzees (*P. troglodytes*) there are sex differences in all these traits, whereas no sex differences in pygmy chimpanzees exist for these traits.

Canine size, also, is a very interesting trait in primates for the study of sexual dimorphism and is directly preserved in the hominid fossil record. In monkeys and apes, canine size often shows marked variation between the sexes and, for a group of thirty-five species of monkeys and apes, correlates with body size dimorphism (correlation coefficient r = 0.76). Body size dimorphism is apparently influenced by more factors than is canine size and is therefore more variable (Leutenegger and Kelly 1977). Factors that seem to influence selection on canine size include predator defense, extent of social role differentiation between the sexes, and visibility within the habitat. Selective pressures on body size relate to predator defense and avoidance, territorial availability, food availability, diet, habitat and locomotion, and social role differentiation (Leutenegger and Kelly 1977).

Canine size dimorphism does correlate with social role differentiation among living monkeys and apes, so small canine size and the absence of dimorphism in this trait among early hominids may offer clues to their social behavior. In monkeys and apes, absolute as well as relative canine size differences between the sexes do correlate with sociability but not with mating pattern per se. For example, female monkeys in multifemale/one-male groups have the smallest canines relative to body size, and females who live in pairs, the largest (Harvey et al. 1978*a,b*). In a small-bodied ape, the gibbon, *large* canine teeth exist in *both* females and males; gibbons live in small family groups of one adult female, an adult male, and their subadult offspring; there is high intolerance among adults, even between the male and female pair. The offspring are expelled when they approach adulthood. Competition for food does exist among members of the family group, related to their small home range. The suggested function for large canines in the adult female is her effective competition for food with the adult male (Ellefson 1968).

Standing in contrast to this example are pygmy chimpanzees (*P. paniscus*). Canine teeth are relatively small for both sexes, though slightly larger for males (Johanson 1974). Both females and males are quite social; they live in mixed groups of males and females of about twenty individuals (Kuroda 1979). This is quite different from common chimpanzees (*P. troglodytes*, with moderate body size and canine size dimorphism), where females tend to forage with their offspring and males travel in company of other males (Wrangham 1979), behaviors considered to reflect less sociability and greater social differentiation (i.e., male-male competition) than occurs in the closely related pygmy chimpanzees. There is then a correlation between canine size and social organization that reflects the patterns of actual social interaction between individuals. Frequency and intensity of interaction, competition, and relations among classes of individuals are reflected in canine morphology.

In turning to the fossil record and the problem of sexual dimorphism of now extinct species, it is essential to discover, from fossil fragments of bones and teeth, the range of body size that can be reconstructed from this evidence. The fossil bones of three million years ago indicate a size range among individuals, and one explanation for this variability may be sexual dimorphism (Johanson and White 1979). If so, body size dimorphism was probably no more than moderate (as in both species of chimpanzees and humans), though could have been extreme, as in gorilla and orangutan. The evidence is not yet clear. However, the early hominids of two million years ago show no dimorphism in canine size. Moderate to extreme body size differences, in combination with no functional difference in canine size, may have been a pattern unlike that found in living apes or modern humans. From estimates of body weight, Leutenegger (1977) argues that both species of early hominids (*Australopithecus africanus* and *A. robustus*) were dimorphic and therefore that their mating systems were probably polygynous. This may not have been the situation, given the example of the two chimpanzee species, both with moderate body weight dimorphism but with different social organizations.

Canine tooth size may be more helpful in inferring social behavior. The fact that they are small and nondimorphic among early hominids could reflect greater sociability among individuals, between males and females, females and females, and a reduction of male-male competition and aggression, similar to, and even an extension of, that found among pygmy chimpanzees. This behavioral interpretation of an anatomical character fits with two hypotheses presented in this chapter and discussed by others regarding early human social life: (1) Food sharing has long been considered a new and integral part of economic and social life of the human species (Washburn and DeVore 1961; Tanner and Zihlman 1976; Isaac 1978). Decreasing competition and other changes in male-male interaction would be expressed in sharing food between males and females and intense social interaction among kin and community members. (2) With regard to kin investment by males, females preferred as sexual partners those males who were more social and less aggressive toward them and who contributed to the welfare of their own kin group (Tanner and Zihlman 1976; Zihlman 1978*a*). Both hypotheses are more recently borne out by studies on sharing patterns and sexual behavior of pygmy and common chimpanzees. Common chimpanzee females apparently avoid mating with males aggressive toward them (Sugiyama 1973; McGinnis 1973), and among pygmy chimpanzees a high degree of food sharing is closely interwoven with copulation (Savage and Bakeman 1978).

The increased sociability of early hominid males toward their kin and other social group members may be expressed anatomically in the small size of their canine teeth. In addition to the social function of canine teeth, other selective pressures could also be operating to reduce canine teeth in both sexes of early hominids. Because one correlate of marked canine dimorphism is antipredator behavior, among early hominids tool using for predator defense might have replaced large canines in males, assuming that early hominids inherited large canines from their ape ancestor. In fact, there is evidence to suggest that these ancestral apes' canine teeth were not much larger than those of pygmy chimpanzees (Zihlman et al. 1978). Another function of natural selection for reduction of canines in both sexes may have been to increase the effectiveness of the food-grinding mechanism for processing large quantities of tough, gritty foods.

In summary, size and weight differences between the sexes no doubt existed in the early hominids, though such differences have yet to be delineated in any but the most general way. Absence of canine dimorphism, a diagnostic primate character for social behavior, may safely be interpreted to indicate frequent and relatively nonaggressive social interaction between males and females. This by no means suggests "monogamy" or "polygyny" in mating strategies or an absence of aggression. The function of sexually dimorphic characters is not always apparent and in fact may not exist for all characters (Caspari 1978). For example, because degree of body size and weight dimorphism varies so widely among human populations—and in part can be attributed to nutritional differences (Tobias 1975)—the possibility must be considered that variation in such characters may not have direct behavioral significance (contra Alexander et al. 1979).

There is no specific character in male or female physique in ancient or modern humans that can be interpreted to signify that only males must hunt and females gather. Considerations regarding child care and the limitations it imposes on females are another variable and a factor distinct from physical strength per se. A division of labor probably evolved late in human evolution and has never been absolute. Sexual dimorphism is not sufficient to conclude the necessity of a division of labor by sex, of a particular mating pattern, or of nurturing behavior confined to one sex.

The Relation of Gathering to Hunting

A major assumption with significant impact on the interpretation of the division of labor of early hominids centers upon the emergence of hunting and gathering together. Recent emphasis has been placed on the sharing of both plant and animal resources, a "mixed" economy, in which women gather and men hunt (Isaac 1978; Lancaster 1978; R. E. F. Leakey and Lewin 1978). These "newer" views of early hominid behavior attempt to integrate females into human evolution and into the social and economic systems by emphasizing gathering and the division of labor by sex. This is merely a *superimposition of gathering onto the traditional hunting model.* If hunting and gathering did arise simultaneously in the distant past, or hunting before gathering, then a system in which males hunted and females gathered probably would have been the main way to divide the labor. When viewed in this way, the division of labor and sex roles related to subsistence seem very deterministic, thereby reinforcing the supposed biological base for very different roles between the sexes. This minimizes the unique and central contribution of women, not only to economics, but also to reproduction, and undermines the behavioral flexibility of both sexes. Even within a feminist perspective, "man the hunter" and male dominance unfortunately can prevail as the unifying framework of human behavior, past and present (e.g., Friedl 1975, 1978).

What is the evidence that hunting arose early? or later? My conclusions that hunting arose relatively late in evolution and grew out of the technological and social bases in gathering derive from archaeological and paleontological evidence, or its absence, from behavior of living peoples, from the anatomy and ecology of early hominids, and from the principles of evolutionary continuity and "recombination." Modern gatherer-hunters represent an integrated adaptation of gathering with hunting and a highly developed technology, such as bow and poisoned arrows, and may not extend beyond the last one hundred thousand years, as opposed to the three or four million years I am discussing here. We cannot assume a division of labor such as occurs in living peoples to apply automatically to the ancient past.

Before proceeding to the evidence, it is important to define "hunting" properly. Much of the debate about its origin might be eliminated by making proper distinctions among a variety of behaviors. The term is often used interchangeably with carnivore killing for food (by tooth and claw), chimpanzee predatory behavior (by use of hands), killing with tools, scavenging, butchering, taking big game or small, acting alone or in groups. These are all ways of obtaining meat, but they differ markedly in the behaviors and technology involved and in what members of society carry out the behavior. For example, butchering requires good cutting tools, makes available for sharing a meat source of large animals that cannot be torn limb from limb with hands or teeth, and is easily performed by either females or males. The comparison of carnivore with human hunting confuses rather than clarifies because it is a mixture of behavioral, technical, and dietary analogies with no consistent evolutionary or genetic framework. Human hunting, as we know it, is a composite of behaviors: stalking, pursuing, bringing down, killing, and butchering, and various tools are tied in with some parts. Each part may have developed prior to the crystallization of the whole pattern. And depending on the prey and the environment and the social organization of the "predators," these behaviors may vary radically.

There are difficulties in interpreting the archaeological evidence on hunting origins; questions remain concerning (1) the appearance of stone tools and their continuity with prior tools, (2) the meaning of bone accumulations and their association with stone tools, and (3) the behavioral/technical means for killing large animals and the frequency of such kills.

There is ample evidence that the hominids were on the scene for almost two million years prior to the appearance of stone tools and butchering sites (Zihlman 1978a); as has been remarked, however, organic tools and plant remains do not preserve as readily as stones and bones. Chimpanzee tool use suggests that a long period of organic tool using could have preceded the invention of tools made of stone (Lancaster 1968; Teleki 1974). And organic tools in the beginning were more likely to have been digging types. It is not difficult to imagine the step necessary to develop a digging tool from a probing type of grass stem or twig as used by chimpanzees (see chapter 1, this volume).

Of the stone tools that first appeared about two million years ago, many are simple "choppers" and are not extensively modified. Early choppers may have been preceded by earlier use of unmodified flakes or cores to improve the manufacture of tools from organic materials. This suggestion arises from the fact that tools similar to these early choppers are still used today. Among the !Kung San, women carry a stone "chopper" to sharpen their digging sticks (Marshall 1976), and choppers continue to be used among Australian Aborigines, whose technology is largely based upon organic tools manufactured with stone tools (Mulvany 1975; Hayden 1977). The use of materials of one type to make/process materials of another involves a number of conceptual connections and a "sophistication" regarding tool use and manufacture further supported by the rapid changes in tool types, including the bifaces, which occurred by 1.5 million years ago.

In the archaeological and paleontological records, concentrations of fragmented bones have been interpreted as tools and as evidence of hunting. Dart (1957) and Ardrey (1961) treated the large number of bones at Makapansgat Cave in the Transvaal of South Africa as evidence of toolmaking, hunting, and meat eating by early hominids. Dart suggested that early man had fashioned tools out of the bones, teeth, and horns of the animals they had killed and eaten. Washburn (1957) long ago questioned this evidence; he interpreted the bone accumulations as hyena meals, and recent studies (Shipman and Phillips-Conroy 1977) confirm his suspicion. Bones may accumulate by natural processes, such as water action that selectively deposits them some distance away depending on density and shape, and by carnivore scavenging (Brain 1970; Behrensmeyer 1976). Bone accumulations once considered hominid meals can be explained by mechanisms more plausible than hunting. Even when stone tools do occur with animal bones, careful study must establish whether or not the association is fortuitous.

Evidence of tools used in connection with meat comes from several sites dated between 1.6 and 1.8 million years ago (Isaac et al. 1971; M. D. Leakey 1971). Although hominids may have butchered the hippo and elephants at these sites, there is little evidence that they actually killed them. The animals were uncovered in what were once ancient swamps, where they could have become mired, a suggestion made by Mary Leakey and illustrated in modern swamps today (Johnson et al. 1977). The archaeological finds are important, however, because they indicate that hominids had "discovered" small sharp flake tools, which would have enabled them to cut up and share large animals more efficiently, presumably, than tearing them apart with hands or teeth. Even so, the butchering sites indicate less efficient utilization of the meat than occurs later. Furthermore, butchering, as opposed to chasing after an animal, could as easily have been done by women with children as by men. The association of these tools with animal bones by no means proves "the hunting hypothesis."

The anatomy of the hominids themselves is another line of evidence that points to the importance of plant foods. For their body size, early hominids had relatively large teeth which show a great deal of wear and chipping. Markings on the fossil skulls and jawbones indicate well-developed muscles for grinding food, a chewing mechanism typical of omnivores and herbivores (Crompton and Hiiemäe 1969; DuBrul 1977). Thus the anatomy suggests a high proportion of gritty and tough material in the diet. The kinds of food that need extensive processing in the mouth are the tougher vegetable foods, some fruits and nuts, or foods found on or under the ground. It may be no coincidence that the chronic disorders today associated with a diet high in fat and animal protein suggest that one composed principally of vegetables rich in dietary fiber represents better the "natural" condition of the species (Mendeloff 1977).

Finally, the combined evidence suggests that the early hominid diet can be best described as omnivorous: meat would be included but would be of less importance than the popular hunting hypothesis proclaims. As yet no explanation for the origin of hunting takes into account evolutionary continuity: there is no simple extension from chimpanzee-like predation (catching small animals without tools) to throwing at, trapping, driving, or stalking and killing animals of all sizes with the use of tools. Further, any explanation must take into account the archaeological evidence, or lack of it. All components—anatomical, social, technical, ecological—of hunting must be delineated; until then the development of hunting cannot be reconstructed step by step as it must have emerged in evolution.

Questions remain regarding the emergence of hunting, but the gap narrows when we recognize the continuity and similarities between gathering and hunting. Gathering may have laid the social and technological foundations for the emergence of hunting. For example, behaviors attributed to hunting can as easily be explained by gathering: long-distance walking, use of tools, sharing resources, large home range, home base, low population density, detailed knowledge of the environment, and cognitive mapping. Sharing patterns established between mothers and offspring continued into adulthood and expanded to include other adult males and nonrelated individuals. Actual hunting probably built upon these existing sharing patterns. Individuals engaged in obtaining raw materials for tools or pursuing unpredictable game could gather for themselves while traveling, and if they did not succeed in the capture they would be assured of shared food gained from others' effort.

Technology of hunting could have developed from tools initially invented for gathering activities and plant food preparation. As aspects of evolutionary continuity, wooden spears and, later, hafted tools, fishing nets, and the like may have developed from digging sticks or "bags" for collecting and carrying, in the same way that digging sticks may have emerged from an ape's termiting stick. Tools invented for food preparation, such as those used to pound and pulverize tough plant foods or to cut up large fruits and vegetables for consumption and sharing, may have been the basis for inventing stone tools for cutting up animals or pounding meat prior to eating. One might also make a case for hunting as a specialized form of gathering—"gathering" small reptiles, conies, rodents, and so on, and building on this to go after small and young herbivores, and on to larger herbivores. The interrelation of gathering with the later emergence of hunting must have expanded considerably the feeding and foraging strategies of the early hominids for utilizing an ever wider range of dispersed and varied food types, both plant and animal; this in turn would contribute to reproductive success of those individuals and social groups so engaged.

A firm foundation in a gathering way of life would then have enabled the hominids' successful exploitation of more extreme habitats as they moved out of the tropical areas of Africa and Asia into the temperate regions, where plants were not available year around. The hominids of half a million years ago living in the temperate climates must have utilized a great deal of meat (Butzer 1977). However, there are few clues in the archaeological record of how frequently and by what means the animals were killed. Initially, it may have been close-range killing with a digging type of tool that could knock out a small animal; later, more effective tools for close-range killing of medium-sized to large animals would have been used. Such killing might be contrasted with predation—killing of smaller animals by hand—and the distinction between the two indicates a higher level of social, technical, economic, and cognitive organization.

Conclusions

In the origin of the human way of life, women's roles in feeding, carrying, and caring for their nursing and weaned young were critical for species survival. Men's roles also were geared to investing time and energy in the next generation, for their own offspring as well as their "kin." The female contribution to reproductive success included an active role in production and subsistence. Gathering and preparing food with tools made it possible for the early hominids, especially the mothers, to exploit the abundant savanna resources: it was a new feeding pattern in a new environment for obtaining, transporting, and preparing foods to share. Foods obtained in this way, which are mostly although not exclusively plant, require less energy than going after mobile animals, an important consideration for a female with dependent young.

At the earliest stages of human evolution, a pronounced division of labor by sex is unlikely, though there was probably a tendency for males, or even females without young, to range in groups more widely for food than those mothers with young. In this way, resources could be efficiently utilized over a wide area. Males became more involved in the survival and well-being of their kin, and so contributed to the gene pool through kin selection and by being chosen as mates for females who preferred more social, food-sharing, nurturing males. Hunting, emerging later and utilizing male mobility and female information "banks" and gathering as security, further provided means for exploiting more effectively another food source of moderate-to-large-sized animals. This in turn provided the basis for developing wider sharing networks that included non-kin. This broader definition of both women's and men's roles in this long time frame gives us greater insight into the development of the division of labor by sex, and hunting in relation to gathering, and the complementarity of the nurturing roles of both sexes.

The flexibility of the human adaptation over the long haul allowed exploitation of a wide variety of plant, animal, and fish species, through the invention of tools and new behavioral patterns. Ultimately, the success of human reproduction means producing and socializing offspring that not only survive but also in turn have offspring of their own. Women's critical contribution to shaping the human adaptation must be integrated into an evolutionary picture in order to explore their interrelation with men's roles. If we are to advance our understanding of sex roles in prehistory, which in turn may further understanding of the sexes today, we must ask questions in ways not previously asked, and most importantly we must break away from the traditional "man the hunter" formulation. Only then can we begin to redress the imbalance of history and embark on new avenues of research to broaden our insights into human behavior.

Acknowledgments

For comments and discussion, I thank Catherine Borchert, Meg Conkey, Karen Janszen, and Jerry Lowenstein. For the photograph, I thank Richard Lee. I acknowledge research support from the Wenner-Gren Foundation for Anthropological Research and the Faculty Research Committee, University of California, Santa Cruz.

References

Alexander, Richard D. 1974. The evolution of social behavior. *Annual Review of Ecology and Systematics* 5:325–83.
Alexander, Richard D., John L. Hoogland, Richard D. Howard, Katherine M. Noonan, and Paul W. Sherman. 1979. Sexual dimorphisms and breeding systems in pinnipeds, ungulates, primates and humans. In *Evolutionary biology and human social behavior,*

ed. Napoleon A. Chagnon and William Irons, pp. 402–35. North Scituate, Mass.: Duxbury Press.

Ardrey, Robert. 1961. *African genesis: a personal investigation into the animal origins and nature of man.* New York: Atheneum.

———. 1976. *The hunting hypothesis: a personal conclusion concerning the evolutionary nature of man.* New York: Atheneum.

Behrensmeyer, Anna K. 1976. Taphonomy and paleoecology in the hominid fossil record. *Yearbook of Physical Anthropology* 19:36–50.

Bicchieri, M. G. 1972. *Hunters and gatherers today.* New York: Holt, Rinehart and Winston.

Bourlière, François. 1963. Observations on the ecology of some large African mammals. In *African ecology and human evolution,* ed. Francis Clark Howell and François Bourlière, pp. 43–54. Chicago: Aldine.

Brain, C. K. 1970. New finds at the Swartkrans australopithecine site. *Nature* 225:1112–19.

Butzer, Karl W. 1977. Environment, culture, and human evolution. *American Scientist* 65:572–84.

Campbell, Bernard, ed. 1972. *Sexual selection and the descent of man 1871–1971.* Chicago: Aldine.

Caspari, Ernst W. 1978. The biological basis of female hierarchies. In *Female hierarchies,* ed. Lionel Tiger and Heather T. Fowler, pp. 87–122. Chicago: Beresford Book Service.

Chagnon, Napoleon A., and Raymond B. Hames. 1979. Protein deficiency and tribal warfare in Amazonia: new data. *Science* 203:910–13.

Cramer, D. L., and Adrienne L. Zihlman. 1978. Sexual dimorphism in the pygmy chimpanzee, *Pan paniscus.* In *Recent advances in primatology,* vol. 3, *Evolution,* ed. D. J. Chivers and K. A. Joysey, pp. 487–90. London: Academic Press.

Crompton, A. W., and K. Hiiemäe. 1969. How mammalian molar teeth work. *Discovery* 5(1):23–34.

Crook, John Hurrell. 1972. Sexual selection, dimorphism and social organization in the primates. In *Sexual selection and the descent of man 1871–1971,* ed. Bernard Campbell, pp. 231–81. Chicago: Aldine.

Crook, John Hurrell, and J. S. Gartlan. 1966. The evolution of primate societies. *Nature* 210:1200–03.

Dart, Raymond A. 1955. Cultural status of the South African man-apes. Annual Report, Smithsonian Institution.

————. 1957. *The osteodontokeratic culture of* Australopithecus prometheus. Memoir No. 10. Pretoria: Transvaal Museum.

Darwin, Charles. 1859. *The origin of species by means of natural selection or the preservation of favored races in the struggle for life.* New York: Modern Library.

————. 1871. *The descent of man and selection in relation to sex.* New York: Modern Library.

DeVore, Irven. 1963. A comparison of the ecology and behavior of monkeys and apes. In *Classification and human evolution,* ed. Sherwood L. Washburn, pp. 301–19. Chicago: Aldine.

————. 1965. Male dominance and mating behavior in baboons. In *Sex and behavior,* ed. Frank Beach, pp. 266–89. New York: Wiley.

DuBrul, E. Lloyd. 1977. Early hominid feeding mechanisms. *American Journal of Physical Anthropology* 47(2):305–20.

Eaton, G. Gary. 1976. The social order of Japanese macaques. *Scientific American* 235(4):97–106.

Ellefson, John O. 1968. Territorial behavior in the common white-handed gibbon, *Hylobates lar Linn.* In *Primates: studies in adaptation and variability,* ed. Phyllis C. Jay, pp. 180–99. New York: Holt, Rinehart and Winston.

Fox, Robin. 1972. Alliance and constraint: sexual selection and the evolution of human kinship systems. In *Sexual selection and the descent of man 1871–1971,* ed. Bernard Campbell, pp. 282–331. Chicago: Aldine.

Friedl, Ernestine. 1975. *Women and men: an anthropologist's view.* New York: Holt, Rinehart and Winston.

————. 1978. Society and sex roles. *Human Nature* 1(4):68–75.

Gale, Fay, ed. 1970. *Woman's role in Aboriginal society.* Australian Aboriginal Studies No. 36. Social Anthropology Series No. 6. Canberra: Australian Institute of Aboriginal Studies.

Garn, Stanley M., Rose S. Kerewsky, and Doris R. Swindler. 1966. Canine "field" in sexual dimorphism of tooth size. *Nature* 212:1501–02.

Gartlan, J. S. 1968. Structure and function in primate society. *Folia Primatologica* 8(2):89–120.

Goodall, Jane van Lawick-. 1968. The behavior of free-living chimpanzees in the Gombe Stream Reserve. *Animal Behavior Monographs* 1:165–311.

Grand, T. I. 1978. The head of *macaca:* its relative weight and tissue composition throughout development. Manuscript.

Hamilton, W. D. 1964. The genetical evolution of social behavior. *Journal of Theoretical Biology* 7:1–52.

Haraway, Donna. 1978a. Animal sociology and a natural economy of the body politic. Part I: A political physiology of dominance. *Signs: Journal of Women in Culture and Society* 4(1):21–36.

———. 1978b. Animal sociology and a natural economy of the body politic. Part II: The past is the contested zone: human nature and theories of production and reproduction in primate behavior studies. *Signs: Journal of Women in Culture and Society* 4(1):37–60.

Harvey, Paul H., Michael Kavanaugh, and T. H. Clutton-Brock. 1978a. Canine tooth size in female primates. *Nature* 276:817–18.

———. 1978b. Sexual dimorphism in primate teeth. *Journal of Zoology* 186: 475–85.

Hayden, Brian. 1977. Sticks and stones and ground edge axes: the Upper Palaeolithic in Southeast Asia? In *Sunda and Sahul: prehistoric studies in Southeast Asia, Melanesia and Australia*, ed. J. Allen, J. Golson, and R. Jones. New York: Academic Press.

Howell, F. Clark. 1978. Hominidae. In *The evolution of African mammals*, vol. 3, ed. Vincent Maglio and H. B. S. Cooke. Cambridge, Mass.: Harvard University Press.

Howell, Nancy. 1979. *Demography of the Dobe !Kung*. New York: Academic Press.

Huxley, Thomas H. 1863. *Evidence as to man's place in nature*. Ann Arbor, Mich.: University of Michigan Press, 1959.

Isaac, Glynn L. 1978. The food sharing behavior of protohuman hominids. *Scientific American* 238:90–108.

Isaac, Glynn L., Richard E. F. Leakey, and Anna K. Behrensmeyer. 1971. Archeological traces of early hominids, east of Lake Rudolf, Kenya. *Science* 173:1129–34.

Janszen, Karen. 1978. Sexual dimorphism: female and male size and proportion. Senior thesis, University of California, Santa Cruz.

Janszen, Karen, and Adrienne L. Zihlman. 1979. Sexual dimorphism in crested langurs, *Presbytis cristata*. Manuscript.

Johanson, D. Carl. 1974. Some metric aspects of the permanent and deciduous dentition of the pygmy chimpanzee *(Pan paniscus)*. *American Journal of Physical Anthropology* 41:39–48.

Johanson, D. Carl, and T. D. White. 1979. A systematic assessment of early African hominids. *Science* 203:321–30.

Johnson, P., A. Bannister, and C. Bond. 1977. *Okavango, sea of land, land of water*. Cape Town, South Africa: C. Struik.

King, Glenn E. 1976. Society and territory in human evolution. *Journal of Human Evolution* 5:323–32.

King, Mary-Claire, and A. C. Wilson. 1975. Evolution at two levels in humans and chimpanzees. *Science* 188:107–16.

Kleiman, Devra G. 1977. Review of E. O. Wilson's *Sociobiology: the new synthesis*. *Signs: Journal of Women in Culture and Society* 3(2):493–95.

Koyama, Naoki. 1967. On dominance rank and kinship of a wild Japanese monkey troup in Arashiyama. *Primates* 8:189–216.

Kruuk, Hans. 1972. *The spotted hyena*. Chicago: University of Chicago Press.

Kummer, Hans. 1971. *Primate societies: group techniques of ecological adaptation*. Chicago: Aldine.

Kuroda, Suehisa. 1979. Grouping of the pygmy chimpanzees. *Primates* 20(2):161–83.

Lancaster, Jane B. 1968. On the evolution of tool-using behavior. *American Anthropologist* 70:56–66.

———. 1978. Carrying and sharing in human evolution. *Human Nature* 1(2):82–89.

Laughlin, William S. 1968. Hunting: an integrating biobehavior system and its evolutionary implications. In *Man the hunter*, ed. Richard B. Lee and Irven DeVore, pp. 304–20. Chicago: Aldine.

Leakey, M. D. 1971. *Olduvai Gorge*, vol. 3: *Excavations in Beds I and II, 1960–1963*. Cambridge: Cambridge University Press.

Leakey, M. D., and R. L. Hay. 1979. Pliocene footprints in the Laetolil Beds at Laetoli, northern Tanzania. *Nature* 278:317–23.

Leakey, M. D., R. L. Hay, G. H. Curtis, R. E. Drake, M. K. Jackes, and T. D. White. 1976. Fossil hominids from the Laetolil Beds. *Nature* 262:460–66.

Leakey, Richard E., and Roger Lewin. 1978. *People of the lake: mankind and its beginnings*. New York: Doubleday.

Lee, Richard B. 1965. Subsistence ecology of the !Kung Bushmen. Ph.D. dissertation, University of California, Berkeley.

———. 1968a. What hunters do for a living, or how to make out on scarce resources. In *Man the hunter*, ed. Richard B. Lee and Irven DeVore, pp. 30–48. Chicago: Aldine.

———. 1968b. Comments. In *New perspectives in archeology*, ed. Sally R. Binford and Lewis R. Binford, pp. 343–46. Chicago: Aldine.

Lee, Richard B., and Irven DeVore, eds. 1968a. *Man the hunter*. Chicago: Aldine.

————. 1968*b*. Problems in the study of hunters and gatherers. In *Man the hunter,* ed. Lee and DeVore, pp. 3–12. Chicago: Aldine.

————. 1976. *Kalahari hunter-gatherers: studies of the !Kung San and their neighbors.* Cambridge, Mass.: Harvard University Press.

Leibowitz, Lila. 1978. *Females, males, families: a biosocial approach.* North Scituate, Mass.: Duxbury Press.

Leutenegger, Walter. 1974. Functional aspects of pelvic morphology of simian primates. *Journal of Human Evolution* 3:207–22.

————. 1977. Sociobiological correlates of sexual dimorphism in body weight in South Africa australopiths. *South African Journal of Science* 73:143–44.

Leutenegger, Walter, and James T. Kelly. 1977. Relationship of sexual dimorphism in canine size and body size to social, behavioral, and ecological correlates in anthropoid primates. *Primates* 18:117–36.

Lévi-Strauss, Claude. 1949. *Les Structures élémentaires de la parenté.* Paris: Presses Universitaires de France.

Linton, Sally. 1971. Woman the gatherer: male bias in anthropology. In *Women in cross-cultural perspective,* ed. Sue-Ellen Jacobs. Champaign, Ill.: University of Illinois Press. Reprinted under Sally Slocum in *Toward an anthropology of women,* ed. Rayna R. Reiter, pp. 36–50. New York: Monthly Review Press, 1975.

McGinnis, P. 1973. Patterns of sexual behavior in a community of free-living chimpanzees. Ph.D. dissertation, Cambridge University.

McGrew, W. C. 1977. Socialization and object manipulation of wild chimpanzees. In *Primate bio-social development,* ed. Suzanne Chevalier-Skolnikoff and Frank E. Poirier, pp. 261–88. New York: Garland.

McGrew, W. C., C. E. G. Tutin, and P. J. Baldwin. 1979. New data on meat eating by wild chimpanzees. *Current Anthropology* 20(1):238–39.

Mann, A. 1975. Paleodemographic aspects of the South African australopithecines. *Anthropology* No. 1, University of Pennsylvania, Philadelphia.

Marshall, Lorna. 1976. *The !Kung of Nyae Nyae.* Cambridge, Mass.: Harvard University Press.

Martin, M. Kay, and Barbara Voorhies. 1975. *Female of the species.* New York: Columbia University Press.

Meehan, Betty. 1977*a*. Hunters by the seashore. *Journal of Human Evolution* 6:363–70.

———. 1977*b*. Man does not live by calories alone: the role of shellfish in a coastal cuisine. In *Sunda and Sahul: prehistoric studies in Southeast Asia, Melanesia and Australia*, ed. J. Allen, J. Golson, and R. Jones, pp. 493–531. New York: Academic Press.

Mendeloff, Albert I. 1977. Dietary fiber and human health. *New England Journal of Medicine* 297(15):811–14.

Morris, Desmond. 1967. *The naked ape.* New York: McGraw-Hill.

Mulvaney, D. J. 1975. *The prehistory of Australia,* 2nd ed. Victoria: Penguin.

Nishida, Toshisada, Shigeo Uehara, and Ramadhani Nyundo. 1979. Predatory behavior among wild chimpanzees of the Mahale Mountains. *Primates* 20(1):1–20.

Peters, R., and L. D. Mech. 1975. Behavioral and intellectual adaptations of selected mammalian predators to the problem of hunting large animals. In *Socioecology and psychology of primates*, ed. Russell H. Tuttle, pp. 279–300. The Hague: Mouton.

Rowell, Thelma E. 1966. Forest living baboons in Uganda. *Journal of Zoology* 149:344–64.

———. 1967. Variability in the social organization of primates. In *Primate ethology*, ed. Desmond Morris, pp. 283–305. London: Weidenfeld and Nicolson.

———. 1974. The concept of social dominance. *Behavioral Biology* 11:131–54.

Sade, Donald Stone. 1967. Determinants of dominance in a group of free-ranging rhesus monkeys. In *Social communication among primates*, ed. Stuart A. Altmann, pp. 99–114. Chicago: University of Chicago Press.

———. 1972. A longitudinal study of social behavior of rhesus monkeys. In *The functional and evolutionary biology of primates*, ed. Russell H. Tuttle, pp. 378–98. Chicago: Aldine.

Sarich, Vincent M., and John E. Cronin. 1976. Molecular systematics of the primates. In *Molecular anthropology*, ed. Morris Goodman and Richard E. Tashian. New York: Plenum.

Savage, S., and R. Bakeman. 1978. Sexual morphology and behavior in *Pan paniscus.* In *Recent advances in primatology*, vol. 1, *Behaviour*, ed. D. J. Chivers and J. Herbert, pp. 613–16. London: Academic Press.

Schaller, George. 1972. *The Serengeti lion.* Chicago: University of Chicago Press.

Schaller, George B., and Gordon Lowther. 1969. The relevance of carnivore behavior to the study of early hominids. *Southwestern Journal of Anthropology* 25(4):307–41.

Shipman, Pat, and Jane Phillips-Conroy. 1977. Hominid toolmaking versus carnivore scavenging. *American Journal of Physical Anthropology* 46:77–86.

Shostak, Marjorie. 1976. A !Kung woman's memories of childhood. In *Kalahari hunter-gatherers: studies of the !Kung San and their neighbors,* ed. Richard B. Lee and Irven DeVore, pp. 246–78. Cambridge, Mass.: Harvard University Press.

Sugiyama, Yukimaru. 1973. The social structure of wild chimpanzees, a review of field studies. In *Comparative ecology and behavior of primates,* ed. Richard P. Michael and John H. Crook, pp. 375–410. New York: Academic Press.

Tanaka, Jiro. 1976. Subsistence ecology of Central Kalahari San. In *Kalahari hunter-gatherers: studies of the !Kung San and their neighbors,* ed. Richard B. Lee and Irven DeVore, pp. 98–119. Cambridge, Mass.: Harvard University Press.

Tanner, Nancy, and Adrienne L. Zihlman. 1976. Women in evolution. Part I: Innovation and selection in human origins. *Signs: Journal of Women in Culture and Society* 1(3, pt. 1):585–608.

Teleki, Geza. 1974. Chimpanzee subsistence technology: materials and skills. *Journal of Human Evolution* 3:575–94.

Thompson, Philip R. 1975. A cross species analysis of carnivore, primate, and hominid behavior. *Journal of Human Evolution* 4:113–24.

Tiger, Lionel. 1969. *Men in groups.* New York: Random House.

Tiger, Lionel, and Robin Fox. 1971. *The imperial animal.* New York: Holt, Rinehart and Winston.

Tobias, Phillip V. 1975. Brain evolution in the Hominoidea. In *Primate functional morphology and evolution,* ed. Russell H. Tuttle, pp. 353–92. The Hague: Mouton.

Trivers, Robert L. 1972. Parental investment and sexual selection. In *Sexual selection and the descent of man, 1871–1971,* ed. Bernard Campbell, pp. 136–79. Chicago: Aldine.

Truswell, A. Stewart, and John D. L. Hansen. 1976. Medical research among the !Kung. In *Kalahari hunter-gatherers: studies of the*

!Kung San and their neighbors, ed. Richard B. Lee and Irven De-
Vore, pp. 166–94. Cambridge, Mass.: Harvard University Press.

Washburn, Sherwood L. 1957. Australopithecines: the hunters or
the hunted? *American Anthropologist* 59:107–09.

———. 1968. One hundred years of biological anthropology. In *One
hundred years of anthropology,* ed. J. O. Brew, pp. 97–115. Cambridge, Mass.: Harvard University Press.

Washburn, Sherwood L., and Irven DeVore. 1961. Social behavior
of baboons and early man. In *Social life of early man,* ed. Sherwood L. Washburn, pp. 91–105. Chicago: Aldine.

Washburn, Sherwood L., and C. S. Lancaster. 1968. The evolution
of hunting. In *Man the hunter,* ed. Richard B. Lee and Irven De-
Vore, pp. 293–303. Chicago: Aldine.

Wilson, Edward O. 1975. *Sociobiology: the new synthesis.* Cambridge,
Mass.: Harvard University Press, Belknap Press.

Wrangham, Richard W. 1979. Sex differences in chimpanzee dispersion. In *The great apes,* ed. David A. Hamburg and Elizabeth R.
McCown. Menlo Park, Calif.: Benjamin/Cummings.

Zihlman, Adrienne L. 1973. Review of *The imperial animal,* Lionel
Tiger and Robin Fox. *American Journal of Physical Anthropology*
38(1):145–46.

———. 1974. Review of *Sexual selection and the descent of man,
1871–1971,* ed. Bernard Campbell. *American Anthropologist*
76(2):475–78.

———. 1976. Sexual dimorphism and its behavioral implications in
early hominids. In *Les plus anciens hominidés,* Colloque VI, IXe
Congrès. Union Internationale des Sciences Préhistoriques et
Protohistoriques, ed. P. V. Tobias and Y. Coppens, pp. 268–93.
Paris: CNRS.

———. 1978a. Women in evolution. Part II. Subsistence and social
organization among early hominids. *Signs: Journal of Women in
Culture and Society* 4(1):4–20.

———. 1978b. Motherhood in transition: from ape to human. In *The
first child and family formation,* ed. Warren B. Miller and Lucile F.
Newman, pp. 35–50. Chapel Hill, N.C.: Carolina Population
Center Publications, University of North Carolina.

———. 1979. Pygmy chimpanzee morphology and the interpretation of early hominids. *South African Journal of Science* 75:165–68.

Zihlman, Adrienne L., John E. Cronin, Douglas L. Cramer, and Vincent M. Sarich. 1978. Pygmy chimpanzee as a possible prototype for the common ancestor of humans, chimpanzees, and gorillas. *Nature* 275:744–46.

Zihlman, Adrienne L., and Nancy Tanner. 1978. Gathering and hominid adaptation. In *Female hierarchies,* ed. Lionel Tiger and Heather Fowler, pp. 163–94. Chicago: Beresford Book Service.

Zuckerman, Sol. 1932. *The social life of monkeys and apes.* London: Routledge & Kegan Paul.

3 WOMAN THE HUNTER:
THE AGTA
Agnes Estioko-Griffin and P. Bion Griffin

Among Agta Negritos of northeastern Luzon, the Philippines, women are of special interest to anthropology because of their position in the organization of subsistence. They are substantial contributors to the daily subsistence of their families and have considerable authority in decision making in the family and in residential groups. In addition, and in contradiction to one of the sacred canons of anthropology, women in one area frequently hunt game animals. They also fish in the rivers with men and barter with lowland Filipinos for goods and services.[1]

In this chapter, we describe women's roles in Agta subsistence economy and discuss the relationship of subsistence activities, authority allocation, and egalitarianism. With this may come an indication of the importance of the Agta research to the anthropology of women and of hunter-gatherers in general. We also consider implications for modeling Pliocene-Pleistocene hominid cultural evolution.

Women, especially women in hunting-gathering societies, have been a neglected domain of anthropological research. The recent volume edited by Richard Lee and Irven DeVore (1976) and the *!Kung of Nyae Nyae* (Marshall 1976) begin to remedy the lack but focus solely on the !Kung San of southern Africa. Other works are either general or synthetic (Friedl 1975; Martin and Voorhies 1975), or report narrowly bounded topics (Rosaldo and Lamphere 1974). Sally Slocum, writing in *Toward an Anthropology of Women* (Reiter 1975), has provided impetus for the Agta study. Slocum points out a male bias in studying hunter-gatherers, showing how approaching subsistence from a female view gives a new picture. From the insights of Slocum we have sought to focus on Agta women, to compare the several dialect groups, and to begin investigating the nature and implications of women as not "merely" gatherers but also hunters.

The Agta

The Agta are Negrito peoples found throughout eastern Luzon, generally along the Pacific coast and up rivers into the Sierra Madre interior (fig. 3.1). Although perhaps fewer in numbers, they are also located on the western side of the mountains, especially on the tributary rivers feeding the Cagayan. In general terms, the Agta of Isabela and Cagayan provinces are not dissimilar to other present and past Philippine Negritos. (See Vanoverbergh 1925, 1929–30, 1937–38; Fox 1952; Garvan 1964; and Maceda 1964 for information on Negritos outside the present study area.) In the more remote locales, hunting forest game, especially wild pig, deer, and monkey, is still important. Everywhere, collection of forest plant foods has been eclipsed by exchange of meat for corn, rice, and cultivated root crops. Fishing is usually important throughout the dry season, while collection of the starch of the caryota palm (*Caryota cumingii*) is common in the rainy season. An earlier paper (Estioko and Griffin 1975) gives some detail concerning the less settled Agta; both Bennagen (1976) and Peterson (1974, 1978*a,b*, n.d.) closely examine aspects of subsistence among Agta in the municipality of Palanan.

A brief review of Agta economic organization will be sufficient for later discussion of women's activities. Centuries ago all Agta may have been strictly hunter-gatherers. Since at least A.D. 1900 the groups near the towns of Casiguran (Headland and Headland 1974) and Palanan have been sporadic, part-time horticulturalists, supplementing wild

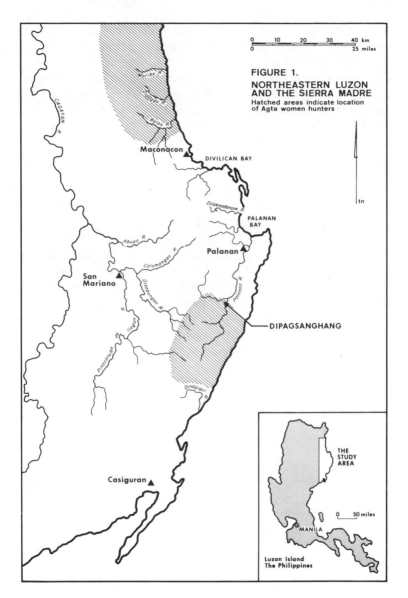

Figure 3.1. Northeastern Luzon and the Sierra Madre.

plant foods with sweet potatoes, corn, cassava, and rice. The more remote, interior Agta, sometimes referred to as *ebuked* (Estioko and Griffin 1975), plant small plots of roots, a few square meters of corn, and a banana stalk or two. They usually plant only in the wet season, harvesting an almost immature crop when staples are difficult to obtain by trade. *Ebuked* neglect crop production, preferring to trade meat for grains and roots.

Lee and DeVore (1968:7) argue that women produce much of the typical hunter-gatherers' diet and that in the tropics vegetable foods far outweigh meat in reliability and frequency of consumption. The Dipagsanghang and Dianggu-Malibu Agta strikingly contradict this idea. They are superb hunters, eat animal protein almost daily, and, as noted above, may have both men and women hunting. (The Tasaday, to the south in Mindanao, may represent an extreme nonhunting adaptation, one in which plant food collection is very dominant [Yen 1976].) Hunting varies seasonally and by techniques used among various groups, but is basically a bow and arrow technology for killing wild pig and deer, the only large game in the Luzon dipterocarp forests. Monkey, although not large, is a reliable rainy season prey. Among Agta close to Palanan and Casiguran, hunting is a male domain. Many hunters pride themselves on skill with bow and arrow; less able hunters may use traps. Dogs to drive game are very desirable in the dry season when the forest is too noisy for daylight stalking of animals.

The collecting of wild plant food is not a daily task. Most Agta prefer to eat corn, cassava, and sweet potatoes, and neglect the several varieties of roots, palm hearts, and greens procurable in the forest. Reasons behind the shift have been explored in another paper (Estioko-Griffin and Griffin, in press). Briefly stated, forest foods are difficult to collect, necessitate residence moves over long distances, and do not taste as good as cultivated foods. Emphasis of trade networks with lowland farmers favors deemphasis of forest exploitation of plants. Only in the rainy season do Agta actively process a traditional resource, the sago-like caryota palm. Fruits are often picked on the spur of the moment; seldom do parties leave camp solely for their collection.

Trade with farmers is practiced by all Agta known to us. Rumors of Agta "farther into the mountains" who never trade (or cultivate) seem to be without substance. In the report of the Philippine Commission (1908:334), evidence of lowland-Agta trade around 1900 indicates the *ibay* trade partner relationship to have some antiquity. As the lowlander population has increased since World War II, trade has also increased. Agta are more and more dependent on goods and foodstuffs gained from farmers; adjustments of Agta economic behavior continue to be made, with labor on farms being one aspect of change. Agta formerly simply traded meat for carbohydrates. Around Palanan they may now work for cash or kind when residing close to farmers' settlements. Hunting decreases as the demands of cultivation are met. A cycle is created, and further withdrawal from forest subsistence occurs. Farmers live in areas once solely owned by Agta. Debts to farmers increase with economic dependence; freedom of mobility and choice of activity decrease; and Agta in farming areas become landless laborers.

At the same time, Agta seek to get out of the cycle by emulating the farmers. Many Agta within ten kilometers of Palanan Centro are attempting to become farmers themselves. While the success rate is slow, the attempt is real. Again, when questioned by an early American anthropologist, Agta close to Palanan Centro claimed to be planting small rainy season plots with corn, roots, and upland rice (Worcester 1912:841). Living informants confirm the long practice of cultivation, but suggest a recent expansion of Agta fields and commitment to abandoning forest nomadism (especially over the last fifteen years). Around the areas of Disuked-Dilaknadinum and Kahanayan-Diabut in Palanan, Agta are well known for their interest in swidden cultivation. Even the most unsettled Agta farther upriver claim small fields and sporadically plant along the rivers well upstream of lowland farmsteads.

The horticultural efforts of the Agta appear less than is the case, since the social organization and settlement patterns are very different from those of the farmers. Agta throughout Isabela and Cagayan are loosely organized into extended family residential groups. A group, called a *pisan,* is seldom less than two nuclear families and very rarely more than five (in the dry season—perhaps slightly higher average during the wet season). The nuclear family is the basic unit of Agta society, being potentially self-sufficient under usual circumstances. The residential group is organized as a cluster of nuclear families united either through a common parent or by sibling ties. Non-kin friends may be visitors for several weeks, and any nuclear family is able to leave and join another group of relatives at will.

As is typical of hunting-gathering societies, no formal, institutionalized authority base exists. The nuclear family is the decision maker concerning residence, work, and relations with other people. Older, respected individuals, often parents and grandparents of group members, may be consulted, but their opinions are not binding. Often group consensus is desired; people who disagree are free to grumble or to leave.

The settlement pattern is determined, in part, by the seasonal cycle of rains and sunny weather, and by these influences on the flora and fauna exploited for food. Rainy season flooding restricts forest travel, brings hardships in exchange, but is compensated by good condition of the game animals. The dry season permits travel over greater distances and into the remote mountains. Predictable fish resources enhance the advantages of human dispersal; only the need to carry trade meats to farmers inhibits distant residence placement.

Women's Activities

Women participate in all the subsistence activities that men do. Women trade with farmers, fish in the rivers, collect forest plant foods, and may even hunt game animals. Tasks are not identical, however; a modest sexual division of labor does

Figure 3.2. An Agta nuclear family at Dianggu.

exist. Furthermore, considerable variation is found among the groups of Agta of Isabela and Cagayan provinces. These differences may possibly be ascribed to degree of adjustment of Agta to lowland Filipino culture. Some differences may be due to unique culture histories and to little contact.

Although in Isabela most Agta women do not hunt with bow and arrows, with machetes, or by use of traps, most are willing to assist men in the hunt. Not uncommonly, women help carry game out of the forest. Since mature pig and deer are heavy and the terrain is difficult, this is no small accomplishment. Even in areas around Palanan and Casiguran, women are known to accompany men and dogs into the forest and to guide the dogs in the game drive. Some women are famous for their abilities to handle dogs; one informant, a girl about fifteen years of age, was especially skilled. In Palanan and Casiguran, women and men laugh at the idea of women hunting. Such a practice would be a custom of wild, uncivilized Agta (*ebuked*) far in the mountains, they say. Many of the attributes of *ebuked* seem to be old-fashioned customs still practiced by interior groups.

Two groups studied as part of the present research do have women who hunt. Among the Dipagsanghang Agta, several mature women claim to have hunting skills; they learned these in their unmarried teen years. They only hunt under extreme circumstances, such as low food supplies or great distances from farmers and a supply of corn. All these Agta are found in southern Isabela between Dipagsanghang and Dinapiqui.

In the northernmost section of Isabela and well into Cagayan province, women are active and proficient hunters. While we have termed the Agta here as the Dianggu-Malibu group, we are actually referring to speakers of the southeast Cagayan dialect who live on the river drainage areas of the Dianggu and Malibu rivers.[2] Both the dialect and women who hunt are found over a considerably greater territory, according to informants, reaching north to Baggao, Cagayan, and at least to the Taboan River.

Among the Dianggu-Malibu women some variation, perhaps localized, perhaps personal, is found. On the Dianggu, some of the women questioned, and observed hunting, carried machetes and were accompanied by dogs. They claim to prefer the machete to the bow and arrow, allowing dogs to corner and hold pigs for sticking with the knife. Our sample of actual observations is too small to argue that only immature pigs are killed, but we do know that in the dry season adult male pigs are dangerous in the extreme. Dogs may be killed during hunts. Since Agta dogs are seldom strong animals, we wonder if mature pigs are acquired only occasionally. On the other hand, so many dogs are owned by these Agta that sheer numbers may favor large kills. We have observed two Agta women with as many as fifteen dogs. Other Dianggu women prefer the bow.

On the Malibu River, Agta women are expert bow and arrow hunters. On both of our brief visits to this group, women were observed hunting. They claim to use bows always, and they seek the full range of prey animals. Wild pig is most desired, while deer are often killed. Future work must quantify the hunting details, but women seem to vary slightly from men in their hunting strategies. Informants say they hunt only with dogs. On closer questioning they admit to knowing techniques that do not involve dogs—for example, they may climb trees and lie in wait for an animal to approach to feed on fallen fruit. Among all Agta, hunting practices vary considerably between the rainy and dry seasons. Our fieldwork in Malibu has been confined to the dry season, when dogs are important. In the rainy season solitary stalking is practiced. Field observations should eventually provide quantitative data on women hunting in this season; we must stress that our data are primarily from interview and brief observation. We have not resided among Cagayan Agta long enough to advance quantitatively based generalizations.

Women not only hunt but appear to hunt frequently. Like men, some enjoy hunting more than others. The more remotely located Agta seem most to favor hunting. Even among Agta certain males and females are considered lacking in initiative, a fault that may not be confined to hunting.

Informant data indicate that while women may make their own arrows, the actual blacksmithing of the metal projectile points is a male activity. More field research is necessary to

Figure 3.3. A woman hunter of Malibu.

confirm the universality of this detail. Other items of interest
pertain to the composition of hunting parties. Most people in
any one residence group are consanguineally or affinely related. We have observed several combinations of hunting
parties. Men and women hunt together or among themselves.
Often sisters, or mother and daughter, or aunt and niece
hunt together. At Malibu, two sisters, co-wives of one male,
hunt together, and either or both sisters join the husband to
hunt. When young children exist, one of the two wives may
stay at the residence while the husband and the other wife
hunt and fish. Also, sisters and brothers cooperate on the
hunt. A woman would not hunt with, for example, a cousin's
husband unless the cousin were along.

The only real argument, in our opinion, that has been advanced to support the contention that women must gather and men hunt relates to childbearing and nurture. Among the Agta, during late pregnancy and for the first few months of nursing, a woman will not hunt. In spite of the small size of each residential group, however, some females seem always to be around to hunt, although one or more may be temporarily withdrawn from the activity. Women with young children hunt less than teenagers and older women. On the occasion of brief hunts—part of one day—children are cared for by older siblings, by grandparents, and by other relatives. Occasionally a father will tend a child. Only infants are closely tied to mothers.

Girls start hunting shortly after puberty. Before then they are gaining forest knowledge but are not strong. Boys are no different. We have no menopause data, but at least one woman known to us as a hunter must have passed childbearing age. She is considered an older woman, but since she is strong, she hunts. The pattern is typical of men also. As long as strength to travel and to carry game is retained, people hunt. Our best informant, a young grandmother, hunts several times a week.

Both Agta men and women fish. In fact, from early childhood until the infirmity of old age all Agta fish. If most adults are gone on a hunting trip for several days, the remaining adults and children must obtain animal protein by themselves. Only women in late pregnancy, with young infants, or into old age, withdraw from fishing, which makes considerable demands of endurance as well as skill. Some men excel at working in rough, deep, and cold waters. The everyday techniques for fishing are limited to underwater spear fishing. Glass-lensed wooden goggles, a heavy wire spear or rod varying according to size of fish sought, and an inner-tube rubber band complete the equipment. To fish, people simply swim underwater, seeking fish in the various aquatic environments known for each species. Girls in their teens are very capable at fishing. When fishing individually, women may be major contributors to the daily catch.

When group fishing is undertaken, a drive is conducted. In this operation, a long vine is prepared by attaching stones and banners of wild banana stalks. Two people drag the vine, one on each end and on opposite sides of the river, while the people in the water spear fish startled by the stones and stalks. Women join men in the drives, with older men and women dragging the vine while all able-bodied youths and adults work in the water.

Difficulty of fishing may be characterized as a gradient upon which men and women become less and less able as age and debilities increase. The elderly, when mobile, may still be productive, but instead of true fishing, their activities may be termed collecting. Both the coastal reef areas and freshwater rivers and streams have abundant shellfish, shrimp, and amphibians that may be caught by hand. Elderly women and grandchildren are especially eager to harvest these resources. Older men are not ashamed to follow suit, although the enthusiasm of others for the task seldom gives old men incentive. Men are much less eager to give up riverine fishing after middle age than are women. Clearly some emphasis on males securing protein is found among Agta. Women, however, seem to have traditionally been active in fishing. Interestingly, as a few Agta adopt lowland fishing technology, especially nets, women seldom participate. Like their female counterparts in lowland society, women are deemed not appropriate in net fishing.

One might expect that, on the basis of worldwide comparison, tropic hunters would really be gatherers, and that women would be the steady and substantial providers. Agta do not fit the generalizations now accepted. Few Agta women regularly dig roots, gather palm hearts, seek fruit, or pick greens. Most Agta daily consume domesticated staples grown by the farmers. Women are, however, very knowledgeable concerning flora and its use, and among the less settled Agta, young girls are still taught all traditional forest lore. Brides-to-be among these Agta are partially evaluated on the basis of their knowledge, skill, and endurance in collecting jungle plant foods.

Roots are collected by women whenever more desirable food is unobtainable, when several wild pigs have been killed and the men want to eat "forest food" with pig fat, or when a visit to relatives or friends calls for a special treat. The interior groups may actually combine meat and wild roots for weeks when camped so far from farmers that exchange for corn is impossible. Downriver Agta consider such a practice a real hardship, not to be willingly endured. Men are known to dig roots, even though they say it is women's work. On long-distance hunts men do not as a rule carry food, and they may occasionally dig roots to alleviate the all meat-fish diet.

As hunting is thought of as a "sort of" male activity among many Agta (in Isabela), processing the starch of the caryota palm is a female activity. Women cruise the forest searching for trees containing masses of the starch; they also chop down the trees, split the trunks, adze out the pith, and extract the flour. Often parties of women and girls work together, speeding up the laborious task. On occasion, men will assist. Extracting the flour starch is moderately heavy work, and tiring. Husbands may help when wives have a pressing need to complete a task quickly. Since much of the final product is given in gift form, the need for haste occurs frequently. Perhaps most important to note is the male participation. Sexual division of labor is tenuously bounded among all Agta. Emphases may exist, but a man can even build a house (i.e., tie the fronds to the frame—a female task).

As noted at the beginning, trade, exchange, and horticulture are not new to Agta. Informants, early photographs, and writings indicate that all but the most remote Agta were not "pure" hunter-gatherers after about A.D. 1900. Since the mountains have been a final retreat—from the earliest Spanish attempts to conquer the Cagayan Valley until the present—Agta must have been in contact with former farmers/revolutionaries in hiding. Keesing (1962), summarizing the peoples of northern Luzon, documents several societies of pagan swiddeners adjacent to or in Negrito territory. The Palanan River drainage area was inhabited by farmers before Spanish contact in the sixteenth century. Doubtless, Agta have participated in economic exchange and social intercourse for centuries. Agta now have institutionalized trade partnerships, at least in Palanan and Casiguran municipalities. Trade partners are called *ibay* (Peterson [1978*a,b*] discussed the *ibay* relationship in detail), and partnerships may last between two families over two or more generations. *Ibay* exchange meat for grains and roots, or meat for cloth, metal, tobacco, beads, and other goods. Services may be exchanged, especially in downriver areas. Fields may be worked by Agta, who then borrow a carabao, receive corn or rice, and satisfy any of a number of needs. What is important in relation to this chapter is that Agta women may engage in *ibay* partnerships. Among the lowland farmers almost all *ibay* are males. An Agta woman may be an *ibay* with a lowland man. According to our data, an Agta husband often is not also *ibay* with his wife's *ibay*, but he must treat the farmer as he would his own *ibay*. Of course Agta men and women trade with any farmer they choose, but such exchange is without the consideration given to an *ibay*. (Considerations include credit, acts of friendship, and first choice/best deal on goods.) Not only do women have *ibay*, but they very frequently are the most active agents of exchange. In areas where the trade rests mostly on meat and where men do most of the hunting, women are likely to carry out the dried meat and bring back the staple. They therefore gain experience in dealing with the farmers. We should note that many farmers attempt to cheat the Agta by shortchanging them on counts or weights, but they do so on the basis of gullibility or naiveté of the Agta, not on the basis of sex. Agta women are actually more aggressive traders than are men, who do not like confrontation.

Among the Dipagsanghang Agta, women seldom hunt today, and infrequently dig roots. They do carry out meat to trade. They seem to have an easier life, with emphasis on corn, rice, and roots instead of gathering wild foods. However, downriver, close to farmers, Agta women have reversed this trend, and are working harder and longer hours.[3] Intensification of the *ibay* relationship and need to own and cultivate land has forced women to become horticulturalists and wage laborers for farmers. On their own family plots (family-owned, not male- or female-owned) they, together with adult males and youths, clear land, break soil, plant, weed, and harvest. When clearing virgin forest of large trees, women do not participate. They do clear secondary growth in fallowed fields.

In the families that reside close to Palanan (see Estioko-Griffin and Griffin, in press, for details) men and women work almost daily in the fields of farmers. Women go to the forest to collect the lighter raw materials for house construction, mats, betel chews, medicines, and so on. Men follow a similar pattern, giving up hunting for field labor and a corn ' and sweet potato diet supplemented by small fish. Again we see a remarkable parallel in the activities of males and females.

Looking more closely at specialized women's activities, one may suggest increasing importance in downriver areas. Women have several domains that they use to gain cash or kind income. As just stated, income from labor in fields adds to the economic power of women. A small-scale traditional pursuit, shared by men and women, is the gathering of copal, a tree resin common to trees (*Agathis philippinensis*) found scattered in the Sierra Madre. Women often collect and carry the resin out to lowland "middlemen," who sell it to the depot in town. While corn and cash may be sought in exchange, cloth is desired in order to make skirts. Medicine and medical treatments for ailing children may be paid for by copal collection. Another example of entrepreneurship by females is a small-scale mobile variety store effort. After working in fields for cash and building a surplus, families may cross the Sierra Madre to the towns of San Mariano, Cauayan, and Ilagan. There Agta, often women, purchase in markets and stores goods for use and resale in Palanan. Palanan Centro itself has no real market, only several small general stores selling goods at highly marked up prices. Since no road reaches Palanan, all manufactured supplies must enter town by airplane from Cauayan or boat from Baler. Freight costs are high. Some Agta women are very eager to hike outside to get tobacco, which always commands a high price and a ready market.

Discussion

The role of women in Agta economic activities has been reviewed. Assessment of an hypothesized egalitarian position of women may be more difficult, and rests on assertions and interpretations drawn from the economic roles. First, drawing in part from Friedl (1975), an argument can be made that women in Agta society have equality with men because they have similar authority in decision making. The authority could be based on the equal contribution to the subsistence resources. Working back, we see that among many Agta, women do contribute heavily to the daily food supply, do perform maintenance tasks with men, and may initiate food acquisition efforts through their own skills. They do control the distribution of their acquired food, sharing first with their own nuclear family and extended family, then trading as they see fit. They may procure nonfood goods as they desire. Men may do the same; generally spouses discuss what work to do, what needs should be satisfied, and who will do what. Whole residential groups frequently together decide courses of action. Women are as vocal and as critical in reaching decisions as are men. Further examples could strongly validate the hypothesis that women do supply a substantial portion of foods, and the assertion that women have authority in major decision making. Two questions arise. May we accept a causal relationship between percentage of food production and equality? Certainly there are cases to the contrary. According to Richard A. Gould (personal communication), Australian Aboriginal women in various areas collected the bulk of the food, yet remained less than equal (as we will define equality). Second, we may ask if Agta males and females are actually "equal."

Two avenues may suffice in answering this question. First, one might explore a definition of equality, surely a culturally loaded concept. Since Agta women have authority or control of the economic gain of their own labor, they may be equal in this critical domain. Equality must surely be equated with decision-making power and control of one's own production. The second avenue of equality validation by the scientist may be to examine the female's control over herself in noneconomic matters. These could include selection of marriage partner, lack of premarital sexual intercourse proscription, spacing of children, ease of divorce, and polygyny rules.

In marriage, two forms are typical of Agta. One, the less common, is elopement by young lovers. While such marriages admittedly are fragile, elopement is not uncommon. In this case both partners must be willing. Rape and abduction are rare. Rape by Agta men is not known to the authors. Abduction must involve a slightly willing female, and is not done by young people. A mature man might abduct a married woman, crossing the mountains to a safe locale. To abduct a young girl would be difficult. Parents of eloping couples may be enraged, but usually reconcile themselves to the marriage. If the newlyweds stay together, no more is made of it.

The proper form of marriage is one arranged by customary meetings and discussions, as well as exchange of goods between two families. Often neither the bride nor the groom has had much say in the matter, although serious dislike by either would probably kill the negotiations before the marriage. Mothers are the most important in choosing who will marry whom. Even when their children are young, they are looking about for good partners. Word filters around when a young girl is marriageable, and efforts are made to get the appropriate young man and his family into negotiations before an undesirable family appears. Once any family with a prospective groom formally asks, a rejection is given only for strong and good reasons, since the denied family loses considerable face and may be angry enough to seek revenge.[4]

Criteria for choice of a marriage partner are varied. Often a young man in his early twenties marries a girl about fifteen. Girls entering marriage before puberty are not uncommon. In such cases the husband may help raise the girl until the time the marriage is consummated and full wifehood is recognized. Other combinations are seen. One much discussed case was the marriage of a woman in her forties to a man in his mid-twenties. The couple seemed very happy, with the wife paying rather special attention to her husband. The man's mother, a friend of the wife's, decided that the marriage was peculiar but acceptable.

Premarital female chastity is not an ideal of much currency. Agta close to farmers will pay lip service to the idea, but should a girl become pregnant she will take a husband. There are no illegitimate Agta children, although an occasional rape of an Agta by a lowland male may produce a child. Since by the time a girl is fertile she likely will be married, illegitimacy is not the issue. Although some data are difficult to collect concerning sex, almost certainly girls are able to engage in sexual activity with relative ease; promiscuity is not favored in any circumstance. Males may have as little or great difficulty in engaging in sex as females. The Agta are widely dispersed in extended family groups; hence appropriate sexual partners are seldom seen. No homosexuality is known to exist.

Agta gossip suggests that many Agta, male and female, married and unmarried, constantly carry on extramarital sexual relations. This may be a function of gossip, and a gross exaggeration. Whatever reality, neither males nor females seem to be especially singled out for criticism.

Women say they space their children. The practice certainly varies hugely from person to person, as does fecundity and luck in keeping children alive. The Agta use various herbal concoctions that supposedly prevent conception, cause abortions shortly after conception, and have several functions related to menstruation. These medicines are known to all Agta and are frequently used. Our census data indicate that some women seem to be successful in spacing births. Other cases note high infant mortality yet no infanticide, female or male. All Agta abhor the idea.

Divorce is infrequent among Agta, with elopement being more prone to failure than are arranged marriages. Divorce does happen often enough, however, for us to look at the causes and relate them to an inquiry into female equality. First, either sex may divorce the other with equal ease. Agta have no possessions. Some gift giving between the two families establishes the marriage, but most of the gifts are food. Cloth, kettles, and minor items make up the rest. Return of marriage gifts is unlikely. Spouses simply take their personal possessions and return to the residential group of close relatives.

Causes for divorce are mainly laziness or improvidence, excessive adultery, or personality clashes and incompatibility, usually caused by a combination of the first two conditions. Skill and success in subsistence activities is of primary importance to marriage. While some Agta are less industrious and less skilled than others, all Agta expect a mate to work hard at all appropriate tasks. Should a mate fail, divorce is likely. Occasionally, very young couples experience extra difficulties. These may be accentuated by displeased parents of either party.

Polygamy is not found in most of Isabela. Census data collected to date reveal only monogamy or serial monogamy. That is, spouses may be divorced or widow(er)ed several times in a lifetime. In Cagayan the data are incomplete but startling. Probably some of the strongest support for the equality of women hypothesis, when added to the facts of women as hunters, comes from a study of Agta polygamy. We noted earlier that two co-wives, sisters, hunted together in Malibu. South of Malibu at Blos, another husband and two sisters/co-wives arrangement was found. In the same residential unit we recorded a woman residing with her two co-husbands.

They were not brothers; one was older than the wife, one younger. The other women considered this arrangement as humorous, but acceptable. An insight into the male sexual jealousy found in many societies worldwide is the comment of a Palanan Agta man. This old man, when told of the polyandrous marriage to the north, thought for a moment and commented, "Well, perhaps one man with two wives is OK, but a woman with two husbands? I find that totally bad." The women laughed at him.

Conclusions and Implications for Further Research

The case must be rested that Agta women are equal to men. They do have authority, and they do regularly contribute a significant portion of the subsistence resources. Their freedom of choice in sex and marriage seem to support the hypothesis of an egalitarian society.

Clearly only a beginning has been made in understanding women's position in the Agta society. The current study is based on inadequately quantified data, on questions incompletely answered, and an insufficient length of participant observation in the field. Perhaps the best that can be done is to discuss the importance of continued investigation of Agta women and to summarize the importance of the research to the anthropology of hunting-gathering societies, to the anthropology of women,[5] and to understanding hominid biocultural evolution in the early Pleistocene.

Three main implications come to mind after reviewing the Agta data. First, we may need to examine again the available ethnographic literature concerning hunter-gatherers worldwide. We may have overlooked off-the-cuff comments which suggest that women were hunting in many situations. Several publications discuss some form of female hunting (Jenness 1923; Flannery 1932, 1935; Landes 1938; Fox 1952; Goodale 1971; Briggs 1974; Hammond and Jablow 1976). In unpublished data, Richard Nelson, Florence Shipek, and Richard A. Gould indicate that in their experiences, women hunters have been known. These include people as far out of the humid tropics as Alaskan and southern California Indians and Australian Aborigines. Part of the problem is in the definition of hunting itself and in an ill-defined separation of big from small game. This is very evident in looking at data concerning Mbuti of the Ituri forest in Zaire (Turnbull 1965; Harako 1976; Tanno 1976). No hint was given that women use bow and arrow or spear, or that they kill buffalo or elephant. However, one might ask again. Mbuti women do hunt among the net hunters. Their activity is part of a team effort but cannot be called gathering. That they also collect plant foods is beside the point. Men do, too.

Among the Aboriginal peoples of Western Australia, women hunt and gather (Richard Gould, personal communication). Game is not large—kangaroos (occasionally) and lizards are the usual fare. Friedl (1975:12) would call this gathering, but classification seems only to force artificial boundaries. The Australian women's recent adoption of dogs as successful hunting companions remains an unexplained anomaly. Agta hunt mid-range-sized game, the largest found in Luzon. The adult boar, deer (as big as mule deer), and (formerly) feral water buffalo are prey of Agta predators. Size and strength of the hunters may depend less on size of prey than on the environment. Small people seem suited to exploiting humid tropics game; drier, more open biomes may favor larger, stronger hunters. Sex differences as to size and strength cannot now be clearly asserted as relevant. We remain in need of quantified data collected in field situations detailing exertion in hunting, the effect of pregnancy and lactation, and the context of gathered plant foods in opposition to animal protein.

A serious handicap is a major cultural bias. Hunting is a valued activity among males of much of Europe, Asia, and Africa—men in nation states. American women do hunt with men, but a quick glance at the sport's journals shows that no status is ascribed to successful women hunters. Anthropologists have, as has been superbly discussed by Slocum

(1975), been certain of the robust Paleolithic male hunter-provider. Only since Lee and DeVore's *Man the Hunter* (1968) have we known that women gather and may be the steady, no-nonsense providers of plant foods. The man-the-hunter/woman-the-gatherer dichotomy has become the latest "law." Instead of questioning the basic assumption, anthropology has sought to show that, in being gatherers, females were important in the evolution of culture and in shaping human institutions. This is good, gathering is *important,* but perhaps the time has come to decide to what extent and under what conditions women could have been hunters. Are the Agta an aberrant, inconsequential society, or may they have put us into a new insight? So strong are our biases against the idea of females hunting that we have allowed the hunting division of labor to creep into both our scientific inquiry and our artistic representations. (See the well-known pictures of australopithecines in Howell 1973:62–69 for a case in point.) The Agta case is clearly anomalous. Even if literature searches and field surveys locate more women hunters, the atypical nature of significant nonmale hunting must be explained. We may not ignore the importance of gathering, nor may we overstate the critical contribution of hunting by either sex. By understanding the causal influences in the generation of women hunters in any foraging society, we may state when, why, and under what conditions women hunt. Only through isolation of generating pressures may we confound regularities now established explaining sexual division of labor in preagricultural societies.

The main issue to resolve first is just how childbearing influences subsistence activity. As Quinn (1977:187) states:

> Most writers agree that hunting is incompatible with pregnancy, carrying small infants, and child care, although they are not always agreed as to whether it is the actual physical exertion which hunting demands, the danger it involves, or the long-distance travel it engenders which is most critical to this incompatibility.

A simple determinism, based largely on some uncomfortable

negative evidence, seems to be guiding the relationship of hunter-gatherer sexual division of labor and childbearing. The relationship may be accurate; at first glance worldwide data so indicate. As we proceed, two avenues of inquiry are imperative to follow. Quantitative data collectible among the Agta must be structured for maximum value in testing the hypothesis that women are withdrawn from serious hunting because of children. Other hunting groups may be researched; the forests of Southeast Asia alone contain several target populations. We suggest that already the Agta data deny the universality of the woman-the-gatherer model, and go far to advance the concept of hunter-gatherers as incredibly flexible in all their organizational characteristics. Subsistence activities as well as social organization may be so malleable that whatever the environmental pressures for and historical trajectory of culture change, hunters may shift people into whatever food-getting pursuits will keep everybody fed.

Several hypotheses may be developed for the Agta case. First, an ecological approach emphasizing energy resources available to Agta should be detailed. Predator-prey relationships may favor emphasis on animal protein acquisition (by Agta). The short- and long-term availability of wild roots and vegetables is hardly known; they are probably not available in quantities adequate to support the present density of Agta. Wild pig and deer, however, are considered abundant by the interior Agta. One testable hypothesis concerns the advantage of emphasis on consumption of meat. Analysis of caloric and nutrient return on labor invested for hunting and for gathering may partially bear on the hypothesis. One Agta, at Malibu, said we would be welcome to live with them during research if we could live on meat.

Determination of both social and natural environmental effects on the organization of Agta subsistence will enable isolation of possible adaptive pressures favoring women hunters. The availability of lowland farmer-produced roots and grains surely influences Agta close to Palanan. It is no accident that only in remote mountain regions do women hunt. Farmers place considerable pressure on Agta to conform to lowland customs. All lowlanders regard hunting as solely a male activity and ridicule participation by women. Also, perhaps less meat is necessary today than in the past. While Agta trade most meat acquired, eating only a small portion themselves, the trade foods may easily replace formerly necessary animal protein.

We know only that the Agta women are successful hunters. We must yet learn their importance in subsistence. Comparison among at least three groups should allow extrapolation of response to different conditions. A range of variation such as evidenced by Malibu, Dipagsanghang, and Palanan Agta would be the correct preview of upcoming research.

Several interesting and provocative papers have recently built on the male-female sexual division of labor to model a fuller view of basal Pleistocene hominid behavior (Isaac 1969, 1971, 1978; Gough 1975; Tanner and Zihlman 1976; Lancaster 1978; McGrew, chapter 1, this volume). Isaac's 1978 paper, since it advances archaeological data, is especially exciting. As does Lancaster, he sees carrying of tools, materials, and food as critical in the formation of a more "human" type of society. Isaac argues:

> Among extant and recently extinct primitive human societies the transport of food is associated with a division of labor. The society is divided by age and sex into classes that characteristically make different contributions to the total food supply. . . . Could this simple mechanism, a division of the subsistence effort, have initiated food-carrying by early hominids? [1978:100]

The assumption, based on evidence of a "home base," is that males and females collected different sorts of food, carried the goods home, and shared among those present or at least within nuclear families. From rather modest beginnings in labor specialization, the dichotomies of the later Paleolithic big-game hunters developed. "Because females and juveniles may be involved in hunting small creatures, the social organization of big-game hunting would also lead to an intensification of a sexual division of labor" (Washburn and Lancaster 1968:296).

We cannot deny the elegance and attractiveness of this model. We can, however, suggest another for eventual testing. Perhaps what really generates the idea is only a shift away from a "!Kung San model" to an "Agta model." The suitability of tropical forest habitats for hunter-gatherers should be explored, and implications for late Pliocene hominid adaptive radiations hypothesized. First, the primacy of the edge of the savannah environment as maximally suited for all early hominids may be questioned. A wide range of easily secured plant and animal foods is found in the more seasonal tropical forests. Fossil preservation conditions seldom approach the ideal offered by the East African lake edges several million years ago, but a lack of fossils cannot demonstrate the nonexistence of forest-dwelling hominids, as many scholars have pointed out (e.g., Isaac 1969). For decades we have envisioned a development of bipedalism, hunting, and progression onto the game-rich savannah. The generalized ancestors of australopithecines may have diversified into many resource niches. As we become more acquainted with tropical forests and their inhabitants, we learn that they are provident homes indeed (Turnbull 1965).

Next, the disadvantage of early division of labor may be considered. In acquisition of small game, all but the most pregnant females should be competent. Young, including infants, may be quickly handed to siblings or to any weak individual such as an elderly group member. The adaptive value of both carrying and sharing may be as real without males hunting and females gathering as with. In a situation of increased infant dependency, group cooperation may be as adaptive as father-mother-child cooperation. Any single hominid, or combination of hominids, might scavenge a large animal, carrying meat back to a sheltered base camp. Or an entire group might travel to a new location near the kill, together retrieve the meat, and hasten off to safety. Small animals should fall into the same category as gathered plant foods. It can be argued that all mobile members of a group would be out daily collecting everything they could get their hands on. Return to a base camp and sharing is likely, although some foods would be consumed while in the bush. Contemporary hunter-gatherers tend to support the likelihood of this procedure. Not all societies share only big meat kills; Agta share, within the confines of the residential unit, and sometimes more widely, *all* foods. The Tasaday of southwestern Mindanao, a collecting group, find family units foraging together, sharing mainly among themselves, but bringing some foods back to the base camp in a cave (Yen 1976 and personal communication).

The ethnographic data indicate the viability of alternative hypotheses concerning the origins of sexual divisions of labor among early hominids. The archaeological data certainly will permit asking new questions. Permutations of the woman the hunter model may be extended through the Pleistocene and into the present. Mbuti pygmies (male, yet small) are able to kill elephant and buffalo (Harako 1976); surely, western European classic Neanderthal women could have participated in the hunt. Agta Negrito women kill wild pig and deer. Should *Homo erectus* females in Java be assumed unable to do the same? Further investigation of the archaeological record and of present groups coping with the impact of childbearing and nurture may allow us to rethink the whole business of sexual division of labor as a foundation of present human society.

Acknowledgments

The original survey that located the unsettled Agta groups was supported through the generosity of the Wenner-Gren Foundation for Anthropological Research (Grant 2905) and the University of Hawaii. The National Science Foundation (Grant SOC73-09083 A01) funded the longer field visit, which took place between June 1974 and June 1976. The University of Hawaii provided sabbatical salary in 1975–76 and again funded a return to Cagayan in August 1978. The Social Science Research Institute at the University of Hawaii has assisted throughout the research. We gratefully acknowledge these institutions.

The senior author thanks Dr. Arsenio Manuel and Professor Ponciano Bennagen of the Department of Anthropology of the University of the Philippines for their assistance and advice. The junior author thanks the National Museum of the Philippines for their continual support of and interest in the Agta study. Director Godofredo Alcasid, Assistant Director Alfredo Evangelista, Dr. Jesus Peralta, and Dr. Eric Casino are especially thanked. Lieutenant Colonel Ernesto Sacro of NOREASCOM, Armed Forces of the Philippines, Ecague, Isabela, is thanked for his interest and assistance. We are also grateful to the management of Acme Plywood and Veneer, Inc., for their assistance in many ways.

Several people have kindly provided both brief and extended comments that have improved this chapter. We thank all critics, and especially note the assistance of Frances Dahlberg, Jean Peterson, Thomas Headland, David Tuggle, James Eder, Karl Hutterer, and Richard A. Gould, to whom we owe the use of the concept of anomaly. We thank Myra Tomonari-Tuggle for preparation of the map.

The Agta peoples are gratefully acknowledged; their interest and hospitality have made the project possible. We hope our writings properly reflect their pride and importance as one of the cultures of the Republic of the Philippines.

Notes

1. Although the authors have worked among the Agta about fourteen months, visits to the northerly group in the Dianggu-Malibu area have been brief. The practice of women hunting was first observed during a survey trip in 1972. We again visited the Dianggu group in 1975. In August 1978 we returned for one week to Dianggu and Malibu, where we verified in greater detail the subsistence activities of women. Data were collected using the Palanan Agta dialect and Ilokano.

2. Dianggu and Malibu are river names used by Agta and nearby Malay Filipinos. On the Board of Technical Surveys and Maps (Lobod Point, Philippines), the Dianggu is named the Lobod and the Malibu is named the Ilang.

3. Peterson (n.d.) argues that "downriver" Agta women are highly variable in their devotion to labor, older women being hardworking and young mothers not at all industrious.

4. Thomas Headland tells us that rejection of a prospective spouse may be a less serious matter among Casiguran Agta than among those we know.

5. Research in 1979 and 1980 is planned among the unsettled Agta of Isabela and Cagayan. The senior author will emphasize an investigation of the subject covered in this chapter. The junior author will continue his studies of Agta subsistence activities.

References

Bennagen, Ponciano. 1976. Kultura at Kapaligiran: Pangkulturang Pagbabago at Kapanatagan ng mga Agta sa Palanan, Isabela. M. A. thesis, Department of Anthropology, University of the Philippines, Diliman, Quezon City.

Briggs, Jean L. 1974. Eskimo women: makers of men. In *Many sisters: women in cross-cultural perspective,* ed. Carolyn J. Matthiasson, pp. 261–304. New York: Free Press.

Estioko, Agnes A., and P. Bion Griffin. 1975. The *Ebuked* Agta of northeastern Luzon. *Philippines Quarterly of Culture and Society* 3(4):237–44.

————. In press. The beginnings of cultivation among the Agta hunters-gatherers in northeast Luzon. In *Contributions to the study of Philippine shifting cultivation,* ed. Harold Olofson. Laguna, Luzon, Philippines: Forest Research Institute.

Flannery, Regina. 1932. The position of women among the Mescalero-Apache. *Primitive Man* 10:26–32.

————. 1935. The position of women among the eastern Cree. *Primitive Man* 12:81–86.

Fox, Robert B. 1952. The Pinatubo Negritos, their useful plants and material culture. *Philippine Journal of Science* 81:113–414.

Friedl, Ernestine. 1975. *Women and men: an anthropologist's view.* New York: Holt, Rinehart and Winston.

Garvan, John M. 1964. *The Negritos of the Philippines,* ed. Hermann

Hochegger, Weiner beitrage zur kulturgeschichte und linguistik, vol. 14. Horn: F. Berger.

Goodale, Jane C. 1971. *Tiwi wives: a study of the women of Melville Island, north Australia.* Seattle, Wash.: University of Washington Press.

Gough, Kathleen. 1975. The origin of the family. In *Toward an anthropology of women,* ed. Rayna R. Reiter, pp. 51–76. New York: Monthly Review Press.

Hammond, Dorothy, and Alta Jablow. 1976. *Women in cultures of the world.* Menlo Park, Calif.: Benjamin/Cummings.

Harako, Reizo. 1976. The Mbuti as hunters—a study of ecological anthropology of the Mbuti pygmies. *Kyoto University African Studies* 10:37–99.

Headland, Thomas, and Janet D. Headland. 1974. *A Dumagat (Casiguran)-English dictionary.* Pacific Linguistics Series C. No. 28. Australian National University, Canberra: Linguistics Circle of Canberra.

Howell, F. Clark. 1973. *Early man,* rev. ed. New York: Time-Life Books.

Isaac, Glynn L. 1969. Studies of early culture in East Africa. *World Archaeology* 1:1–27.

———. 1971. The diet of early man: aspects of archaeological evidence from lower and middle Pleistocene sites in Africa. *World Archaeology* 2:278–98.

———. 1978. The food-sharing behavior of protohuman hominids. *Scientific American* 238(4):90–109.

Jenness, Diamond. 1922. *The Life of the Copper Eskimos. Report of the Canadian Arctic Expedition 1913–1918,* vol. XII, pt. 9. Ottawa: Acland.

Keesing, Felix. 1962. *The ethnohistory of northern Luzon.* Stanford, Calif.: Stanford University Press.

Lancaster, Jane B. 1978. Carrying and sharing in human evolution. *Human Nature* 1(2):82–89.

Landes, Ruth. 1938. *The Ojibwa woman.* New York: Columbia University Press.

Lee, Richard B., and Irven DeVore. 1968. Problems in the study of hunters and gatherers. In *Man the hunter,* ed. Lee and DeVore. Chicago: Aldine.

———. 1976. *Kalahari hunter-gatherers: studies of the !Kung San and their neighbors.* Cambridge, Mass.: Harvard University Press.

Maceda, Marcelino M. 1964. *The culture of the Mamanuas (northeast Mindanao) as compared with that of the other Negritos of Southeast Asia.* Manila: Catholic Trade School.

Marshall, Lorna. 1976. *The !Kung of Nyae Nyae.* Cambridge, Mass.: Harvard University Press.

Martin, M. Kay, and Barbara Voorhies. 1975. *Female of the species.* New York: Columbia University Press.

Peterson, Jean Treloggen. 1974. An ecological perspective on the economic and social behavior of Agta hunter-gatherers, northeastern Luzon, Philippines. Ph.D. dissertation, University of Hawaii at Manoa.

————. 1978*a*. Hunter-gatherer farmer exchange. *American Anthropologist* 80:335–51.

————. 1978*b*. The ecology of social boundaries: Agta foragers of the Philippines. *Illinois Studies in Anthropology No. 11.* University of Illinois, Urbana-Champaign, Ill.

————. n.d. Hunter mobility, family organization and change. In *Circulation in the Third World,* ed. Murray Chapman and Ralph Mansell Prothero. London: Routledge & Kegan Paul.

Philippine Commission. 1908. *8th Annual Report of the Philippine Commission: 1907.* Bureau of Insular Affairs, War Department. Washington, D.C.: Government Printing Office.

Quinn, Naomi. 1977. Anthropological studies on women's status. In *Annual review of anthropology,* ed. Bernard J. Siegel, pp. 181–225. Palo Alto, Calif.: Annual Reviews.

Reiter, Rayna R., ed. 1975. *Toward an anthropology of women.* New York: Monthly Review Press.

Rosaldo, Michelle Zimbalist, and Louise Lamphere, eds. 1974. *Women, culture and society.* Stanford, Calif.: Stanford University Press.

Slocum, Sally. 1975. Woman the gatherer: male bias in anthropology. In *Toward an anthropology of women,* ed. Rayna R. Reiter, pp. 36–50. New York: Monthly Review Press.

Tanner, Nancy, and Adrienne Zihlman. 1976. Women in evolution. Part I: Innovations and selection in human origins. *Signs: Journal of Women in Culture and Society* 1:585–608.

Tanno, Tadashi. 1976. The Mbuti net-hunters in the Ituri Forest, eastern Zaire—their hunting activities and band composition. *Kyoto University African Studies* 10:101–35.

Turnbull, Colin M. 1965. *Wayward servants: the two worlds of the African pygmies.* Garden City, N.Y.: Natural History Press.

Vanoverberg, Maurice. 1925. Negritos of northern Luzon. *Anthropos* 20:148–99.

———. 1929–30. Negritos of northern Luzon again. *Anthropos* 24:1–75, 897–911; 25:25–71, 527–656.

———. 1937–38. Negritos of eastern Luzon. *Anthropos* 32:905–28; 33:119–64.

Washburn, Sherwood L., and C. S. Lancaster. 1968. The evolution of hunting. In *Man the hunter,* ed. Richard B. Lee and Irven DeVore, pp. 293–303. Chicago: Aldine.

Worcester, Dean C. 1912. Head-hunters of northern Luzon. *National Geographic* 23(9):833–930.

Yen, D. E. 1976. The ethnobotany of the Tasaday: III. Note on the subsistence system. In *Further studies on the Tasaday,* ed. D. E. Yen and John Nance. Makati, Rizal: PANAMIN Foundation Research Series No. 2.

4 INTERPRETATIONS AND "FACTS" IN ABORIGINAL AUSTRALIA
Catherine H. Berndt

The Timeless Image

The label "Australian Aborigines" conjures up for some people a timeless image. Man the hunter strides along with spears and spear-thrower, and maybe a couple of boomerangs. Behind him comes woman the gatherer carrying a digging stick, a firestick, a food container or two (dilly bag, bark basket, or curved wooden dish), with perhaps a wooden dish half full of water balanced on her head, a child under one arm or astride her shoulders and perhaps another at her feet—plus all her worldly possessions. A few dogs run alongside them. The landscape is harsh. They look thin, and any physical defects such as wrinkles or sagging are fully visible. They are part of the landscape, and melt into it, leaving no trace beyond their stone tools, the remains of their fires, and the discarded remnants of meals (animal bones, shell middens), and in some cases, of course, their own skeletal material, for archaeologists and physical anthropologists to study.

There is just enough substance in this kind of image to provide a glimpse of Aboriginal life in Australia before European contact, and in some regions for a long time after that—until a few decades ago, in fact. Of course, it *does* give only a glimpse. It needs to be rounded out with many more "facts" about that life. Also, many of the interpretations of such facts, past and present, need to be looked at again.

The continuities in Aboriginal life appear to be quite striking over a very long period indeed. Archaeological research has revealed material evidence to this effect dating back at least 40,000 years. (See Berndt and Berndt 1977 for a brief comment on this and a range of bibliographical references.) The basic hunting and gathering economy, with dogs coming into the continent a little later than people did, has therefore a lengthy prehistory. What is lacking in such finds, of course, is evidence regarding intangibles: the sphere of nonmaterial culture, of social relations, of speech and dance and the oral literature that have been so significant in the traditional culture of Aborigines as we know it from living people and from others in the relatively recent past. The place of women in the traditional Aboriginal scene is a specific aspect of the question—the question of people generally—in that scene: men, women, and children, how they related to one another in their family living, in broader affairs, in economic and political transactions, and in the sphere of religion. Archaeologists are interested in such matters, as helping to throw light not only on the distant Aboriginal past but on the behavior of early hunting and gathering groups in general. Social and cultural anthropologists, while they may share that interest, are usually more concerned with the near past and the contemporary present, with people living now or within the last hundred or so years.

It is not possible to talk or write about Australian Aborigines as if they had been insulated from all outside influences. The changes, even in the last decade, have been so far-reaching that their hunting and gathering days are virtually over, at least as a way of life or a major preoccupation. In this chapter, I try to give a realistic summary of the present situation, if only to set their traditional life in perspective. And in the course of doing this, I take up several issues of both facts and interpretation which I consider to be crucial in understanding women's role and status in that way of life.

Negative Attitudes

Australian Aborigines[1] generally have had a bad press, especially in the past. They have been disparaged or patronized, or both. The most consistent overall reason was their supposedly simple culture. To many Europeans, the Aborigines' life-style as hunters and gatherers was archaic and obsolete, outside the mainstream of "normal" living. The various points of criticism were spelled out in newspapers, books, official documents, and popular comments about them: that the Aborigines had no obvious permanent settlements, no conspicuous accumulation of material wealth, virtually no clothing (and worst of all, they didn't seem to *mind* going naked), no large-scale political and war-making machinery, and no signs of organized economic competitiveness. All this was summed up under such headings as "primitive" and "savage."

In recent years "primitive" has become a good word, at least among some archaeologists, because it connotes conservation and concern for the natural environment. For others, including some archaeologists, it still carries the implication of "early in time": Paleolithic, Stone Age, and the like. Australian Aborigines particularly are still taken to represent the oldest known surviving examples of early man (and early woman). This was brought home most forcibly to my husband and me when early in 1965 we participated in a conference at the University of Chicago organized by Sol Tax on the subject of the origin of man. Papers and films on Olduvai Gorge skeletal material and studies focusing on nonhuman primate behavior were prominent features in this discussion of the beginnings of human culture, and we were under strong pressure to comment on the pivotal place of Aboriginal Australians in helping toward an understanding of that primal scene.

By 1965 this frankly evolutionary view of Aborigines was being stated more delicately than it had been even a decade or so before, though more explicitly than it tends to be now. In its crudest form it would have been quite congenial to most of the earliest European settlers to Australia and many of the later ones. They believed that Aborigines were much lower in the evolutionary scale. Written evidence over the last couple of centuries suggests that those settlers had quite strong opinions about the place of women, too—women in general—though they seem to have been rather more ambivalent about this than they were about Aborigines. Insofar as they considered the Aboriginal situation at all, they read into it what they supposed were more or less comparable sentiments about the status of Aboriginal women. So Aboriginal women were assumed to be "inferior" on both counts: first, because they were *Aborigines;* and second, because they were *women,* which meant that their own menfolk "naturally" and properly would see them as subordinate and inferior. Of course, there were variations in such attitudes and in the ways they were translated into practice—and into writing. Nevertheless, they were very widespread and very tenacious.

We cannot gauge, now, what effects these views may have had on Aboriginal attitudes regarding women. Aborigines would not have been able to read what was said about them—or not for some time. Language barriers blocked or distorted spoken communication, too, until Aborigines began, of necessity, to learn some sort of English. But one thing is quite certain. Such views had a double relevance. They influenced the actions of the people who held them. Also, a point that has a crucial bearing on the subject matter of this chapter, they influenced the *reporting* of Aboriginal attitudes in this respect, as well as the reporting of other aspects of the Aboriginal scene. And they continue to do so, with far-reaching implications for the intepretation of a number of statements that are becoming attached as "facts" to the "timeless image."

Aborigines, Past and Present

Europeans Came to Stay . . .
Since the beginnings of sustained contact between Aborigines and the outside world, a huge amount of written material has accumulated about them. Almost all of it has been prepared by outsiders, mostly Europeans, or mediated through such outsiders. The fact that the Aborigines were nonliterate put them at a disadvantage in recording their reactions and experiences, and their rules and ideals. Their normal systems of

oral transmission were not geared to cope with the succession of crises as European settlement spread from the south of the continent to the center and north.

Of course, that is a long and complicated story.[2] But several things need to be remembered, in this preliminary overview, before we turn specifically to the topic of women.

It is important to remember that the process of subduing, disorganizing, and reorganizing the Aboriginal population took quite a long time. In some places the full impact was delayed until after World War II, whereas in others it was early in the sequence and quite drastic. Even so, all were affected to some extent. Captain Cook's first landing in the southeastern corner of the continent in 1770 was more than a symbolic step in the takeover process. But in the 1950s there were still groups of Aborigines who spoke and understood only their own languages and were oriented toward their own traditions. Apart from a few pockets here and there, in the Kimberley area of Western Australia, in northern Queensland, and in parts of central Australia, most were in Arnhem Land and in the arid region that is often called collectively the Western Desert. The main reason was that such regions appeared to have no economic or political usefulness to anyone else. The establishing and sustaining of Aboriginal reserves (i.e., reservations) in those locations needs to be seen within that framework.

. . . And Changed the Landscape

By the 1960s, the assessment of the usefulness of these lands to people other than Aborigines was being substantially redefined. Bauxite and alumina and other mining projects were making inroads into these once-remote areas, on a scale and at a speed that the local people had never envisaged even as a possibility. Liquor problems were intensifying. By the 1970s, massive uranium-mining developments in and close to western Arnhem Land were well under way, with planning for a sizable township. Northeastern Arnhem Land already had the third largest town in the Northern Territory, near a mission station that had been set up in the mid-1930s to cater for people who were then still leading seminomadic lives.

"Seminomadic" is a way of saying that the northeastern Arnhem Landers, like other Aborigines, traditionally moved about within recognized limits. In coastal and riverine areas where food was relatively plentiful, and where they had a range of seasonal base camps where they could expect to find one another at appropriate times, this was like a mobile settlement pattern. In arid regions, seasonal movements were spread more widely but were still fairly predictable. In either case, people's relationship to the land had simultaneously two fundamental facets: ownership and use.

The building of towns and substantially visible settlements in the southeastern and southwestern coastal fringes and in parts of the interior of the continent upset both of these aspects. In the short term, they blocked the Aborigines' customary land-use arrangements. In the long term, conflicts in assumptions and claims about land ownership have become audible and visible on an Australia-wide basis only in the last few years, but they were obvious in many localized crises from time to time throughout the whole period of contact between the two populations. The invading Europeans took it for granted that the land was theirs now, to acquire or buy or sell or dispose of as they wanted. To the Aborigines, land was inalienable, god-given, not a commodity that could be transferred or taken over or seized by people who had no traditionally recognized rights in it. Therefore, they were slow to understand what was happening. When they did, in closely settled regions it was too late to react against it; and in any case, by then, many of them were ill or dead.

In the center and north, small-scale fossicking and small-machine mining were deceptive, and some Aborigines themselves engaged in this (in the eastern goldfields and Pilbara regions of Western Australia, for instance). The development of new iron-ore towns in the Pilbara was disturbing enough to the surviving Aborigines of that area. The arrival of huge mining projects and their work forces and towns was even more traumatic to the Arnhem Landers, although they had had a short breathing space in which to reaffirm their ownership. They could neither stem the tide nor persuade enough other Australians to accept the priority of Aboriginal rights in that land and in its resources. Current agreement on Aboriginal land ownership and restoring of various Aboriginal territories in some regions, notably in parts of the Northern Territory and South Australia, but elsewhere as well, is hedged about with conditions. The plea of "national interest," including fuel-crisis and export-earning demands, and the prospect and actuality of monetary rewards, have persuaded some Aborigines to agree to uranium mining, drilling for oil, and similar enterprises.

In the Kimberley area of Western Australia by 1980, a major crisis was triggered by an international (U.S.-based) company's attempts, backed by the state government, to drill for oil on an Aboriginal pastoral lease at Noonkanbah. In the process, Noonkanbah became a place on the map for people inside and outside Australia who had never heard of it before. The reverberations of this crisis are widespread and long term. They link up with further arguments about diamond drilling in other parts of the Kimberleys. State and federal governments, trade unions, anthropologists, social workers, students, and a variety of others have become embroiled in varying degrees. Interestingly, though, all the publicly visible and publicly audible figures involved have been men. In discussions and confrontations about the identification of sacred sites, for instance, all the official and nearly all the unofficial non-Aboriginal participants have been men. The Aborigines have responded accordingly. Women remain in the background; discussion of sites (almost any sites) becomes a matter for men—with a trend toward becoming "for men only," even on topics that were formerly open to everyone, or to all adults. Some men fear mining for its possible effects on their family life. Women, they say, will be attracted to the miners and form liaisons with them or, worse still, marry them; and the children they bear will be lost to the Aboriginal community, unable to play any serious part in the handing on of traditions and the sustaining of local Aboriginal culture.

The development of towns and cities in the south, even of the smaller townships in the north, must have seemed to the Aborigines to be taking place at an incredible speed. In retrospect they were relatively low key, however drastic they undoubtedly appeared at the time. The mining complexes of the 1970s, even of the 1960s, have dwarfed those earlier events in rapidity and intensity. They not only mushroomed in what had been relatively quiet bushland or undeveloped areas, but in the process they upheaved huge tracts of country, digging enormous (wide and deep) cavities, destroying vegetation, and moving hills and other landmarks.

In the past, much of "outback" Australia was given over to pastoral holdings that had alienated or taken over Aboriginal land. The European settlers introduced cattle and sheep and otherwise interfered with watering places, fenced off areas to which Aborigines formerly had free access, and generally restricted Aborigines' movements and rights. Young Aboriginal women were employed as "stockboys" on some northern stations, mustering and yarding cattle with the stock camps. Nevertheless, in such cases there was not an instant transformation of a known environment into something foreign and previously unimaginable. Even where individual sites were built over, or water holes shut off, named localities were still identifiable. Up to a point, women could still find edible plants that had not been eaten out by introduced animals, and in some places men could still get kangaroos and other meat and fish foods. And although the superimposed structure of authority and power was quite evident, Aborigines in such regions knew very well who were the "real" owners of the country, which sites were the responsibility of which people, the religious associations of all these, and who was "legitimately" entitled to use the natural resources that had been provided by the original creative beings. On all these scores, owners and users were, and are, of *both* sexes.

Owning, and Using

Direct, core ownership of land virtually everywhere rested on patrilineal descent. In practice, for both men and women, "my own country" meant "my father's country" (or, "my fathers' country") and, by implication, "my father's father's (fathers' fathers') country," from *their* fathers, and so on. Or, it could be "where I was born," though still with the idea of "father's country" in the background. Ideally, a person was born in his or her "father's country." There were other kinds of ownership links of a less direct kind, for example with a person's mother's (and mother's brother's) country, and mother's mother's (and mother's mother's brother's) country. Also, the tracks of mythical characters that crisscrossed the whole landscape were significant in regard to so-called conception sites: meaning the place at which a women first realized she was pregnant.

Place of birth, place of reported conception awareness, were especially important in the case of boys, though there were regional differences in assessing that importance. This was because the main responsibility for attending to the sites (and to a lesser extent the intervening stretches) in one's "own country" devolved on adult men who had religious-ritual ties, *ownership* ties, to it and, just as crucially, social ties with others who acknowledged the same bond. So father-son territorial and religious identification was a pivotal feature—more corporately organized than were comparable father-daughter links.

The terms *clan* and *sib* can be confusing because of lack of agreement on what they signify. The label "local descent group" is less ambiguous. It points directly to (1) the local, territorial base, (2) the descent link that was seen as a major criterion of relationship with that base, and of relationships between the persons involved in (3) the *group* (not merely category) of people deriving from the combination of (1) and (2). It was a small, always-exogamous unit. Its members shared the same language or the same dialect of one language, even though, since most Aborigines were bilingual or multilingual, they would normally speak and understand at least one other. They acknowledged full, close, and nominal kinship with members of other such units within a certain regional and social range, and interacted with them in a variety of contexts: cooperation in religious ritual affairs, in marriage arrangements, in trade and gift exchanges, for instance.

As far as everyday land use went, the main socioeconomic unit was what used to be called a horde, now sometimes called a band. It was a land-utilizing, land-occupying unit, a co-resident or at least co-camping unit, or potentially so. Not all its members would necessarily be camped in the same place at the same time, because of seasonal movements, which took the form of gathering and dispersal according to the availability of resources. Religious ritual events were also influenced by this last factor. The core members of any such unit were adult male members of one or more local descent groups, plus their wives and unmarried daughters, together with other close relatives. They moved over and used the territories of several local descent groups, drawing on the natural resources of those territories. And they collaborated in what they saw as the necessary ritual work for the spiritual maintenance and renewal of their resources, work in which women had a positive part to play.

Questions of land use as well as land ownership have become critical in the preparation of land rights claims. Aborigines themselves knew, but many others did not realize, that two aspects (at least two) are involved. One is the prior claim of local descent group members to a particular territory that it owns. The other is that members of contiguous local descent groups have a special interest in their linked constellation of territories. This special interest is a kind of ownership: a consistent and continuing investment of effort and labor and cooperation in a corporate concern. (For a discussion of Aboriginal relations with the land, including references to some of the controversies surrounding it, see Berndt and Berndt 1977: e.g., 91–97, 135–49.)

Woman the Forager

Even though Aboriginal women at marriage usually moved out of their own parents' camps to live with their husbands, this was very rarely the drastic break that some writers have suggested. Marriage took place between kin, in many cases between very close kin; and always, traditionally, within a certain territorial range. A young wife learning about the vegetation and terrain in her new home area, if she did not already know that area from earlier visits to it, could always expect to be taught and helped by other women: especially her husband's own mother and others he called "mother" (who were her own relatives, too, in varying degrees of closeness), or her co-wife or co-wives. Because women often went food collecting in small groups, she could "earn as she learned" (to transpose her work situation into a different verbal setting). In the *Aboriginal* work situation, a woman could combine the tasks of getting a living, bearing and rearing children, and enjoying the company of other adults—instead of either being shut away in a single-family enclosure in a suburb or city or isolated farm, or separated from her family in some kind of paid employment. Her work and her family relationships belonged together.

Hoebel and Frost (1976:108) use the label "intensive foraging" for a subsistence economy that relies basically on plant foods, with meat as a supplement. (By the way, central Australians never used "dried root meal" as Hoebel and Frost suggest in their figure 6.2, p. 109; it is seed meal that is being winnowed here.) That was the basic Aboriginal pattern, although it varied regionally and seasonally. At some times and in some regions, larger meat sources (kangaroos, wallabies, emus) were scarce; fish and turtles were likely to be more plentiful in coastal regions, especially throughout the north, with occasionally whales and dugongs and the like. Meat and fish (and turtles) were highly appreciated, but the staple was usually an assortment of vegetable foods, with smaller game as an almost equally basic resource; and such smaller game, marsupials and goannas, even wallabies in some areas, like crabs and shellfish in others, could be and was obtained by women. Women valued men's contributions of large red-meat animals but did not depend on men for economic support. Men, however, did depend on women in that regard. Women were foragers and small-scale hunters; men were large-scale hunters, with some foraging, for the wild honey that either sex could collect.

Hoebel and Frost's comment that intensive foragers "have not yet domesticated plants" is unrealistic if applied to Australia. Parts of the continent are fairly fertile, but much of it is not. As we have pointed out elsewhere (Berndt and Berndt 1978:12), "Their foraging life was hard, in many ways. But life as cultivators would have been even harder for them in most regions—poor soil and irregular rainfall pose problems even for people who can draw on a range of technical aids, crop-boosting fertilisers, insect repellents and large-scale irrigation." In many respects, they were much better off as foragers and hunters. This life was possible because their populations were relatively small scale, and their regional range was bounded by mutual understandings between neighboring sociolinguistic constellations. The fact that land was not a contentious issue, that ownership was firmly recognized and not disputed, supported the type of coexistence that was characteristic of Aboriginal life throughout the continent. This continental similarity of life-style was important. The kind of generalization that Lewis (1976:171) makes, for example, is not relevant here: "In hunting and gathering, a band is, to an extent varying with population pressures, constrained by the movements of other bands and by surrounding sedentary peoples." The "sedentary peoples" as far as the Aborigines were concerned were all outside the continent— until Europeans arrived. Even the "Macassan" (Indonesian) traders who visited the north coast were seafaring voyagers who did not settle there permanently.

In some areas, Aborigines have been in continuous occupation up to and including the present day, and until only a few years ago maintained a fair amount of their traditional practices and beliefs—including foraging and hunting techniques. Reports from early European explorers note an Aboriginal presence in areas they visited; and archaeological evidence, from a different perspective, makes the same claim. They do not identify such Aborigines personally or socially, in such a way that they can demonstrate continuity with the occupants of those areas in more recent times. Nevertheless, we can postulate continuity of occupation by broadly similar populations, to complement the statements made by members of such populations looking back at their own past. That is as far as most of us can go. Controversies about whether and how, and how much, the climate and landscape have changed through the millennia of such occupation, and whether Aboriginal hunters (and their dogs) helped to induce some of these changes (e.g., through seasonal burning-off procedures, and through reducing the animal population), are beyond the scope of this chapter. In any event, what they did in this respect was of minimal significance compared with the impact of Europeans. They were fairly adaptable people, moderately innovative, on a conservative basis, and must have been able to cope reasonably well with small changes in their natural environment. Women's foraging skills must have helped considerably in ensuring the survival of their families in all but severe droughts and disasters. However, that was not enough to sustain their way of life when Europeans came.

The Traditional Past in the Present
Like other hunting-gathering people, the Aborigines were highly vulnerable when it came to confrontation with waves of much more aggressive and better equipped invaders. Not that Aborigines were *un*aggressive, but in this respect they were no match for Europeans. (For a short overview, see C. H. Berndt 1978.) Their wars involved only small groups. They were never aimed at conquest, and were more like feuds designed to achieve revenge or specific ends; or they were individually prompted attacks for the purpose of punishing an eloping couple or, in some areas and in some circumstances, acquiring

a wife by force. (The combatants in such cases were always men; and there appear to be no examples of acquiring husbands by such means.)

Their lack of central political authority and formal chief-style leadership made it harder for unimaginative and cross-culturally inexperienced Europeans to know how to deal with them. The fact that they did not have a single, continent-wide language and culture meant that the more conscientious of the newcomers could not just learn a single language and code of conduct and use them for coping with the entire population. There were many similarities in culture throughout the continent, but there was also a fair amount of diversity, including linguistic diversity. And although trade routes and mythical tracks extended so widely, the zones of interaction had regional limits: communication extended only so far. Aboriginal sociocultural constellations were partly interdependent but relatively *in*dependent, interconnected but locally oriented. This in itself was in one sense a source of protection for the people who survived the first onslaught. They were able to keep something of their own traditions in the face of considerable pressures.

Nonetheless, erosion of traditional Aboriginal culture was inevitable as non-Aboriginal elements intruded more and more strongly. This reflected what was happening to the Aboriginal population itself. Especially in the south, but through much of the north as well, a mixed population was developing, partly Aboriginal and partly something else, mostly European. Many half-Aboriginal children were forcibly taken away from their Aboriginal mothers and put into institutions or foster homes, the official idea being that by this means they would be more easily assimilated into the wider society. At the same time, in the various states and in the Northern Territory different regulations and laws defined who were to be regarded as Aboriginal and (ostensibly in order to protect such people) what they were not allowed to do. They were separated out even when they did not want to be—although some of them did. Numbers of light-skinned persons who would have merged into the general population were legally defined as Aborigines or "natives" and were subject to various restrictions. In this respect, in many areas, "being Aboriginal" had negative connotations. And the people defined in those terms did not necessarily have much or any firsthand knowledge of traditional Aboriginal culture.

Those conditions no longer apply. Discriminatory legislation of this sort was repealed some years ago, with dramatic changes in the official position of Aborigines. Some prejudice against them remains, but this may be outweighed by the more positive benefits of "being Aboriginal." Currently, people of Aboriginal descent have been working to establish a sense of national unity which they did not have before, with a sense of common identity and expectations. This development has been encouraged officially through the establishment of state and national advisory, consultative, and decision-making Aboriginal bodies. Unofficially, people of Aboriginal descent have become much more mobile. Even in "outback" areas, all but a few of the oldest people have become more articulate in English—which is now a *lingua franca* for Aborigines from different areas. "Urban" and "tribal" Aborigines have been discovering that they have more in common sociopolitically than some of them would admit before. And urban Aborigines are using the *idea* of Aboriginal culture, or selected bits of it, as a symbol of this shared identification. Some of them try to build up a picture of what their particular Aboriginal background was, or might have been, drawing on written material and on surviving oral traditions.

Traditional is always a relative term. Certainly, "Aboriginal culture" means something different now from what it meant even twenty or thirty years ago. In urban areas particularly, it has come to mean the culture of people who identify as Aborigines and are so identified by others. The content is not entirely irrelevant, but it is "Aboriginal" because it is what people defined as Aboriginal are saying and doing. Partly as a heritage of past restrictions, the label now covers a very wide

range of appearance, experience, and information about
what the distinctively Aboriginal (*traditional* Aboriginal) past
was like. This is another source of misunderstanding in interpreting Aboriginal materials and will lead to more such misunderstandings in the future as the traditional-Aboriginal
base recedes into the past.

More Interpretations than "Facts"

Gaps in the Evidence
Information about traditional Aboriginal life is regionally
very patchy and very uneven in quality. There are several reasons for this over and above the Aborigines' dependence on
oral transmission—a system that was quite sophisticated and
could have been turned to better advantage in recording by
people who put more emphasis on written traditions and
writing skills. Great distances, difficult terrain, poor transport
and communications, lack of interest in Aboriginal culture or
of competence or opportunity to explore it systematically,
and the diversity and spread of languages and culture
generally—all combined in varying degrees to discourage
serious inquiry. Detailed accounts of specific regional groups
are rare, and they suffer from various handicaps: language
and other communication problems, for instance, or consistent bias from missionary or other points of view. Given the
circumstances, it is probably remarkable that there is not even
less information extant.

By the time better training became available, as well as
more funds for research and more interest in the realities of
Aboriginal life (as contrasted with speculation at a distance),
Aboriginal culture was no longer a going concern in most
parts of Australia. The areas where traditionally oriented
people were still concentrated (oriented toward their own,
Aboriginal life systems, although increasingly influenced by
outsiders) were getting fewer and smaller. In fact, expressions
of interest in Aboriginal culture(s), including interest in re-

search, seem to have increased in inverse proportion to the survival of that culture.

All told, then, there are formidable gaps in the surviving information and many topics on which virtually nothing is known—either by outsiders *or* by the descendants of people who originally knew and lived in those cultures. What they— and we (the rest of us)—have lost is only hinted at in the material that survived long enough to be put on record in notebooks if not in print. A rough gauge of the loss in quantity, if not in quality or content, can be arrived at through two preliminary procedures: (1) looking at the amount of published material for the whole continent, taking into account all the groups that are very poorly represented in that material; and (2) considering the detailed information available for some groups, especially in central and northern areas and especially (but not only) in recent years, as against the tantalizingly slight information that commemorates so many others, especially in the zones of first contact.

That applies to the specific focus of this chapter (Aboriginal women) and to the broader context which is significant for understanding who these women are, what they do and say, and how they relate to other women and to men and children. In much of the early literature, there are glimpses here and there but very little more—either of individual women or of women in a range of interrelationships and roles, in a setting of emotions and activities, with their own comments on these. The sex of the inquirer-reporter is, of course, not the only criterion here. Daisy Bates, legendary and controversial amateur anthropologist and welfare worker,[3] is a notorious example. In general, she assumed the legitimate authority and superiority of men over women. Accordingly, she attached little value, and paid scant attention, to the positive aspects of Aboriginal women's activities and status.

Aside from the issue of what earlier writers did, or might have done, or should have done, I know from my own experience some of the information that has not been recorded and is no longer accessible. This personal comment is necessary, to emphasize the point I want to make. I first carried out field research in Aboriginal Australia in 1941, at Ooldea in South Australia on the edge of the Great Victoria Desert (anthropologically and linguistically regarded as the southeastern corner of the Western Desert), near the Transcontinental railway line. Since then I have spent varying periods at other places: especially, northern South Australia and the Lower River Murray, Adelaide city, eastern and western Arnhem Land; the Victoria River district, including Wave Hill; the Daly River; the wartime Army Aboriginal settlements in the Northern Territory; east Kimberley and the north of the Western Desert, in Western Australia. In all of these, and others, I concentrated on working with women. I was fortunate in being able to do this because my husband was concentrating, simultaneously, on working with men. Within that frame, I tried to narrow down the range of topics I wanted to explore most consistently, without being too inflexible about this. They were: women in the sphere of religion, including myth and ritual and other kinds of participation; marital relations; family and other socioeconomic responsibilities; and the socialization of children, including the teaching of stories (e.g., myths for children), parent-child (child-parent) relations, and so on.

Before World War II, anthropological fieldworkers in Aboriginal Australia had been scarce enough. During the war and immediately after it there were virtually none. Funds were still short, interest was still minimal, and where there was such interest it still centered on men. We were acutely aware of the changes that were very visible in all the areas and among all the people we came to know. Aboriginal populations were small; and in the traditional open-style camps it was possible to observe, and hear, a great deal of what went on in a group setting. Even so, the limits to what one person (or even two persons) could do were painfully obvious. There was no chance of following up a great deal of what I saw and heard and was told. The choice of one situation or event or set of persons, paying closer attention to this rather than that, meant either missing out on "that" or just being on the edges of it. Although I tried to find out something about what I was missing, when missing was unavoidable, that was a poor substitute. Particularly in earlier years when we had no mechanical recording aids (or even ball-point pens, only lead pencils), it was not feasible to do more.

Over the years, I have accumulated an enormous amount of information, which includes checking and cross-checking and considering variations and continuities through time. Nevertheless, I know very well what I was not able to do: how much was lost, not only in the fields of my special interests but in every field of Aboriginal culture and not only in the regions I am acquainted with but in others. The time span involved is not really very long, relatively speaking. Yet so much has gone, even from the level of "memory culture" when no living person remembers the content of some things that were traditionally there, or even recalls that they *were* there. The new mythologies or the new ideologies that have been growing up in those regions—almost all regions, although more conspicuously in some—are helping to redefine the traditional picture, developing new, reframed traditions. Probably this was always a feature of the ongoing scene, in the pre-European past as well as since. But the transformations that have been taking place in the last couple of decades would appear to have no close precedents. The nearest parallel is the cultural turmoil (as it was from the Aborigines' perspective) that followed the first waves of invasion in the south.

Gaps between Evidence and Assertions
The nexus between "facts" and generalizations is a matter of prime concern in social science methodology. In everyday speech and in writing on almost any topic, anywhere, shortage of "facts" is no bar to making assertions, drawing conclusions, taking a stance.

Two examples that bear on the status of women meet on common ground in this respect, although they diverge sharply in their approaches to what Radcliffe-Brown called "conjectural history." The more recent of the two (Leacock 1978) is constructed around a simple formula: band societies were egalitarian, and (p. 247) "their egalitarianism applied as fully to women as to men"; "women were autonomous in egalitarian society—that is, . . . they held decision-making power over their lives and activities to the same extent that men did over theirs." Insofar as the scenes presented in the ethnographic literature differ from this, the reason is that imperialist/colonial powers have forced radical changes in the structure of such societies, and/or the anthropologists or other reporters involved have been so blinded by their own class-society-derived, male-dominated ethnocentric imperialist/colonial bias that they have failed to understand the true situation. This applies to all band societies; they were egalitarian by definition, and are now (p. 247) "virtually all in some measure incorporated into world economic and political systems that oppress women"; accordingly (p. 248), "a public domain becomes defined, . . . as counterposed to a private 'familial' sphere. Furthermore, the public domain, associated with men, is either the economically and politically more significant one or is rapidly becoming so." Australian Aboriginal societies were band societies; therefore they were (had to be) egalitarian societies; women had an autonomous place in them before the European invasion imposed on them a new, male-dominated social order.

This is even more tricky than seeking information on the "traditional Aboriginal" situation. It raises the question, How do we know what Aboriginal culture, and specifically the position and "degree of autonomy" of women in that culture, was like before the coming of Europeans? The answer is that we don't and can't know. We can only surmise.

"This is how things should be," or "could be," or "how they should have been," becomes "this is how they may have been," and finally, dogmatically, "this is how they *were*." And much of the literature on Aboriginal women is either oriented along such lines or influenced in some measure by the selection of clues to fit a prearranged pattern. There are plenty of fairly recent cases of this, but the most glaring are those that provided the data for Malinowski's study, the second of our two examples.

Malinowski's early volume (1913) was titled *The Family among the Australian Aborigines;* but, inevitably, he has a lot to say about relations between husbands and wives and, by extension, between men and women generally. Preparation of the study was evidently a sort of exercise, before his visit to Australia and his subsequent Papua New Guinea research. He relied wholly on written sources; and a major part of his contribution as he saw it (pp. vii–ix)[4] was not only the "unprejudiced" collection of "facts," without "preconceived ideas" about them, but also a critical assessment of them. He acknowledged (p. ix) that some of the evidence he used came from "older sources whose trustworthiness might be disputed," but he believed he could handle that problem because "many of their observations are highly valuable if properly interpreted." In his final, summing-up chapter he repeats (pp. 292, 293–94) that his "chief practical difficulties lay in the methodological treatment of the evidence," which involved "contradictions, incompleteness and lack of precision," and "speculative inference." He could not "use the statements in their crude form," and had "to use caution and method in drawing inferences" from them. They included "a great deal of inaccuracy," and some were "quite or nearly useless owing to complete confusion." "Furthermore, all qualifying expressions referring to the treatment of husband and wife, expressions referring to sexual morality, etc., were in the highest degree inexact."

He appears to have been satisfied that through his "critical" interpretations he had sifted the evidence well enough to provide a comprehensive statement of the "factual" situation as it stood at the time he wrote it. His own assessment and interpretations, however, and his opinions, were very much a product of his time, his sociocultural background, and his personal perspectives. For instance, it was reasonable enough

for him to raise the questions of how far the Aborigines in the
sources he quotes were influenced by contact with outsiders,
and how competent the writers concerned were to cope with
that aspect; but his framing of these questions reveals one sort
of bias: "In general, it may be taken as a rule that all writers
who were in any close contact with aborigines had to do with
fairly degenerated specimens. They were usually squatters or
missionaries, and had to do with blacks hanging round farms
or with remnants of tribes gathered in missions" (p. 20).
Aborigines "in their natural uncorrupted state," "their really
savage state," were "extremely shy . . . and inaccessible" (p. 20,
n. 2). The others were "degenerate," "corrupt," "in an advanced state of decay" (pp. 20, 21). And specifically as regards
women, he more or less accepts as proven the view he originally set out to explore, that women were "slaves" and the
"property" of their husbands (e.g., chapter 3), even though he
contends (p. 297) that "in general—allowing for a natural
variety of feelings—the preponderance of feelings of attachment appears to be the rule."

Malinowski's study does contain a number of useful points
and, as he himself suggested (p. ix), it is a convenient compi-
lation of reference sources. Otherwise, it is very far from
being the objective, scientific analysis he claimed it to be. It is
certainly neither positive nor carefully balanced. We could
and should apply to it the kind of critical assessment he ideally
attempted to apply to his own sources. In my view, the same
process should be adopted also in regard to *all* the evidence
that is now available on the subject of Aboriginal women.

Domestically Speaking

Woman the Breadwinner
In a field that has for so long been permeated with mildly or
potentially contentious issues, there is one major point on
which virtually all sources agree. Even the sources used by
Malinowski emphasized it, in varying contexts and with varying amounts of detail in their description. Malinowski sums it

up briefly (1913:283; his italics): "the woman's share in labour was of much more *vital importance* to the maintenance of the household than the man's work. . . . But even the food supply, contributed by the women, was far more important than the man's share. . . . So that it appears fairly probable that, on the whole, food collected by women was the staple food of the natives." And (p. 288), "The woman's work appears as the chief basis of the economy of the Australian [Aboriginal] household."

Reports to the same effect came from all over the continent, regardless of the writers' possible bias in other directions. Without going over any of the sources used by Malinowski, or others like them, it is enough for us here to look at a couple of short references. From a missionary in the northwest of Western Australia (Love 1936:66): "The women of the Worora are pre-eminently the food providers, and the firewood providers." "[They] provide the staple foods." From an archaeologist-anthropologist, about the Warburton Range area of the Western Desert (Gould 1969:18): "Kuka [meat] is always preferred over mirka [plant foods], but on most days . . . mirka is actually more important in the total diet. Since it is the women who collect and prepare most of the mirka, they are thus the mainstay of the economy. For all their talk about this or that kangaroo they once killed, . . . the men contribute relatively little to the subsistence of the group."

All such references underline a salient characteristic of Aboriginal society (societies): the division of labor in terms of sex. They link different kinds of edible materials with one or other of the two sexes, in what was in many cases a separate operation for each. Recognition of a *two*-sex model (C. H. Berndt 1974*a*) at the level of practical affairs was expressed, often in overtones, sometimes in undertones, through a wide range of relationships and tasks, both socioeconomic and religious. There were always cross-linkages, though some were thinner or less numerous than others. There were joint enterprises, as in fish-trap drives or the roundup of edible creatures when grass or scrub was fired; collaborative activities of a less visible kind, as in certain religious ritual affairs; and tasks that could be performed by members of either sex, such as catching goannas and chopping out wild honey. But the division was a social reality, not a fictional construct.

Most of the statements about women's food contribution versus men's are (were) based on impressions, personal observations plus verbal reports and comments from Aborigines, and so on. They rarely count or weigh or measure, for instance. Betty Hiatt (1974:9–13) summarizes the evidence from a number of sources in her "attempt to show that in hunting societies women are more important than men as food providers in areas where gatherable foods occur in abundance" (p. 4).

A point that comes up in the Gould quotation is the matter of preferences. To many Aborigines, meat is what they like best; plant foods are the basis (the "bread," the "rice"), but meat is more than a garnish or a useful extra. Not that plant foods were viewed as invariably dull or monotonous. Many were eagerly sought after, and had their own attractive and varied taste qualities that make comparison with bread and rice untenable in that respect. Also, the small animals, reptiles, shellfish (oysters, crabs, cockles, and so on), eggs, and other nonvegetable foods that women obtained as a routine procedure in appropriate places and seasons were far from being regarded as boring. And although the process of getting them lacked the strenuous excitement of hunting larger creatures, it was not necessarily dull and monotonous either. It was slower-paced—which did not mean that able-bodied women actually moved slowly on all occasions; they could show speed as well as stamina when the occasion demanded. But monotony is a relative concept. On the other hand, to writers such as Malinowski (1913:282–83) it was not only hard work (as it undoubtedly was in some circumstances, in arid areas and in bad seasons): it was also lacking in "sport and amusement," which he ascribed to men's hunting activities; women's work had no "excitement or variety," only "system and regularity," the kind of thing that was "usually done only

under a strong compulsion"; it was "the most repulsive" work
(p. 257); nobody would do it voluntarily; women, "the weaker
sex," were forced to do it "by the 'brutal' half of society," that
is, men (p. 288). In fact, Malinowski was expressing and anti-
cipating the downgrading of, and antipathy to, domestic work
that has become even more evident in the years since he
wrote.

Another point in relation to women's food-collecting tasks
is that they were undertaken in conjunction with childrearing.
Even where women could share their child-minding activities,
between co-wives, or with grandparents who stayed at a base
camp during the day (more customary in coastal or other relatively fertile regions), the socialization of young children was
predominantly their responsibility, and one just as demand-
ing as their food-getting tasks.

Woman the Incubator

In studies of Aborigines, two controversies have gathered
around this topic of pregnancy: how did the embryo/fetus/
baby get there (into the "incubator") in the first place; and is
the woman concerned *more* than just an incubator—a place in
which the child can develop? The last point has almost ceased
to be an issue since Kaberry (1939:43,54–61) took up Ashley
Montague's argument that Australian Aborigines did not recognize physical maternity. The physical as well as the social
bond between mother and child is acknowledged plainly in
other regions where information is available, not only among
the Kimberley people Kaberry studied. The other point continues to be controversial: that is, whether and how
Aborigines recognize physical (or physiological) paternity, the
role of the genitor in procreation. The discussion has not
been helped by the muddled statements in a recent article
(Hippler 1978:226–27).

This is not the place to go into the question. But the fundamental premise among Aborigines generally is that human
beings are composed of two kinds of substance: the physical
or material, which is transient and mortal, and the soul or

spirit, which provides continuity of life. The physical cannot grow or develop without the spiritual: an embryo cannot become an embryo unless the physical-material potential is spiritually animated. The conditions of spiritual animation, the transmission of this quality, have to be right. The relation between a prospective father and the child-to-be may be highlighted in the dream revelation to him of the spirit-child-animator; but other relatives may be involved in comparable messages. (See Berndt and Berndt 1977:150–53 for some comments on this; also Strehlow 1971:596.)

Mothering Roles, Continued
The role of fathers is less visible at the beginning of a child's physical life; it becomes more so later on. A mother's role is visible almost from the beginning, or at least it is suspected with the cessation of menstrual periods ("watching the moon," as one western Arnhem Land woman put it, and counting) when no other cause such as illness or extreme weakness could be held responsible.

The nurturing, mothering role begins in pregnancy, and not merely on a personal-choice basis. Depending on the area, there are (were) specific rules to be observed: food tabus; avoidance of specified activities or places, such as billabongs, for instance, where a rainbow snake could endanger the child. The aim in such rules is to ensure the child's healthy, normal growth: and the mother is responsible for this. It is true that in some cases sorcery is blamed for unintended miscarriages and the like, but in general terms the responsibility is clearly acknowledged as hers. And that goes for the child's well-being after its birth, too. The mother is (expects to be) helped by other people; but it is up to her to ensure that the child is kept safe from *all* kinds of danger, which includes "dangerous" or "strong" or ritually prohibited foods as well as potentially hostile creatures. She is expected to be affectionate, not merely conscientious; but the sanctions in the background, traditionally, included punishment from the child's father and in some areas from her own brothers (the child's mother's brothers) if she was careless or neglectful. The image of a "good mother" was reflected in myths and stories as a good example to follow, just as the image of a "bad mother" was partly reflected there and was used to indicate the bad example, what *not* to do.

Positive, Negative

Not a great deal of material has been published about women in family and socialization contexts, except in terms of formal systems of kinship and marriage. Kaberry's 1939 volume was the first to give a personal, human picture of relations between mothers and children (and grandmothers, etc.). (See also Berndt and Berndt 1977:153–66, for a general overview; Berndt and Berndt 1970:154–67, for reference to western Arnhem Land; and C. H. Berndt 1978:144–60, in regard to "learning non-aggression.")

It is all the more unfortunate, therefore, that Hippler's recent article gives such a negative and distorted view of (among other things) the mother-child relationship in northeastern Arnhem Land. The tone of his comments is illustrated in his claim (p. 229) that the father "is . . . the one person who can and sometimes does force the mother to care for the infant or reduce the physical attacks on him," because "the care of children under 6 months of age can be described as hostile, aggressive and careless; it is often routinely brutal."

There are always mothers who treat their small children roughly, just as there are men who tend to beat their wives if they can get away with it. Such items are more than "trouble cases": they are news. Traditionally, there were various sanctions that could be imposed in both kinds of situation, and they seem to have been successful in varying degrees. But this is one of the hazards in reporting on current conditions of life in Aboriginal Australia. Annette Hamilton's (1970) material that Hippler cites came, not from northeastern Arnhem Land, but from an adjacent region: it was an honest attempt to describe the then-current picture at the government settlement of Maningrida, in north-central Arnhem Land, where socialization and adult-child relations had been drastically affected by the new life-style that was developing there. Similarly in northeastern Arnhem Land, and not only at Elcho Island settlement, the tremendous stresses the Aboriginal people were experiencing included a sudden population surge that enlarged the bottom of the age pyramid to unprecedented proportions. Traditional child-spacing procedures had been lapsing. And intrafamily discipline was becoming a problem by the late 1950s, as mothers found they had more children to cope with, in a large-settlement environment where other adults were being deflected from potential helping roles, and the impact of a growing non-Aboriginal population and the values and materials being introduced from outside were having visible effects. The advantages of medical care were offset by disadvantages of a more comprehensive, less easily summarized kind. Women were not the

Figure 4.1. Women and children at Balgo, on the northern fringe of the Western Desert, Western Australia, 1960. Casually constructed shelters such as the one in the background were often preferred to new-style houses. Photo R. M. Berndt.

only ones affected, of course, but they bore much of the brunt of what was happening.

Negative assessments of women's role are of longer standing, as Malinowski's study shows. Róheim, for instance, acknowledges the importance of women's food contributions in central Australia, but he still manages to assert (1933:208) that "the women are, on the whole, more greedy and selfish than the men." Writing more generally, Maddock (1972:25) follows Malinowski in conceding that women's labor is "productive," but he goes on to denigrate it as a *type* of work. It is, he claims, "pedestrian" and "menial": its main advantage is that it supports, or makes possible, the "aristocratic," "higher activities of men." Even in *his* evaluation, this would represent a formidable support base, in underpinning the welfare of the communities concerned. And Maddock follows Róheim in adding (p. 155), "Women's cults are centered on narrow, divisive and personal interests, such as making love magic and reacting to physiological crises." His later admission (p. 188), speaking more moderately about complementarity, with "neither [sex] established as subordinate," does not fit with his other statements. These include the claim (p. 59) that "a woman starts off under her father's control and finishes under her son's"—which (as I noted in a review: C. H. Berndt 1974*b*) makes nonsense of the whole socializing process, including the role of mothers: we could just as well say that a man starts life under the control of his mother. In Maddock's presentation, Aboriginal societies were two-class, or two-tier, societies, with women as the "working class." He affirms Malinowski's interpretation and spells it out explicitly.

The positive aspects of women's domestic and mothering roles have yet to be put into clearer perspective. Items of what could be called submerged evidence have yet to be assembled and discussed in a wider frame. For instance, (1) the almost complete absence of evidence of women-as-sorcerers, as contrasted with women-as-healers; (2) the reports noting the traditional authority of women in the southwest of the continent (R. M. Berndt 1979:86) and in the lower River Murray region of South Australia; (3) the usually overlooked fact that as a rule "small children were introduced to religion most directly and most consistently through women, especially their mothers" (C. H. Berndt 1978:152); and (4) Strehlow's (1971:596) point that "in the Aranda-speaking area . . . the conception site of every person was determined solely by an experience of his mother which could happen to her only at a time when she was already pregnant beyond any possible doubt"—it was for *her* to "make her official declaration," reporting the place at which or near which she first realized she was pregnant, on a matter (spiritual links with sacred sites, mythical tracks) which was so ritually critical for men's religious roles in that area.

Of course, to return to the problem of interpretation, presentation of "facts" is never enough. The domestic contributions of Aboriginal women in the traditional scene were perhaps *too* basic—a comment that could be thrown on to a wider screen.

Marriage[5]

Women as "Objects"

Traditionally, marriages in Aboriginal Australia were arranged. They were set within a framework of rules about the proper social categories and groups that should be involved, the proper kin relationships, and other specific requirements, such as the fact that in certain circumstances a man could accumulate wives, but in no circumstances could a woman accumulate husbands—or not simultaneously. (For an outline, with further references, see, e.g., Berndt and Berndt 1977:188–298; also Berndt and Berndt 1978:50–60; and in regard to western Arnhem Land, Berndt and Berndt 1970: e.g., 93–101.)

Marriage as such was accepted as a normal state for everyone. Ideally, there was no room for personal choice between getting married or remaining single. The only questions were who a person's spouse or spouses would be, and who would decide; or, to turn it around, who would do the arranging, and who was "being arranged." If we were to accept most of the literature on the subject, it was mainly females who were being organized and deployed in what can be called the marriage-planning game (Berndt and Berndt 1978:50).

Up to a point, this image coincides with local-Aboriginal statements and actions, where the emphasis is more on "giving women" than on "giving men" in making marriage arrangements. Relative age was one factor in this: girls were more likely to be betrothed at or before birth or in early childhood than boys were, and a girl's first husband was likely to be much older than she was. The accepted dominance of older (i.e., able-bodied and mentally alert older) over younger people included or supported the authority of older men *and women* to deploy younger people, assuming they were in the appropriate categories. Also, the largely implicit value placed on women's ability as food providers made them useful acquisitions.

Some writers interpret this to mean that women as food suppliers are such a valuable resource or commodity that they have to be managed and controlled, as other resources are. Cawte (1974:142) takes this view, in line with his contention that Aboriginal men are dominant in virtually all respects.[6] Peterson suggests almost the same thing, but in a more limited way, proposing that this desire to make use of women's food-getting capacity is a major factor in band organization. He suggests (1974:22–24) that a factor in band composition is "the need for older men to have access to the labour of younger women"; and that they try to do this by keeping their young daughters and daughters' husbands with them as long as they can, to benefit from the labor of both daughters and sons-in-law, and by marrying additional, young wives.

What Peterson does not say is that in the area he was discussing the "band" was not an uncomplicated-traditional phenomenon, even though the people concerned were traditionally oriented. That group was one of the early examples

of the "outstation" development which has since escalated
into the "homeland" movement, as Aborigines move out from
overcrowded settlements to form smaller, more homogene-
ous communities, mostly on their own traditional lands. In
this particular instance, the outstation was started on the initiative of the missionary then in charge at Elcho Island. He
piloted his small mission plane to ferry people and supplies,
establish an airstrip, and assist those families who wanted to
stay there rather than at the main mission station. This was
the first of several outstations that were repopulated from
Elcho Island. Now, Arnhem Land is dotted with outstations
that have fanned out from other settlements, from (for instance) Oenpelli in the west, Maningrida on the north-central
coast, and Milingimbi and Yirrkalla on the northeastern side.
All of these are small settlements themselves, more static than
their traditional counterparts. Another point of difference is
the nature of their population. Together, they no longer represent the total universe of population in their region. Many
of their potential members have moved to other places, including Darwin. Also, other people have moved in. The impact of outsiders is evident in their food-getting patterns:
much of their food is imported, along with other material
things they now consider essential. And their communication
links with the rest of the Australian continent are quite different from what they were before. So is the mobility of their
members, with airplane and other links between their fixed
base and the outside world. Their marriage arrangements
reflect this changed pattern. In other words, there are hints of
the traditional band composition of only a few years ago: but
the current situation cannot be taken as providing clear
examples of it.

In these altered circumstances, it is harder for men to indulge in another preference that is made much more explicit:
that is, a preference for young women as sexual partners. In
the northeastern Arnhem Land areas that Peterson wrote
about, the cultural emphasis on fertility meant that both men
and women put a high value on childbearing. Young wives

were an asset to a man in this respect. Much of the local fighting that went on in that area was about women, especially younger women. All these factors probably came into it; but sexual attractiveness was a topic that received a great deal of attention, in song and story as well as in everyday living.

There is plenty of evidence throughout the continent generally about physical preferences for younger people in sexual affairs. The usual way of putting it was that older men liked adolescent or preadolescent girls; but just as often, young women expressed the same kind of preference—in their case, for men of the same age or only a little older. The physical attractiveness of young men made them seem desirable as sweethearts, especially to women who were married to elderly men. Young men, therefore, were a potential threat to jealous husbands. One advantage of polygyny, for men, was that they could acquire new wives without having to discard the wives they already had. (Women could not do this. They could change husbands sequentially, in appropriate circumstances, but not openly collect them.) This in itself could aggravate any tension between older men in positions of authority and younger men, who had to defer to them in most situations, not only in the sphere of religion.

There were, then, men who tended to treat women (girls) as objects in trying to achieve their own marriage aims, whether they wanted the girls for themselves or were attempting to use one or more of their own close relatives (e.g., a sister's daughter) in an exchange arrangement. The use of young men in this kind of game was less obvious. But non-Aboriginal writers have gone beyond Aboriginal usage, in this respect. According to some, Aboriginal men regarded women as commodities, as items of exchange between "consanguineous groups of men." That particular reference comes from Lévi-Strauss (1960:283), from a chapter in which he was looking at the topic more generally. In other publications he has applied this approach to Aboriginal marriage systems in particular. He has been one of the principal exponents of this view. In that chapter, however, he offers an alternative sug-

gestion to appease women readers "who may be shocked" by
what he has said. Hypothetically, he indicates (p. 284), there
could be "a still different (but in that case slightly more complicated) formulation of the game, whereby it could be said
that consanguineous groups of both men and women are engaged in exchanging together bonds of relationship"—and,
he might have added, engaged in planning the social dimensions of the future population in their particular communities. It is certainly a more acceptable and, in my view, a
more realistic formulation. It doesn't get around the problem
of "who is deploying (trying to deploy) whom," but it establishes a more neutral framework for enquiry.

Women were active in negotiating and discussing and decision making in the preliminaries and in the final stages of any
marriage arrangement. It is, and was, never just a matter of
who was involved in the *final* decision; but the processes of
decision making were (it seems) rarely simple and clear cut,
and could be quite long-drawn-out. Not much published material is available in regard to them. Retrospective accounts
are not plentiful either; and they vary in their reliability as
well as in their validity, although Hamilton's (1974) study is a
useful source of data on a neglected subject. Women and men
could be expected to perceive their own participation in such
transactions rather differently, especially when there was a
conflict of opinion. (For reference to one western Arnhem
Land example, see Berndt and Berndt 1970:97–99). But
there is no question about women's involvement, which included decisions about other, usually *younger* women.

Betrothal, or Bestowal?

One English word that has often been used for a preliminary
or a binding marriage contract is "betrothal," although
"promise" is more usual in Aboriginal-English. It does not
specify who is involved, but (like the Lévi-Strauss quotation
already noted) it does leave the options open as far as balance
is concerned. However, another term has become popular
among non-Aboriginal writers: "bestowal." Shapiro (1969:

e.g., 629–30) reported having discovered a system in north-eastern Arnhem Land which went further than "the bestowal of girls as wives," and emphasized "mother-in-law bestowal." He drew, for this, on a minor rite which has locally been long discontinued (Shapiro 1970) and which actually played a relatively small part in marriage-arranging decisions in that area. Over and above the marriage rules based on social categories and kin and other affiliations, including the ideal of a women's marriage to a patri-cross-cousin (it is usually framed, in the literature, as a man's marriage to a matri-cross-cousin), other considerations came into play. It was an area of "wife-collectors," and of more stress on payment in goods and services than was found in, say, central and Western Desert regions. (See, e. g., C. H. Berndt 1970:39–41.) Early Indonesian ("Macassan") trading contacts possibly intensified this material-interest emphasis.

However, "bestowal" does connote a one-way transaction, to an even greater extent than the once-popular contrast between "wife-givers and wife-receivers," just because it stresses a single type of transaction. And it is now being used more frequently in place of "betrothal" (perhaps because it sounds more important?). It is also being used, although it need not be, to obscure the processes of decision making, not only in regard to who the marriage partners will be but also in regard to who is *the* chosen mother-in-law for a man, the woman who will (should) give birth to his prospective wife or wives. The suggestion is that this procedure is or was more widely applicable to regions other than northeastern Arnhem Land. In other words, in this conceptual scheme it is not only a prospective wife who has little or no say in her own marriage arrangements; her mother has no choice, either. The options open to women are defined as being even more circumscribed than they originally seemed to be—and, I would contend, far more circumscribed than they in fact were.

Women could not always choose their marital partners or their sexual partners. That was true of men, too, though there was to some extent a double standard favoring men at the expense of women; but that needs further consideration. What is clear is that in many marriages there was love and affection between husband and wife, in polygynous as well as in monogamous unions; that relations between them were more evenly balanced than some descriptions make them appear to be (the "what's news?", trouble-reporting tendency conceals this); that there was scope for romantic love, if not invariably within marriage, then to some extent outside it.

Sacred, Profane, Mundane?

Probably the hottest debate has built up around the subject of women's place in religion. Negative statements, mainly from men, are in oversupply here. Some still restrict the term *sacred* to transactions on a men-only basis: if women participate, even on a small scale, or know anything about what is going on, the term is *secular* or *nonsacred*.

Elkin was a long-term exponent of that view. (In saying this, I should add that during his lifetime we agreed to disagree in our differing perspectives on women and/in religion. He had a very strong sense of religious hierarchy and strong opinions about the place of women in any such hierarchy.) He put it most succinctly in his Introduction to Kaberry's volume (1939:xxx), when he underlined the "sacred character of the men"; "We must remember that women may be independent, powerful, and yet be profane, or outside of that sphere of sacred belief and ritual, admission to which is by religious initiation." He was unmoved by Kaberry's arguments on this score—though she does use "profane" in some cases as a synonym for "mundane" and not in the Durkheimian sense.

Maddock follows Elkin in this respect (in line with his choice of a title): for instance, about men as "persons born male and translated from childhood to manly status. It is by undergoing this change that one qualifies to act ritually" (1972:135). He could have added, but didn't, "in certain contexts," or some such qualification, whereas his statement ostensibly excludes women from serious ritual participation. In other statements, too, he denigrates women's place in religious affairs. Women and men are, in this respect, he says, separated by a great chasm, and that separation is ritually dramatized. He quotes Elkin, and virtually goes beyond Elkin, in outlining and interpreting the Jabuduruwa (Yabuduruwa) sequence (Maddock 1972:147–49; italics in original) in which, he suggests, "women have penetrated the secret area without looking at the secret things before their eyes. Despite being so *close* to secret things, they are as *far* as ever from knowledge of them." He has already put this as, "Were the women to look they would see . . . sights forbidden to them. It is possible of course that they are dazzled" by the flames springing up as they walk around the edge of the ritual ground, using cylindrical bark emblems to beat at the fire there. Note that he does not say, "They did not see," or "could not see," but implies that they would not or could not. This is a dubious assumption. (From my personal experience of a comparable though not ritually identical event, I know that other female participants as well as myself were able to, and did, glimpse a great deal of what went on beyond the firelight.)

Warner (1958) in his northeastern Arnhem Land research, adopted much the same standpoint. He embraced uncritically the framework that Durkheim had arrived at in his volume *The Elementary Forms of the Religious Life* (1915)—except that he did not look carefully enough at the *range* of sacredness Durkheim had postulated, a range that includes the profane (though he called it negative-sacred) as contrasted with the mundane or secular. Warner denies that women's dreams were ritually significant, since "the world of the extraordinary is largely experienced by men" (1958:511). In reference to dreams of spirit-children, he confines them to prospective fathers, although in that area fathers' sisters were also eligible to have such dreams. His overall orientation is summed up in one sweeping claim (p. 26): "No woman knows the sacred name of a well, or, for that matter, anything else that has to do with the sacred tribal life." He does qualify this by admitting (p. 265), "Even the women have a minimum of maraiin [translated, however, on p. 264, as "powerful, sacred, taboo, or spiritual; it is used to describe anything that is taboo to the women and uninitiated boys"]: they know a part of the ritual tradition."

A rewriting of Warner's study in regard to women, perhaps retaining a Durkheimian approach but scrutinizing it more carefully, would present a very different picture. (For a brief comment, see C. H. Berndt 1965: 279–80.)

Aboriginal religion was for and about and including all the people within a community, women and children as well as men. Women participated responsibly in it, in a great variety of ways, while leaving a predefined amount of such ritual "work" to men. The sexual division of labor is a necessary ingredient in understanding Aboriginal religion, even in regions where it appears to be least obtrusive (as at Bathurst and Melville islands). But it is not a *sufficient* ingredient in achieving such an understanding. Aboriginal religion is not to be

Figure 4.2. Preparing for a women's *yawalyu* ritual. One of the two main "owners" of this *yawalyu* series is singing as she paints the appropriate designs. Balgo, northern fringe of the Western Desert, Western Australia, 1958. Photo C. H. Berndt.

circumscribed within such divided limits. (For an introductory statement on Aboriginal religion, including references, and a comment on women and myth, see Berndt and Berndt 1977:227–303, especially 256–58, 295–99; also, White 1975:123–42, for a provocative and thoughtful discussion of sex antagonism and nonantagonism in myth and in ordinary living in central Australia.)

Róheim began his account of women in central Australia like this: "Biologists have often called the female infantile in comparison to the male. This point of view is, at any rate sociologically, accepted by the Australians, for society is divided into two sections, the initiated and the uninitiated. The latter comprises children and women, although here and there we find exceptions and some women are admitted to the secrets of the male world" (1933:207). Along the way, he commented on a woman who "is what we shall call absolutely normal. From beginning to end she is dominated by the fear of . . . the aggression of the father," "a typically female attitude of sexuality" (p. 234). And he concluded with an observation about "fears, anxieties"; ". . . it is only this phase of religion that is open to the women" (p. 259).

Responsibility for young children, being in the company of and caring for them, becomes from some perspectives alignment with and then identification with children—identification in a negative sense: exclusion not merely from matters that are handled by men, secret to adult men (and secret from others), but from the sphere of religion as a living force. Fortunately for the study of religion, as well as of women, more people are looking again at the available material, including Aboriginal comments and behavior. This does not mean belittling men's role in religion, but it does mean seeing it in a more rounded perspective. Even T. G. H. Strehlow, with his firm views on such matters, pointed out that in two series of rites, among the northern Aranda, *tjurunga* (highly sacred objects) were used, and "women and children *must* be present and the sacred *tjurunga must* be shown to them" (1971:xxxi–xxxii; his italics).

Women, like men, were part of the Eternal Dreaming, "firmly inside it, part of the sacred lifestream," in which the division into two sexes "was almost irrelevant" outside the "narrow span" of physical life (Berndt and Berndt 1978:79).

In a few regions, such as northeastern Arnhem Land, there has been a partial relaxation of some of the rules of secrecy governing public displays of ritually significant objects and public participation in ritual events. In others, such as the Pilbara area of Western Australia and in the Western Desert, there has been a tightening of male solidarity. In one sense, this is a retreat from the demands of the outside world. In another it is a positive affirmation of the continuation of their traditional culture—but of traditional culture focused on a religious core: that core being the special responsibility of men to maintain and preserve and guard against encroachment and attack. In some cases this has meant exclusion of Aboriginal women—to an extent that was not the case traditionally, even at the level of exaggerated public claims about this by men who overstated that aspect of religion but knew that their hearers could put those claims in context. (See, e.g., C. H. Berndt 1973.)

Independence and Interdependence

"Autonomy" (Leacock 1978:247,268) is not a word that Aboriginal Australians would, ideally, apply to themselves as a desirable attribute. They were, and are, too deeply conscious of the importance of cooperation. They were, and are, sociable people, and realistically aware of the need for collaboration in social, political, economic, and religious affairs. And they did not confuse "equality" with "similarity." (See Berndt and Berndt 1978: chap. 7.)

Women *were* valued for what they contributed—valued by other Aborigines. Their economic-support role, their childbearing (population replenishment) role, their childrearing role, may have been taken very much for granted, not celebrated in words; but at the same time, they were not openly disparaged as they have been by outsiders. Verbally, men have tended to put more emphasis on their own contributions in the spiritual dimension, in sustaining and replenishing life forms. Some writers have claimed that men resent women's childbearing ability and their maternal bond with their small children and therefore work toward strengthening their own dominance, using the initiation of boys to weaken that bond and strengthen their male solidarity. This kind of interpretation is accepted most readily by people who see it as confirming their own opinions. It is partial, tentative, and incomplete, and needs further discussion. Women were (in my experience), relatively speaking, more diffident or less vocal about their achievements as a sex, although individual women were not always so modest about their personal claims to attention; and, again with individual exceptions, they appear to have been more secure, emotionally as well as economically. They felt, and were, disadvantaged at times; but that was also true of men, old as well as young. They may have been "junior partners" (White 1974) in some respects, but they certainly were not so in others.[7]

I suggested once (1974a:75) that "women seem to have endorsed the ritual division of labour more easily, accepting their formal subordination in the religious sphere, because in other spheres they were not so subordinated" and because (p. 76) they "were, basically, independent of men economically. . . . And they did have areas of authority, not *only* in the domestic sphere."

In the current scene, women and men serve together on committees and councils, participate in meetings, are elected and appointed members of federal and state bodies concerned with Aboriginal affairs. They have translated their traditional cooperation into a different dimension, with different facets—not excluding conflicts, of course, but adding new avenues of cooperation and understanding. This, however, is a gloss over a situation that becomes more complex every day in "facts" and in interpretations: and that *is* another story.

Breathing Life into the "Timeless Image"

Archaeological research in Australia provides evidence of the very early existence, and use, of tools and weapons, among other things. But *who* made them, or used them? The archaeological record does not reveal this, and there are no written documents or inscriptions to supply even tentative answers. Rock and cave art offers some clues regarding possible use, where male figures are shown with such items as spears or boomerangs, female figures with baskets. We know, however, that in the recent past Aboriginal women did not normally, in most areas, make durable tools or weapons. Among the exceptions were (in some cases) their own digging sticks, bark baskets, woven dilly bags, and the conical *ngainmara* mats of northeastern Arnhem Land. Women prepared twine and other such substances; they collected and crushed ochres and clay for body painting and similar purposes. But when it came to more substantial equipment, they expected their menfolk to make this for them—just as some of women's secret wooden (and other) objects were made and ritually consecrated for them by men. This was regarded as men's job, part of the accepted division of labor that permeated all aspects of their lives. In that understanding, men were responsible for organizing and supervising the major religious rituals on which the welfare of *everyone* in their community depended. Even on Bathurst and Melville islands, preparation of the large, heavy mortuary posts was men's work, not women's.

Much of the paraphernalia of such rituals, like so many other items that Aborigines made and used, was ephemeral. Their preparation and disposal or natural decay were actually part of the ritual sequence. But even supposing that more of *this* kind of material had survived, and even where artifact patterns and assemblages reveal change through time (or similarities through time), they lack the essential ingredients: where time enters, it does so only at the level of physical, material objects and remains. These essential ingredients, which together bring the world of things to life, are social-personal-cultural identification tags, the action dimension, and the speech and the nonverbal symbols, the spoken and unspoken commentaries through which people explain and define and identify, and express views about, themselves and their social and personal, natural and supernatural environment. There is a parallel here with Aboriginal concepts of the relation between physical and spiritual aspects of living: a human fetus does not become such without an animating spirit; a human body without that spirit (without a soul, to translate it in that way) is lifeless, "only a body."

The largely invisible, intangible ingredients are the most ephemeral of all among a nonliterate people such as the Australian Aborigines were. And where "facts" are in short supply, there is a strong tendency for speculation to take over. Or some "facts" are invoked and put forward as if they represented a total picture. Interpretations are asserted rather than suggested; they are closed, with full stops, rather than left open with question marks. The image (or images) of Aboriginal woman in the literature to date is still only an incomplete outline: some bits are sketched-in fairly consistently, others not at all, and much of it is like a tangle of heavy lines attempting to blot out or override alternative interpretations or the possibility of taking into account further factual evidence.

In this chapter, I have not discussed, except in passing, the topic of myth and story in relation to Aboriginal women. It is of course directly and indirectly relevant, as regards both content and context; but it would lead us into too many other areas of concern, including the sphere of religion. Women figure prominently in the content of Aboriginal myths and stories. They range from minor characters to major creative beings who make their own notable contributions to shaping and peopling the landscape. Some are almost "straight" reflections of their human counterparts, bearing and raising children, attending to domestic affairs, living peaceably or otherwise with their husbands, and so on, even if they display extra (e.g., magical) qualities or powers as well. Others are, in one or more respects, very different indeed. In parts of the Western Desert and central Australia, some myths tell of women who keep apart from men, rejecting the normal style of human-family living arrangements. Another and much more widespread mythical theme, especially in central and northern Australia, contends that in the creative era women owned and controlled all or some of the most secret-sacred songs, rites, myths, and objects, to the exclusion or partial exclusion of men, but that men reversed this situation through trickery, theft, or persuasion. Another, related example of role reversal in myth, from northeastern Arnhem Land, claims that in the beginning it was men, not women, who breast-fed children and carried out the ordinary domestic tasks now handled by women. Such accounts, like others, are variously interpreted by Aborigines in the particular areas concerned, and even more variously interpreted by others (non-Aborigines).

The field of myth, and myth interpretation, constitutes one kind of data that can so easily be lost from the record in a nonliterate society when the oral-transmission links are broken or disturbed. That is what has been happening over a large part of the continent. In any event, we would expect that its content as well as interpretations would have changed through time.

Myth statements about oppositions and conflicts between men and women must be considered in conjunction with myth statements about cooperation and harmony between them—and with the real-life situation of oppositions and conflicts, cooperation and harmony between them. All through the continent, the Australian Aborigines were family-oriented. Men and women cooperated in domestic tasks, in food getting and in the making and rearing of children, and in the complexity of religious affairs. In this collaboration, they worked on traditionally defined lines, in a diversity of ways, some on a sex-linked basis and some not. There was no supposition that all types of task had to be similar, in the Aboriginal conception of interdependence.

Archaeological finds in Australia are *neutral* when it comes to evaluation of the contributions of men and women, respectively, and their own assessments and attitudes in that or in any other aspect of their lives. The assessments and evaluations regarding differential authority, superiority or inferiority, and the like, are imposed on such finds, from within other frames of reference.

The image (or images) of Aboriginal woman illustrates very well a combination of some facts and even *more* interpretation, or speculation from a distance. It is a distant view, enlivened by a few close-ups. This applies to two fields of inquiry and reporting. One is the conventional archaeological-evolutionary frame that focuses on the distant past, interpreting that distant past on the basis of evidence derived from the traditional past of more recent times. The other is the field of inquiry and reporting focused on Aboriginal woman in a traditional or near-traditional setting, in the recent past or in the present. Much of this is "at a distance" from empirical actualities in a different sense, in that it draws upon *pieces* of evidence, or incomplete information. The second of these statements has implications for the first. If the reporting of "facts" about the situation in the *recent* past, let alone the matter of interpretation and evaluation, is so fraught with controversies and disagreements, it must surely be even more difficult to transpose such reports and interpretations into the far-distant past. And regional diversity in culture—in ephemeral, intangible facets of culture—compounds those difficulties. Even allowing for fundamental similarities and continuities in such spheres as food collecting and hunting, tools and weapons, social organization including kinship, religious ritual and myth, or music and language and the arts generally, regional variation is just as marked. And the greater part of such variation, like the intangibles that relate specifically to women vis-à-vis men and vis-à-vis one another, cannot be deduced from the material remains alone.

More people these days than in the past are studying or making comments on the current circumstances of Aborigines in Australia. Many of them are doing so from either or both of two perspectives. In one, they are attempting to *read the past into the present* (i.e., the Aboriginal past). They try to use this to throw light on the present, or to give content and substance to definitions and assertions of Aboriginal identity and Aboriginal rights in the land. In the other, they are attempting to *read the present into the past*—the Aboriginal present, or near-present, into the far-distant Aboriginal past: to infuse life into the timeless image, linking the soulless material of that distant past with the vitality of the living traditional scene. Both of these approaches have their own facts-and-interpretations problems. In both of them, however, the fundamental core of the timeless image—woman the gatherer, homemaker, mother, and childrearer, supported by man the hunter in a cooperative enterprise to ensure their survival—is an inevitable and significant point of departure.

Notes

1. "Aborigines" as a plural noun and "Aboriginal" as an adjective and a singular noun are spelled with a capital A to distinguish Australian Aborigines from aboriginal people as a general, locally undifferentiated term.

2. It is impossible to note even in outline the changing situation in Aboriginal affairs, or to list here even a fraction of the written material now available. I mention only two in which I was partly involved; both include other bibliographical references. These are R. M. Berndt 1977 and R. M. Berndt and C. H. Berndt 1979.

3. *The Great White Queen of the Never Never* is the subtitle of Elizabeth Salter's biographical study, *Daisy Bates* (Corgi Books, 1973; first published by Angus and Robertson, Sydney, 1971). Irish-born author of *The Passing of the Aborigines* (1938), labeled "Saint Daisy" in one television program, she was about ninety years old when she died in 1951. Her travels in remote areas, her maternal, later grandmotherly, concern with Aboriginal groups in Western and South Australia, her "uncompromising opinions" and "ceaseless

conflicts with State and Federal Authorities" (as the back cover of the Salter book puts it), the stiff-collared long-skirted nineteenth-century clothing she continued to wear even in hot semidesert conditions—these helped to build up the eccentric image she was not averse to cultivating. Her writings are a prime example of the mixture of facts, interpretations, and *mis*interpretations that have dogged the ethnography of Australian Aborigines, and especially of Aboriginal women.

4. I drew attention to this in a chapter (C. H. Berndt 1979) where I quoted and discussed several statements from earlier and more recent writers about Aboriginal women with particular reference to Western Australia.

5. Every account of betrothal and marriage (and kinship) in Aboriginal Australia involves the female population just as much as the male population. I shan't mention any of these, therefore, except to note two chapters (Gale 1970; Long 1970) as examples of different areas influenced in varying degrees by contact with the outside world.

6. It would take another chapter to discuss Cawte's contentions in his chapter, "The Control of Women" (1974: chap. 9). It is a mixture of fact and interpretation from a particular angle. He takes the dominance of men as a given. Even (pp. 143–44) the subsection system, which emphasizes matrilineal descent, in his opinion "appears to favor social solidarity amongst males"; and (p. 144), also specifically in regard to Walbiri women in central Australia, he reports that some seemed to regard sexual relations as "a perfunctory matter," or expressed "disinclination" or "sexual coldness." Other points, too, differ considerably from my own findings in regard to Walbiri women (in the mid-1940s).

7. It would be hard to find any discussion of Australian Aborigines that does not mention women or at least imply that it concerns women as well as men. But there is still very little that concentrates on women, as Kaberry's now-classic study (1939) did—remembering that she endeavored to study some aspects of men's life as well, to see her material in better balance. My own earlier statements on women's ceremonies and rituals (1950, 1965) are of a very preliminary kind. Marie Reay's (1963) account of her own role, as Aboriginal women envisaged it in the rather depressed Borroloola area in the Northern Territory, provides an unusual slant on this aspect.

On the whole, there is more serious interest now in Aboriginal women as part of an increased interest in Aborigines in general, though less in their traditional culture than in welfare and sociopolitical terms. But more women—and men—are involved in studies focusing on the subject, or taking Aboriginal women more obviously into account. One sign of this is a volume currently being edited by I. M. White, D. Barwick, and B. Meehan (B. Hiatt), tentatively titled "In the Company of Women," consisting of short biographical and autobiographical chapters on Aboriginal women, including urban Aborigines—a gloss for what some people might call non-"tribal," and not necessarily of full Aboriginal descent. (My chapter, "Mondalmi: 'one of the saltwater people,'" is about a Maung woman from South Goulburn Island, sister to Lamilami, whose autobiographical volume was published by Ure Smith, Sydney, in 1974.) Women of Aboriginal descent are not only talking more widely about their own experiences and interpretations of what is going on, but are also writing about them, in a growing range of publications. The program for the 1980 ANZAAS Conference (Australian and New Zealand Association for the Advancement of Science) included a symposium on "The Changing Roles of Aboriginal Women in Australia Today." One of the preliminary documents relating to this program noted (letter to me from Fay Gale, 19 September 1979) that "the Aboriginal women's committee in Canberra is contacting all Aboriginal women who have published and all official Aboriginal organizations inviting Aboriginal women to participate in the discussion"; and "papers are being invited from Aboriginal as well as academics concerned with the theme"; and the initial proposal for "a volume of essays" had met with "a tremendous response." Because so many Aboriginal women, not all of them urban Aborigines, expressed an interest in the ANZAAS symposium, it was extended to cover three days instead of one (including a one-and-a-half-day workshop discussion among Aboriginal women themselves. This project alone is a pointer to the dramatic change in opinions and in participation on a formerly neglected topic.

References

Bates, Daisy. 1938. *The passing of the aborigines.* London: Murray. Second edition, 1966. Melbourne: Heinemann.

Berndt, Catherine H. 1950. *Women's changing ceremonies in Northern Australia.* Paris: L'Homme.

———. 1965. Women and the "secret life." In *Aboriginal man in Australia,* ed. R. M. Berndt and C. H. Berndt. Sydney: Angus & Robertson.

———. 1970. Prolegomena to a study of genealogies in northeastern Arnhem Land. In *Australian Aboriginal anthropology: Modern studies in social anthropology of the Australian Aborigines,* ed. R. M. Berndt. Perth: University of Western Australia Press.

———. 1973. Women as outsiders: a partial parallel. *Aboriginal News* 1:7-8, 21.

———. 1974*a*. Digging sticks and spears, or the two-sex model. In *Woman's role in Aboriginal society,* ed. Fay Gale. Canberra: Australian Institute of Aboriginal Studies.

———. 1974*b*. Some Aboriginal definitional double-talk. *National Review,* March 8, 14.

———. 1978. In Aboriginal Australia. In *Learning non-aggression,* ed. Ashley Montague. New York: Oxford University Press.

———. 1979. Aboriginal woman and the notion of "the marginal man." In *Aborigines of the West: their past and their present,* ed. R. M. Berndt and C. H. Berndt. Perth: University of Western Australia Press.

Berndt, Catherine H., and Ronald M. Berndt. 1978. *Pioneers and settlers: the Aboriginal Australians.* Melbourne: Pitman.

Berndt, Ronald M. 1977. *Aborigines and change: Australia in the 70's.* Canberra: Australian Institute of Aboriginal Studies.

———. 1979. Aborigines of the Southwest. In *Aborigines of the West: their past and their present,* ed. R. M. Berndt and C. H. Berndt. Perth: University of Western Australia Press.

Berndt, Ronald M., and Catherine H. Berndt. 1970. *Man, land and myth in North Australia: the Gunwinggu people.* Sydney: Ure Smith.

———. 1977. *The world of the first Australians.* Sydney: Ure Smith. First published 1964.

———. 1979. *Aborigines of the West: their past and their present.* Perth: University of Western Australia Press.

Cawte, John. 1974. *Medicine is the law: studies in the psychiatric anthropology of Australian tribal societies.* Honolulu: University Press of Hawaii.

Durkheim, Emile. 1976 (1915). *The elementary forms of religious life.* Winchester, Mass.: Allen and Unwin.

Elkin, A. P. 1939. Introduction. In *Aboriginal woman: sacred and profane*, ed. P. Kaberry. London: Routledge & Kegan Paul.

Gale, Fay. 1970. The impact of urbanization on aboriginal marriage patterns. In *Australian aboriginal anthropology: modern studies in social anthropology of the Australian aborigines*, ed. Ronald M. Berndt. Perth: University of Western Australia Press.

Gould, Richard A. 1969. *Yiwara*. New York: Scribner's.

Hamilton, A. 1970. Nature and nurture: child rearing in north-central Arnhem Land. M.A. thesis, University of Sydney.

———. 1974. The role of women in aboriginal marriage arrangements. In *Woman's role in Aboriginal society*, ed. Fay Gale. Canberra: Australian Institute of Aboriginal Studies.

Hiatt, Betty. 1974. Woman the gatherer. In *Woman's role in Aboriginal society*, ed. Fay Gale. Canberra: Australian Institute of Aboriginal Studies.

Hippler, Arthur E. 1978. Culture and personality of the Yolngu of northeastern Arnhem Land. Part I. Early socialization. *Journal of Psychological Anthropology*, vol. 1, 221–44.

Hoebel, Edward A., and E. L. Frost. 1976. *Cultural and social anthropology*. New York: McGraw-Hill.

Kaberry, Phyllis M. 1939. *Aboriginal woman: sacred and profane*. London: Routledge & Kegan Paul.

Leacock, Eleanor. 1978. Women's status in egalitarian society: implications for social evolution. *Current Anthropology* 19:247–75.

Lévi-Strauss, Claude. 1960. The family. In *Man, culture and society*, ed. H. L. Shapiro, pp. 261–85. New York: Oxford University Press.

Lewis, I. M. 1976. *Social anthropology in perspective*. Harmondsworth, Middlesex: Penguin.

Long, J. 1970. Polygyny, acculturation and contact: aspects of aboriginal marriage in Central Australia. In *Australian Aboriginal anthropology: Modern studies in social anthropology of the Australian Aborigines*, ed. Ronald M. Berndt. Perth: University of Western Australia Press.

Love, J. R. B. 1936. *Stone Age bushmen of today*. London: Blackie.

Maddock, Kenneth. 1972. *The Australian Aborigines: a portrait of their society*. London: Penguin.

Malinowski, Bronislaw. 1913. *The family among the Australian Aborigines*. London: University of London Press.

Peterson, N. 1974. The importance of women in determining the composition of residential groups in Australia. In *Woman's role in*

Aboriginal society, ed. Fay Gale. Canberra: Australian Institute of Aboriginal Studies.

Reay, Marie. 1963. The social position of women (with commentary by C. H. Berndt). In *Australia Aboriginal studies*, ed. Helen Sheils. Melbourne: Oxford University Press.

Róheim, G. 1933. Women and their life in central Australia. *Journal of the Royal Anthropological Institute* 63:207–68.

Salter, Elizabeth. 1971. *The great white queen of the never never*. Sydney: Angus and Robertson.

Shapiro, Warren. 1969. Semi-moiety organization and mother-in-law bestowal in northeast Arnhem Land. *Man* 4(4): 629–40.

———. 1970. Local exogamy and the wife's mother. In *Australian Aboriginal anthropology: Modern studies in social anthropology of the Australian aborigines*, ed. Ronald M. Berndt. Perth: University of Western Australia Press.

Strehlow, T. G. H. 1971. *Songs of central Australia*. Sydney: Angus & Robertson.

Warner, W. Lloyd. 1958. *A black civilization*. New York: Harper. First published 1937.

White, I. M. 1974. Aboriginal women's status: a paradox resolved. In *Woman's role in Aboriginal society*, ed. Fay Gale. Canberra: Australian Institute of Aboriginal Studies.

———. 1975. Sexual conquest and submission in the myths of central Australia. In *Australian Aboriginal mythology*, ed. Lester Richard Hiatt. Canberra: Australian Institute of Aboriginal Studies.

5 MBUTI WOMANHOOD
Colin M. Turnbull

As anthropologists we should not be bashful about our inadequacies and limitations, but we should at least be aware of them. As a male anthropologist among the Mbuti of northeast Zaire in central Africa, I came to know Mbuti women, necessarily, through the eyes of Mbuti males (Turnbull 1961, 1965). However, since on successive field trips I was classified as a child, a youth, and then finally, after a brief encounter with adulthood, as an elder, so my perspective on womanhood was constantly changing. Other factors encourage me to make the attempt to write on this topic, one being that as an anthropologist and obvious non-Mbuti I was allowed more freedom to associate with women than would be normal for an Mbuti male. Second, when as an adult I was given the role of clown, this meant that I was not only allowed to break the norms but *expected* to do so, which again meant that I was able to associate freely with women and discuss things with them that would otherwise have been improper. Third, and more crucially still, gender is significant in the social organization of the Mbuti only at the adult stage of life; their terms of address and reference distinguish between male and female only at the parental level, and adults most frequently both address and refer to *their* parents, who are elders, as *tata*, which indeed is better translated as "elders" than as grandparents, but in either case without differentiation of gender. Similarly, males and females at any generational level refer to others of the same age as *apua'i*, just as they refer to all those younger as *miki*, both again without gender differentiation. Plainly, then, "womanhood," for the Mbuti, is associated with "mother-hood," and indeed both men and women see themselves as equal in all respects except the supremely vital one that, whereas the woman can (and on occasion does) do almost everything the male does, she can do one thing no male can do: give birth to life. Right at the outset, then, as a male I can say that the Mbuti associate womanhood with the life-giving principle and demonstrate this clearly in their rituals, formal and informal. It is expressed daily as they go through the forest hunting and gathering, or merely on their way from one camp to another: they shout and sing to the forest as they go (an agreeable device, the anthropologist might say, for keeping predators away), and while both male and female sometimes address the forest (which for them represents the supreme creative principle) as *eba* (father), most of the time they refer to it as *ema* (mother). I have found this to be as true among the archers as the net hunters, wherever I have been throughout the Ituri.

But now let me be more specific about the Mbuti I know best, in the central region between Mambasa and Bafwasende, and first let me recount my personal experience of womanhood at each of the four age levels through which I have passed, and of my *apua'i* of the other gender at each of the same levels.

As a child, when I was first taken to live in the forest, I was clearly in need of much instruction. I had to be toilet trained, for one thing. It did not strike me as unusual that I was adopted by a childless woman, Masamba, even though she was about my own age. Her husband had one child by the first of his two previous marriages and was, it turned out, incapable of having more. He seemed pleased to have me as a son, and indeed adoption in such cases is normal. But although I was interested in him and thought he would become a friend and informant, that was not to be the case until, a few years later, I became an older youth, then an adult. As a child, I was under the tutelage not only of Masamba but of all the other adult women, whom I was equally expected to address as *ema*. Further, while I could be, and was, happily dependent upon this plurality of mothers for all my needs, as soon as I began to learn to be a useful child there were corresponding demands. I was expected to help with the gathering and with collecting the raw materials for various uses such as hut building, making bark cloth, and the making of the twine with which the hunting nets are formed. The skills themselves I did not learn, as they were mostly womanly skills, or appropriate to males at other age levels.

I was disciplined by open criticism and by ridicule and by deprivation of food if I did anything wrong, and the discipline was exerted by any of my mothers. When Masamba went to visit another hunting band I could go with her or stay, it made little difference. However, I was a quick learner and in six months graduated to the status of youth.

As a youth, I first became conscious that the other gender existed at the nonparental, nonadult level. While I was a child it made no difference with whom I associated except at the adult level, but now I was living in a bachelor hut, sometimes by myself but frequently with other male youths, whereas girl youths continued to sleep in the hut of their parents. I now began to learn some of the adult male skills and to participate, as an older youth, in youthful activities from which the other sex was excluded, most importantly the handling of the *molimo* trumpet, the main Mbuti symbol of the forest as a spiritual entity. The male youths also had the exclusive right to perform the ceremony of the *molimo madé*, or lesser *molimo*, in which the same trumpet is used to indicate displeasure, usually directed against some adult activity. The trumpet may also be used to penalize a wrongdoer when it is carried from dwelling to dwelling and the youths tear sticks and leaves from the wrongdoer's hut. But while these activities created a difference and distance between male and female youths, there was no accompanying sense of superiority or exclusive authority. It was a simple division of labor, and if we exceeded or abused our authority we in turn were penalized by the adult women who, as gatherers, were the main food providers.

Further, while as male youths we had the *molimo madé,* the girls had the *elima* (the celebration of their puberty), during which *they* had authority over *us.* Among other things, the *elima* is the occasion for courtship. Male youths from nearby hunting bands gather outside the *elima* house every afternoon and wait for the girls to come out. I later learned from the girls that they often deliberately keep the boys waiting to annoy them and show their power. They have an even more telling way of showing their power, for to be invited into the *elima* hut, which of course is what was on every boy's mind, one has to be chosen by a girl, who issues the invitation by delivering a sound whipping to the boy of her choice with a long, supple sapling. Even that did not give us instant access. There were the *elima* songs to be sung, a joint endeavor, in which the boys had the subordinate role of providing a background chorus. When the girls retired back into their hut, those who had been whipped could follow, but now there was another hazard. The moment the girls retired, the mothers all gathered in front of the hut, armed with sticks and stones, some with bows with which they fired small missiles. No one entered unscathed and the mothers were perfectly capable of preventing any undesirable from entering whether he had been whipped or not. The little authority we male youths could exercise during the *molimo madé,* real though it was, paled before this show of physical and psychological power. Even when walking through the forest, boys were likely to be ambushed by the *elima* girls and soundly thrashed. Their only recourse was to fight their way past the mothers later in the day, enter the *elima* hut, and then spurn the girls who had thrashed them. Once inside you were free to sleep with whoever was agreeable.

As youths, then, we learned that both girls and women have considerable power, and that while girls are exquisitely flirtable, it is on their own terms. My own flirtations were strictly limited by several factors, so much of what else I have to say about this age level derives from observation, hearsay, and diligent eavesdropping. The mothers allowed me into the hut with a moderate beating, after I had been whipped by a girl I rather disliked, but they were plainly pleased when I did not stay the night. The incident provoked a lot of discussion about my status as a youth, and the fact that I was overgrown and really should have been married long ago. (I had made no secret of my unmarried condition.) However, since they knew I was not going to stay, they said, it would be wrong for me to take an Mbuti wife, and participation in the *elima* was very definitely considered as serious preparation for marriage. As a youth I had my first contact with the concept that a child *cannot* be born as a result of premarital sexual intercourse, although there is only one restriction on such intercourse that I know of, namely that the partners must hold each other by the shoulders and not embrace fully. The fact that Patrick Putnam (1948, personal communication) in his twenty-five years of residence in the area, and I now with a further twenty-five years in and out of the area, have not between us been able to record one single case of premarital pregnancy might lead one to suppose that other factors are at work. Neither of us has, for instance, even a hint of abortion being the explanation. The significance of the phenomenon for present purposes, however, is that it highlights the sharp focus of attention on legitimate maternity, for even extramarital escapades are subject to the same proscription of full embrace, and again it is said that pregnancy *cannot* ensue.

Thus the youths of both sexes are undaunted, and indulge in premarital sex with enthusiasm and delight. They talk about it openly, with neither shame nor undue bravado; rather, the conversations tend to be exchanges of confidence as to when and where each couple finds the sexual act to be most fulfilling; morning, noon, afternoon, evening, or night; by the river, on a sandy bar in midstream, on dry leaves, moist moss, in sunlight or shade. They bring all their senses into play, and describe with joy the sounds and the smells of the

forest as if they were an integral part of the act. Uncon-
sciously, I was learning, as a youth, that the forest is indeed
the life giver and that women are somehow closer to it than
men.

As an adult, my experience is limited both in terms of time
and in terms of my status as a clown, a role that is given to any
male of adult age who suffers from a disability that prevents
him from being a hunter. I know one clown who had been
crippled by polio; another was addicted to smoking marijuana
that he obtained from the villagers (strictly forbidden to anyone going on the hunt, which is a daily activity); another can
best be described simply as a "loner"; he would wander off
into the depths of the forest on his own, yet never came to
harm. My own disability was multiple. The Mbuti pointed out
I would never make a hunter because I was too tall (6 feet 2
inches against their 4 feet 2 inches); I was white, and therefore highly visible in the dim light of the forest; and my body
smell was enough, they said, to scare away the largest game.
Above all, with my height I was too heavy to learn to move
with the silence essential on the hunt. I was thus a kind of
cripple and was given the traditional role given to all who are
"different." The role usually means that the individual is unmarried, which normalized my marital status, though efforts
were made to secure a villager wife for me, one who would be
acceptable in the forest.

As an adult I learned that adulthood is a time of conflict,
primarily conflict between male and female. One of the functions of the clown is to serve as a scapegoat for any serious
dispute; a skilled clown learns to avert disputes before they
arise and to resolve them amicably if they do erupt. But he
(the clown is always male) has no power. I was very conscious
of this both in my own role and when observing clowns in
other camps. When a dispute does become serious, it always
involves adults, exclusively, and while the clown may be used
as a diversion, if serious criticism is called for this is done first
by the youths with their *molimo madé*, which is impersonal, and
then made explicit in the most personal terms by a female

elder. She has both authority and power. She may be a gentle, loving, and kindly old lady one moment, as many of the older women are, but in a flash she becomes pure power and is heeded by everyone. Ridicule is an important element in all conflict resolution; only the old women come out into the open, in the middle of the camp, and make explicit criticisms. Men may use the same central position, which commands attention, but only to grumble or complain and perhaps make minor and rather petty criticisms that are most likely to be ignored.

My association with married couples at this age level led to another discovery. While youths enjoy sexual intercourse fully and richly, they know that no child will be born. Once the marital hut is built and a couple begins to live and hunt together, however, they equally *know* that children *will* be born. I have heard both young married men and women tell their friends who are still youths that the sexual act which youths think they know and enjoy is totally different for adults; I think it would be fair to say that adults see it as ecstasy rather than mere joy. Yet the only difference in the act is in the nature of the embrace. This clearly stated attitude to marital sex, then, again emphasizes the dominance of the value of motherhood in the lives of the Mbuti.

I have elsewhere (Turnbull 1978) gone into the Mbuti life cycle at some length with special attention to childbearing and child education, but here I have to repeat the essential factors. The Mbuti believe that life starts with conception (hence perhaps their feelings about marital sex as being of a totally different quality to extra- or premarital sex). At five months, the mother composes and begins to sing a lullaby for the child in her womb and to talk to it as an adult. She will never sing that lullaby for any other child, and no other woman may sing it. When she gives birth, it is done easily, usually with the assistance of a close friend she made during her *elima* (such bond friends go through life together from girlhood onward). Three days after birth she presents the child to the camp. For three years she feeds it at her breasts and is in total charge of its education and discipline, though there is very little discipline during this time. She shares the work of education and discipline with other mothers, however, as the child grows older and is able to move from one family hearth to another. When the child is two, there is a significant ritual but so informal that at first it escaped me. In the middle of camp, a mother hands her child to her husband, who puts the child to his breast. The child is, of course, familiar with the father's body, since it sleeps between the two parents. It cries "ema" (mother) as it tries to suckle at the milkless breast. The father then gives the child its first solid food and corrects the child, teaching it to say "eba" (father). Thus all males are first perceived by their children as "another kind of mother," one who cannot give milk but does provide other kinds of food. The importance of this is inestimable (Turnbull 1978). The pattern of dependence that is the child's experience in the womb is continued through the first three years by its total dependence on first one mother, then on other mothers, and then, gradually, by extension, on "male mothers" who, however inadequate at first sight, ultimately prove to have their uses too. Thus is the essential quality of interdependence that characterizes Mbuti social organization firmly established and continually enhanced.

Why, then, should adulthood be characterized by the ever-present potential for conflict between the sexes? Part of it has to do with the proscription against sexual intercourse between husband and wife for the three years of breast feeding. Part of it also has to do with their clear recognition that male and female are indeed different kinds of creatures, and the difference must never become blurred. Much of the conflict, then, is ritual in nature.

Childbearing in no way diminishes the mother's importance in Mbuti economic life. Since they are perfectly capable of giving birth to a child while on the hunt, then rejoining the hunt the same morning, mothers see no reason why they should not continue to participate fully in all adult women's activities. For the first three days following childbirth only do

Figure 5.1. An Mbuti pygmy woman gathering food in the forest.

they remain secluded in the dark shade of their hut, gradually
introducing the infant to the light of the camp outside. They
rarely stay away from the daily hunt longer than this, never in
my records for more than a week. They may take the infant
with them, slung at the side so that it has constant access to the
breast, or they may leave it in the camp with one of the other
mothers; in the larger camps there is nearly always one adult
woman who stays behind for some reason, as well as some of
the elders and children. As well as a plurality of mothers
(female and male), the infant quickly learns that it has a plurality of siblings and grandparents with whom it learns to feel
totally secure. The conflict does not arise, then, from any perceived or real incapacity of the mother; there is no structural
hiatus. On the contrary, as a male I am aware that it is the
males who feel, to some extent, incapacitated.

The male must now, for the first time in his life, face the
fact that the most precious commodity of all, human life, is
exclusively in the hands of women. He is aware of the need
for his physiological cooperation in the act of creation, and
some males significantly try to maximize this by holding to the
belief that continued sexual activity right up to the day of
birth (*with* the woman's agreement) helps make the child
stronger and "hurries it along." Others accept their limitations more gracefully and begin to refrain from intercourse
in the fifth month. If there is jealousy, it does not manifest
itself in any way that I can see. A certain amount of envy there
is, however, and this is most marked during the first two
years, until the child is presented to the father. The father is
free to fondle and play with the child at any time, but the
child naturally prefers the mother with the food, which for
the first two years is exclusively the female mother.

The problem is compounded by the restriction on in-
tramarital intercourse. The male feels this keenly; his biological urges are undiminished, whereas the mothers seem to
sublimate their sexual drive through their almost passionate
concern for their infants. It is not just that they do not wish to
become pregnant again and thus deprive the infant of milk;

the proscription is clear and does *not* forbid extramarital intercourse, which, as they see it, *could* not result in pregnancy. That argument is only adduced if the husband tries to break the rule, something that very rarely happens and when it does is the cause of a major disputation that disrupts the entire hunting band. There are severe limitations on the extent of any field observations, however diligent; all I can say is that despite every effort to discover the contrary I have been unable to document any extramarital escapades on the part of nursing mothers, not even flirtations. For their part, adult men and male youths seem singularly uninterested in such mothers as sexual partners. The men, however, both flirt and have sexual intercourse with other women, frequently returning temporarily to the fold of the youths and flirting with unmarried girls. They also flirt and have sexual intercourse with other married women, nearly always those who are widowed or separated from their husbands. While this is not proscribed, and indeed seems to be carefully allowed for by the specific nature of the restriction on marital sex, it is not exactly condoned, and if a husband is discovered to be having such an affair, a dispute arises. This is the major source of *akami* (noise, conflict) within any camp, together with disputes concerning food (which are often said to derive from marital discord). Such disputation only becomes manifest if the couple cannot resolve the problem themselves, or if their squabbling impinges on the lives of others. It is nearly always only the younger married couples that are involved.

Since "noise" in the sense of *akami* is inimical to the hunt, being disturbing to animals and humans equally, it leads to hunger, which in turn leads to more disputation. Disputes concerning food are generally easily dealt with by ridicule, or by the *molimo madé* if selfishness or greed is suspected. There are informal ritual dances that help to avert such disputes. There are much more dramatic formal rituals that play a major role in averting conflict arising from gender or sex, however. *Ekokomea* is a transvestite dance in which women dress as men and ridicule that sex quite mercilessly, while men dress as women and are equally merciless. It is significant that while women ridicule the male organ, exaggerating its size to grotesque proportions, men ridicule that (for them) strange life-giving phenomenon, menstruation. When a girl first "sees the blood" and enters her *elima*, there is universal rejoicing because "now she can be a mother." Apart from this ritual reversal, there is ritualized conflict in the form of a tug of war in which the sexes are set against each other. However, since the function of this ritual, at least, is to equalize, it would be disastrous if either side were actually to win. So as soon as the women begin to win, one of them leaves and goes and joins the men; when *they* begin to win, one of the men joins the side of the women. As each crosses over he assumes the identity of the other sex in mime or ridicule, until the whole thing becomes so hilarious that both sides fall to the ground in near-hysterics that are far from feigned. Thus conflict itself is ridiculed and shown to be dysfunctional. And at times when such conflict seems to be in the air, members of a camp will inevitably indulge in hunting dances or honey dances that offer positive reinforcement for the sexual status quo, illustrating the essentially complementary nature of men and women.

Finally, while a man's sexual prowess, or lack of it—or even, as in the case of my mother's husband (Njobo), his inability to have children—is not infrequently ridiculed by both children and youths, a childless mother is *never* ridiculed, nor is she ever blamed for that unhappy state. Adoption is used to normalize her status and for all structural purposes does so. I am not qualified to speak of the emotional condition of such a woman, but it would be impossible to single them out in any camp from any trait of appearance or behavior.

As elders both male and female revert to their former, almost asexual state, except that whereas the one has not created life out of his body, the other has, out of hers, and is consequently held in considerable esteem. The male is not without esteem; it is a difference of quality rather than quantity and does not become a source of disaffection or envy, let alone jealousy. The complementarity of their roles is more readily accepted. Elders are considered as being endowed with special spiritual powers because of their proximity to death and the "other world" of the forest, the supreme source of all life force. Consequently, when an occasion (usually death) arises that calls for the "great" *molimo*, the *molimo man-gbo*, it is they who control it, although the actual handling of the *molimo* trumpet is still done by the youths, who take it from its hiding place, care for it, and return it when all is over. At first the festival, which generally lasts a month, seems to be exclusively in the hands of the men. When I first was present during such a *molimo*, as a "child," I was made to hide in a hut with other children and women.

But I was not there for the full month. On the next occasion I was a youth, and went with the other male youths to get the trumpet and sing into it with the voice of the forest. There was no question about the sense of elation and power we all felt, and women had no part of it. However, on a subsequent field trip I was with the same band day and night and was told by an elder not to leave, as I would see something I had never seen before. What I saw was a long festival, with the usual show of apparently total male dominance. This was suddenly shattered one night toward the end, however, by the (in my ignorance) sacrilegious entry of first an old woman, then a group of young *elima* girls, who literally seized the sacred *banja* sticks with which we beat the special *molimo* rhythm, and ritually "killed" our song. This they did by producing a length of *nkusa* twine, with which the hunting net is made, and tying a noose around the neck of each male in turn so that we were all bound together. The moment he was so bound, each male stopped singing and one of the girls took his part so the song never stopped, but was taken over by the women. Thus they had killed not so much the song, but the male control of the song. The women then stopped singing and playing the *banja* and announced that they had now indeed killed the song *and* killed the hunt since we men were immobilized. They then sat and chatted with each other and laughed and ignored us until we made an offering of tribute. But from that moment on, whenever they wanted, they resumed control of "our" *molimo*. Indeed, there are legends which state that the women had it first but the men stole it from them.

With even greater drama, however, the women performed the penultimate and most crucial ritual act of the *molimo mangbo*. The *molimo* fire, built and maintained by males only (but drawn from each family, female, hearth), is never allowed to die out. It must constantly be fed. That is our (male) way of showing that the death we are celebrating will not spread among us. We sing to the fire and dance to it, and through it to the forest. But now, in the last three days, the women who have shown their power over our song also show their power over our fire. The old lady and the "mother of the *elima*" slowly dance around the fire, then with calm deliberation and even more slowly dance right through it, kicking the burning logs to each side and stamping out the embers. The men throw the logs back together and, with a dance that imitates the act of copulation, fan it back to life. The women repeat their act of destruction, perhaps several times, making it more than clear that while the men may have the power, through the *molimo* trumpet, to invoke the beneficial spirit of the forest, the women have the ultimate power over life and death. Finally, when the fire nearly is altogether extinguished, they leave it for the men to build up the flame one last time.

The women's job is done, and they leave. Early the next morning, the youths take the *molimo* trumpet back to its hiding place, and the adult males, as they hear the voice of the trumpet receding far off into the forest, stamp the fire out, assured by the song of the *molimo* as it leaves for the last time that death has passed, that there is no more need for either the fire or the trumpet.

There is a slight danger of my appearing to be a rather mixed-up male/female chauvinist, for it is by contrast with my own society that I see womanhood among the Mbuti accorded such great prestige and infinite respect. I think that would be putting it too strongly for the Mbuti, who work hard at emphasizing the complementarity of the sexes, stressing the difference only at the adult level, beginning with the *elima*. Sexual differentiation is indeed a major principle of social organization, being used—together with age—as a structural means of dividing the labor and authority—but without any sense of superordination or subordination. If anything dominates, it is that prime quality of *interdependence*, in such sharp contrast to the *independence* our own society values so highly.

Perhaps we are really talking about different things; for, having lived with the Mbuti as child, youth, adult, and elder, I have no doubt whatsoever in my mind that they equate womanhood with motherhood.

References

Putnam, Patrick. 1948. The pygmies of the Ituri forest. In *A reader in general anthropology*, ed. Carleton S. Coon, pp. 322–42. New York: Henry Holt and Company.

Turnbull, Colin M. 1961. *The forest people*. New York: Simon and Schuster.

———. 1965. *Wayward servants*. New York: Natural History Press.

———. 1978. The politics of non-aggression. In *Learning non-aggression*, ed. Ashley Montague. New York: Oxford University Press.

6 THE NULL CASE: THE CHIPEWYAN

Henry S. Sharp

The "traditional" life of the "Caribou-Eater" Chipewyan (Smith 1975) raises several questions, both theoretical and ethnographic, about our conventional conceptualization of women as specialists at gathering plant material in hunter-gatherer societies. The Chipewyan were a hunting culture, one of those odd variants on the hunting-gathering pattern, whose diet was more than 90 percent flesh. Cultures with such an extreme dependence upon flesh are rare and are probably found only in subarctic, arctic, or maritime environments. The theoretical significance of this pattern of subsistence derives from the imbalance in food production by the sexes. Virtually all food is obtained by men, women having no significant role in the actual production of food. In this sense they represent a null case with which our growing recognition of the significance of women's roles in subsistence must deal. Beyond this they pose a more general and significant problem: how is the sexual division of labor in food production, the basic interdependence of human society, preserved in the face of this imbalance? We shall examine these questions in this chapter and show that the problem is solved by creating a distinction between food production and food processing that is part of the basic male-female symbolic complementarity that orders Chipewyan culture.

Chipewyan culture is one in which women are "devalued"; their status, as individuals and as a symbolic category, is low, and although I find the concept theoretically noxious, they

are "oppressed." This condition is categorical, a direct consequence of the symbolic system and integral to the smooth operation of the social system (Sharp 1979; Sharp n.d.). Explanations of women's position in societies in terms of the inherent characteristics of women as reflected in symbolic systems,
as Ortner (1974) has done, for example, are sometimes useful
and insightful, especially for cross-cultural comparisons.
However, as Lévi-Strauss (1963), among others, has shown,
explanations of categories[1] in terms of the "intrinsic" characteristics of their content are inadequate and ultimately in-
valid. The "position of women in society" is a function of
human symbolic systems rather than of the nature of women.

This is of consequence to the massive, and largely specious,
debate about the biological/genetic/economic/psychological
(they all seem to merge into an inseparable confusion) differences between males and females. Without a systematic
ethnographic investigation to see if these Western categories
of male and female are used as we understand them, there is
no validity to their cross-cultural use. Whatever the differences between males and females might prove to be, however,
they are no more relevant to an explanation of the symbolic
treatment of the categories male and female than are the "inherent characteristics" of twins and birds relevant to an explanation of their equation in Nuer thought (Evans-Pritchard
1956). This is not to deny the importance of these questions
of possible sexual differences in biology, genetics, or psychology, although economic anthropologists, if not economists,
should know better. But it must be stated that any biological
or psychological differences between male and female remain
unspecifiable at a social level, and hence irrelevant to the
analysis of sociological questions.

The Chipewyan

The Chipewyan are an Athapaskan-speaking people located
in the Northwest Territories, Manitoba, Saskatchewan, and
Alberta in Canada. They are the easternmost people in this

large language grouping, which stretches from Hudson Bay in Canada to the interior of Alaska and also includes some major southwestern tribes and a few Pacific coastal peoples. At the time of contact with European cultures they numbered between 3,000 and 6,000 people and occupied the largest land area of any North American tribe. During the eighteenth century they expanded their range by a factor of two or three, and they currently number somewhere between 10,000 and 15,000. Before the eighteenth century the Chipewyan were centered in the open transition zone of the boreal forest in the Northwest Territories (Sharp 1977*b*). Their yearly cycle took them onto the tundra in summer and into the boreal forest in winter in pursuit of the barren ground caribou (Burch 1972). This single species was their primary food source, but they also made use of other major mammals (musk-ox, moose, etc.), fish, and small game.

The kinship system is bilateral, and the population was dispersed over vast areas; density was somewhere between one person per fifty square miles and one per hundred square miles. Social groups were kin-based and constantly in motion, both social and physical; temporary aggregations of several hundred people did form around particularly successful caribou kills or good food-producing locations for short periods. Leadership was possible only through influence and was exerted by men of known magical power. The political structure was fluid, without offices or recognized positions of authority.

Contact with Europeans occurred in 1715 (Smith 1975), and the Chipewyan entered fur trade with the Hudson's Bay Company. The early fur trade was a period of prosperity and expansion, the Chipewyan pushing south and southwest as far as the Churchill River and on into Alberta (Gillespie 1975). The expanding Chipewyan became heavily involved with the fur trade, adopted a subsistence style akin to the resident Cree groups, and developed a dependence upon fish and moose. The Caribou-Eater, however, remained in and around the transition zone of the boreal forest and did not become heavily involved in the fur trade until the twentieth century. They remained committed to the pursuit of barren ground caribou and underwent relatively few changes in their patterns of subsistence until recently.

By the mid-nineteenth century they had developed a stable pattern of adjustment to Canadian society (Helm and Damas 1963) that was not to be seriously disrupted until the end of World War II. The Caribou-Eater group lived in bush camps throughout the year and made periodic journeys into the trading posts to sell fur and purchase supplies. In the region in which I did fieldwork, two stores, one at Brochet, Manitoba, and the other at Fond-du-Lac, Saskatchewan, serviced an area of roughly 100,000 square miles until the 1920s. Trips to the stores were infrequent, young people often not making their first trip until their teens. There was little contact away from the stores except for the limited journeys of the Oblate missionaries and the Northwest Mounted Police (Royal Canadian Mounted Police).

With the adoption of repeating rifles near the end of the nineteenth century, the Chipewyan ceased regular summer use of the barren grounds. Canvas had replaced caribou hide as a material for making tents, and the repeating rifle allowed the Chipewyan to dispense with traditional techniques for providing the caribou flesh necessary for survival (Sharp 1977*b*). There are few accounts of the period from contact until the present (e.g., Seton 1911; Curtis 1928; Hearne 1971). The analysis in this chapter is limited to bush life of the period from the 1930s to the 1970s in the region around Stony Rapids, Saskatchewan, as it corresponds most closely to aboriginal practice and is less affected by the now immensely strong pressures of Canadian society.

The Ideological Basis of the Division of Labor

To understand the role of women in Chipewyan society we must first consider the values placed upon man as a hunter. The values assigned to male and female are part of a coherent symbolic system shared by both sexes, but food production is one of the factors at the base of this system of values. How deeply this is ingrained in the structure of the Chipewyan language is shown in Carter's (1974) analysis of the Mission Chipewyan dialect, which uncovered a deep-seated abhorrence of scavenging in Chipewyan thought and is compatible with the results of my (1976) analysis of mythical thought. Both show that not obtaining food by direct action upon the environment is negatively valued in both human and animal. No matter how one views symbolic analysis, the fact is that Chipewyan society places great value upon the ability to hunt and conceives of it in humans as a male activity.

Limiting these skills to males is a function of the Chipewyan perception of the universe through a thought system most easily referred to in English as "magic." It is best to realize that the Chipewyan conceptualization is a causal system ordering the universe. It is, in this sense, a thought system such as mechanics (in form, not in content), a self-contained ordering of experience. It is applied to certain spheres of life, just as Newtonian mechanics is applied to certain spheres, but is not relevant as explanation in other spheres, just as we do not explain love, hot-fudge sundaes, or disco dancing in terms of mechanics. The Chipewyan magic system is causal as well as a means of explanation. It presumes the existence of animate beings in possession of power/knowledge over the universe, who may reveal some of that power/knowledge to men in dreams. I stress men because this system is exclusively male in the flesh; women with power/knowledge appear only in myth.

Power/knowledge is exhibited by males in competitive contexts such as races or gambling, and in performance activities such as hunting or trapping. The most significant other contexts are healing, sorcery, and resistance to physical degeneration with age. Our major concern here is its expression in hunting, as that is the male activity par excellence. In the pursuit of game[2] the hunter is in a relationship that is simultaneously natural and supernatural (as we think of it, not as the Chipewyan think of it) in pursuit of a prey that is both natural and supernatural. The relationship is simultaneously with the individual animal (physically and spiritually), the species, and supernatural creatures appearing in the form of an animal.

Animals are killed only by their consent. The necessity for the prey to consent to its death removes hunting solely from the realm of the natural and, more important, makes it a measure of the power/knowledge of the hunter. This turns subsistence activities into a system of measurement of men and provides both an explanation for the success of certain men (they have more power/knowledge) and the causal basis for the success of certain men (they have more power/knowledge). This, in turn, allows the prediction of future success.

Male and Female, as categories in Chipewyan thought, exist in complementary opposition. It is interesting that male-female complementarity should be so strongly developed in this culture, the one reputed to have treated its women worse than any other North American tribe, for the complementarity has direct consequences for the subsistence system. The category Male has power/knowledge, which underlies men's activities. The category Female is nonmagical, the antithesis of power/knowledge, and women as a category are thus more vulnerable to the effects of magic. A root that is smoked to cure a man's headache is an aphrodisiac for a woman; a charm kept in a pillow to give a man strength will kill a woman who sleeps on the pillow; a plant, the top of whose stalk prevents the hemorrhaging of tuberculosis in both sexes, has a bottom that causes hemorrhaging (miscarriages) in women; a magical power fight that a man can counter will kill a woman. But if the category Female is more vulnerable to magic, individual women are a threat to the magic of specific men. The very pollution of her being will destroy the efficacy of a man's magical materials. A woman, simply by touching them, can ruin a man's entire supply of healing plants, can ruin the magic of a dog harness simply by stepping over it (when menstruating), can drive away the caribou by stepping over a carcass, can break the "luck" on a man's rifle simply by picking it up. The power of women to pollute is so strongly developed that it is in fact a form of magical power. It is antithetical to men's power and comes not from supernatural sources but from the very biology of femaleness. To be female is to be power, to be male is to acquire power. Men *may* have power but women *are* power just by being women.

The implications of these symbolic attributes of male and female, expressed as a male association with wolf and a female association with dog (Sharp 1976), are that man is a predator while woman is a scavenger. Man produces food by killing it, engaging in competition with other predators, while woman is fed—dependent upon the power/knowledge of males to feed her. This fits well with the symbolic system of this culture; it allows and causes the greater valuation of males and the control and regimentation of females. But it still poses a problem: how can interdependency be maintained in the face of the symbolic asymmetry between the sexes?

The Division of Labor in Food Production

Mutual interdependency in food production is maintained by an artificial division of the food production process into two parts: procuring and processing. As in our society, the integral tasks of food production are subdivided in a way that does not reflect or derive from the nature of the tasks themselves or from the ability of either sex to perform them. As we consider earning money to buy food "superior" and the actual purchasing and preparing of food "inferior," the Chipewyan regard the killing of game superior to the processing of the game into food. This division is a social division operative in the public sphere. It is a social division that is public because the basic skills of subsistence are possessed by both men and women, and in isolation the public roles often break down. Let us first consider the public roles of the sexes in this matter.

My informants' descriptions of past camp life present a vivid picture of the sexual division of labor in food production. The distinction between procuring and processing was intensified by the magical system that makes the distinction between the camp and the bush itself symbolically important (Sharp 1976). Procuring occurred in the bush; men killed the animals there and they were field-dressed. The meat was then brought to camp and turned over to the women for processing.

Among the contemporary Chipewyan this transfer often involves a series of transitions reflecting the liminality of unprocessed meat in the camp. Meat in the bush is completely under the control of men, but meat in the camp is more ambiguous. The unprocessed meat is normally kept on a stage, constructed by men, until it is ready for use. The stage contains meat for human use as well as that intended for the dogs or other purposes. Although women can take meat from the stage, it is usually brought to them by a male. What is brought to them for processing is theirs and they control its disposition; what remains on the stage is not clearly the "property" of either male or female and is not necessarily destined to become food. It is the actual effort of converting the raw meat into food that gives the woman her right of control and disposition over it, just as it is the man's actual killing and butchering that gives him the right of control and disposition over the animal from which the meat came.

The men kept a careful watch on this process and the final consumption of the meat. All bone had to be removed from the camp or burned in the fire. Violation of this procedure was offensive to the animal being consumed, and it responded to the violation by refusing to be killed or by leaving the area. This prohibition is expressly stated in terms of keeping dogs from gnawing the bones; but because of the general symbolic linkage of dogs and women it is safe to assert that the concern was more general. The picture informants present is of a camp kept clean, all scraps being removed for burning in the bush.[3]

The picture that informants paint of their past is not a reli-

able statement of actual daily life, at least not without archaeological verification, but it is useful as a statement of currently perceived relationships and principles. The picture is
instructive, for it shows the importance of the tension between the sexes in food production, the aspects of exchange
inherent in raw meat, and the intrusion of symbolic elements
into what Western thought tends to perceive as merely an
economic process, as if labeling a process an economic one
somehow was a final explanation based upon some nonsocial
reality.

In contemporary bush life this systemic neatness does not
exist. Little effort is made to keep camps clean; bones of food
animals—but not furbearers, wolves, or bears—are routinely
fed to the dogs; the processing activities of the women are not
supervised; and there are no ritual butchering areas that are
formally prohibited to women. Nevertheless, the major
dynamics of the male-female opposition are kept in practice,
although the barriers that preserve the separation are not
formally stated as rules. The symbolic elements that serve to
keep women in the camp area, as well as the pragmatic elements, serve the necessary function of separating the procuring of game from its processing into food.

Since killing takes place in the bush, the initial division and
butchering of game are male functions. Transportation of the
game to the camp is men's responsibility. This is a major
problem in an environment where everything must ultimately
be packed. The men are adept at judging what parts of a carcass are worth bringing back to camp and what parts are best
consumed or abandoned in the bush. Interestingly, the parts
that are most frequently consumed or abandoned include the
parts around which there is/was ritual significance, and killing
a game animal is almost always accompanied by a roasting of
part of the animal for a meal. I am not sure how far to push
this latter aspect of hunting and control over game, but this
immediate conversion of meat to food in an all-male context,
though not invariable, does seem intimately related to the
process of hunting as a social activity as well as a parallel to
what women do to obtain control over meat.

Since the meat in the bush belongs to men they have the right of disposal over it and may use it for nonconsumption purposes such as bait. This meat can be shared among men, and they are normally exceedingly generous of their supplies. Especially with freshly killed game, men tend to share by giving away entire kills, entire animals, or very large portions of animals, depending upon the context. This sharing is not normal reciprocity (though it can be), generosity, or even indifference. It is a shaming of the recipient, a statement of the superior power/knowledge of the giver.[4] Bringing meat out of the bush, either by transporting it or by bringing the women to it,[5] results in a transfer of ownership, or at the least the establishment of joint rights over it. Although a man could assert a preeminent claim to the meat in the camp and give it away even after it has been processed,[6] he would be opposed (by women). For all practical purposes, once meat is in the camp it is the property of the wife, mother, or other responsible female associated with the hunter.

The symbolic division between male and female extends beyond food to the tools used in their respective tasks. Male hunting, trapping, and bush gear are basically "hands off" items for women. Whenever possible they are kept outside the dwelling in separate storage areas (rifles are kept inside, and the distinction does not apply to bedding, etc.), whereas women's tools are kept inside or in the area where food is processed. Because of the nature of women's tools and their lack of magical associations, they often serve for the entire domestic group (as in the case of pots, plates, or knives). Nevertheless, that the tools of their trade, as it were, belong to one sex is clearly shown in marital disputes where all the tools of one spouse are thrown out by the other. There are clear understandings as to what is his, what is hers, and what is uncertain or joint.

Food Processing: The Public System

The primary role of women in the food production process is the conversion of raw animal tissue into cooked food. The cooking process itself is symbolically important in the culture; the Chipewyan distinguish themselves from animals and Eskimo by their avoidance of raw food. It should be noted that the idea of cooking does not necessarily correspond to Western ideas on the subject. Things we would consider to be raw (e.g., the singed velvet of caribou antlers), they regard as cooked; conversely, they have little taste for oysters Rockefeller or steak tartare. In fact, the actual cooking of meals is a relatively minor aspect of woman's work,[7] especially compared to drying meat and fish for future consumption.

Drying food, whether meat or fish, is a time-consuming task involving skill with a knife, strong hands, a willingness to sit for long periods of time exposed to inclement weather, and a high tolerance of smoke, as well as the exercise of judgment in the allocation of animal tissue to particular cuts and processes to make the best use of the available resources. The judgmental aspects of the process are frequently not terribly significant, because of the abundance of food, but these skills can be crucial when resources are limited.

Figure 6.1. Chipewyan woman preparing caribou meat for drying.

The Chipewyan dry meat and fish by sun and wind. Fires may be kept burning, as smoke helps drive away insects (especially flies) and gives a nuttier taste to the dried food,[8] but the heat of the fire is often not a significant factor in the drying process. Fish are dried in the spring, and a few families dry them in the fall; otherwise they are only dried as an occasional treat. When the fish are spawning in the spring (the local species of sucker is the fish most frequently dried, although grayling are often taken for this purpose) a good net set will provide up to two hundred fish per day at an average weight of 1.5 kilograms. Each fish must be beheaded, gutted, split, and spread open before it can be placed upon the drying rack.[9] Once on the rack, the fish must be turned several times each day and removed before each rainstorm or shower and at night to keep them from becoming damp. If a fire is kept going, as it generally is with fish, wood must be found— children can do this—and the fire supervised. Use of a tepee as a drying tent requires constant supervision to prevent a destructive fire.

The men can provide the fish with one or two hours' work a day, and if the yield is good they can keep several women working continuously. The labor of women is crucial in this activity, as it is the limiting factor. It is usually possible to catch more fish than the women will be able to process. As it is difficult to dry the fish completely there is a strong temptation to store them before they are finished. This results in a high percentage of the fish rotting before they can be consumed. Chipewyan informants speak of drying huge numbers of fish in the spring and catching and freezing large amounts in the fall (2,000 for the fall is considered a minimum number), but I doubt this. Only a few of the Chipewyan who remain in the boreal forest proper put any effort into fall fishing, mostly for dog food, and they rarely take over 1,000 fish. The dry fish I have seen last only a few weeks at best, and they are bulky and difficult to transport. I suspect that there has been an increased emphasis on dried fish in the past twenty years because of the increased sedentarization of village life—which produces large areas with very little wild game—and the access to a freezer that allows the dried fish to be frozen and kept over the summer.

If dried fish is of localized interest and not very significant, the same is not the case for dry meat, especially dried caribou meat. Before 1950, the Chipewyan population lived throughout the region of exploitation and made only intermittent trips into the store that was established at Stony Rapids in the 1920s. Most of the population was more than fifty air miles from the store, a distance that precluded the transport of bulk foodstuffs by canoe before the day of chartered bush planes. This required the Chipewyan to subsist off the land, with store foods serving as a supplement. In order to exploit the environment effectively the population had to be mobile (Burch 1972; Sharp 1977a,b), always willing to leave an area and move to a location where there were caribou (fall, winter, spring) or other large game (summer) or kinsmen who had been successful at killing caribou. The social system was designed to provide caribou, but it was not designed for a sustained yield. The critical periods of the year were the spring and fall migrations, when caribou could be killed in large numbers; they were killed at other times—in fact at any time it was possible—but sustained yield hunting is not reliable enough. The scale of distances and degree of movement involved are simply too great for this type of subsistence to be dependable, even using the other food sources available.

Surprisingly, in a climate this cold, food storage and transport are a serious problem. Most of the summer, spring, and fall are too damp or too hot to make fresh food storage easy. Temporary expedients, such as putting meat in ice-cold water or under moss next to the permafrost, exist, but they merely slow down the deterioration. Dried meat becomes a crucial resource for several reasons: it can be stored for long periods of time merely by keeping it dry, it is a concentrated food source especially as it is normally consumed with dried caribou fat, and it is light and easily transported. These characteristics make it crucial to the operation of the Chipewyan social system. Fresh food can be frozen for the winter, but dry meat can easily be transported in any moves that become necessary and is easily shared with social groups lacking caribou. This is significant because at a regional level (Sharp 1977a,b) the Chipewyan strategy of exploitation, while assuring that enough social groups will obtain caribou to keep the system operating, also assures that some social groups will obtain caribou only in those rare years when the animals are exceptionally abundant. Dry caribou meat processed and controlled by women becomes the crucial resource in times of scarcity. In this context woman's check on man's preemptive right of allocation takes on an added significance.

Drying meat is akin to drying fish, but it occurs at any time of the year when there is surplus meat. Fish may be wasted, but caribou meat is not. The amount made depends on the supplies of dry meat on hand and the anticipated needs as well as the time of the year and the amount of fresh meat available. By preference, dry meat is made from the rump, rear legs, and "tenderloin" strips (muscles paralleling the backbone), but all parts of the carcass can be used. At least as much concern goes into the drying of fat as goes into the drying of meat. Animal fat is absolutely necessary to provide the calories needed to function in the subarctic cold. Each muscle is detached from the bone and cut into flat sheaves about three-eighths inch in thickness. Pieces with bone, such as the ribs, may be deboned before drying, but heavily boned structures such as the pelvis (a favorite because of the fat inside it) and individual organs must be heavily smoked.[10]

As is the case with fish, it takes longer to dry meat than to kill, butcher, and transport it. Drying may not begin until the meat has been killed and transported, so there are long periods when the women have no meat to process followed by periods when they have more meat than they can handle. By my observation, this is an activity that is conducted by each woman responsible for a family, but younger women with families may work under the supervision of senior kinswomen or affines.

The public roles of male and female are quite logical under the environmental circumstances. Man extracts food from the bush, and as long as it remains in the bush it is under his control. Woman processes the animal tissue after it has been transported into the camp, and the control over the disposition of foodstuff is in her hands but subject to preemptive disposition by her husband.[11] Woman is responsible for cooking food for consumption, storage, baking, and packing the husband's food into his hunting sack. The only procurement woman engages in is berry picking. Whatever the past dietary significance of this activity, it is now intermittent and insignificant.

The roles of male and female, in a public sense, place the former in the position of highly valued, active hunter and the latter as low-valued, passive, continuously working drudge. This view is built into the symbolic system and continuously reinforced. In the realm of social practice the situation is often quite different, and it scarcely needs remarking that the responsibilities of the sexes are not limited to the area of food production that we are considering here.

Food Processing: The Private System

The roles of male and female are a great deal more flexible in the private system (which is really a negative category meaning nonpublic—with all the problems of specification that go along with negatively defined categories). Although based upon the same symbolic structures as in the public system, the attributes of the roles are influenced by a great many factors that do not affect that system. The private system generates the flexibility necessary to meet the erratic necessities of subarctic life. Aside from being a face-to-face relationship between two people, in which psychological characteristics, personality factors, and past actions become relevant, the factors of labor, travel, and isolation require a more fluid relationship between the roles.

A good example of this private flexibility is the conflict that can develop about the effort to be put into procuring food. A man, as a function of his belief in his supernatural power/knowledge, is not inclined to worry about the amount of food available until a crisis arises, that is, until there is not enough food. This dominant perspective, the "hunter-gatherer mentality," is fine in public and for males, but it is often a sore point for women. Being divorced from direct participation in the system through the possession of power/knowledge, women are privately far less convinced that something will turn up. They insist that the men get out and hunt. There is a risk in this that the men will balk at hunting. I saw it happen in 1975 when the men of a camp turned to building a cabin instead of hunting. They missed the last caribou migration and killed an inadequate supply of meat. The women are not entirely unreasonable in their feeling that power/knowledge is not an effective substitute for work.

There is a real parallelism between the pressure women bring to bear upon men to hunt and the role they occupy as polluters of magical implements and magical power/knowledge. The opposition between the sexes, in both realms, creates a situation of conflict that forces action. People are not able to rely on fixed social positions or statuses to produce results. The social positions and statuses themselves are the product of a continuous process of resolution of the conflict generated by the ideological structure of the society. A woman's pressure upon her husband to get out and hunt confirms both systems, her private doubts and his public belief, no matter how the ensuing hunt turns out. If he is successful it is proof to him that his power/knowledge works and to her that he should work. If it is a failure it is proof to him that these things are mystical and do not respond to the urging of women or mere physical effort; to her it is proof that power/knowledge is not a substitute for action. The effect is to keep a constant pressure upon men to hunt while at the same time giving them a mechanism to use their judgment of local conditions and game as a check to prevent wasted effort. It is the interplay between the public and private systems that keeps the entire system from becoming fatalistic and passive.[12] The system runs on doubt and disbelief of the opposite sexual category, at the level of specific people in actual situations, as much as belief and trust. All of this serves to keep the system functioning and integrated at the higher level of symbolic relationships between categories.

The contrast between the public and private systems is most visible to an observer when social groups, particularly families, are in isolation. This occurs for short periods when people are on the trail, arrive early at a camp, or move off for a few days for the exploitation of a specific resource. It also occurs as a necessary step for any family wishing to establish social autonomy from their kin. Isolation is a rather frequent situation, and physical isolation is usually rather complete. Parts of the village I studied, as late as 1970, were distributed over 45,000 square miles during the fall of that year. Their population that still went into the bush was so scattered that it was not uncommon for isolated groups to be forty or fifty miles away from their nearest neighbor (ground distance, which is about double the air distance). At this level of isolation it is not always possible to maintain the distinction between the public and private systems in the processes of food production, so only the most basic elements are preserved in private.

This is the reason for the earlier assertion that the distinction between food processing and food production is arbitrary. Members of both sexes have the skills necessary to survive in isolation. Men often live by themselves for weeks or months at a time, either individually (rarely) or in pairs. Women are frequently left alone (with their children, if any) for days and sometimes weeks. Under these circumstances both sexes must both procure and process food for themselves. Ironically, men seem to have a better mastery of women's skills than women do of men's.[13]

The isolation of a single-sex group will certainly call upon a greater range of skills than will be the case when both sexes are represented, but even with heterosexual pairs the public system may not be maintained completely. During periods of isolation, both partners become aware of each other's skills. There are also certain times when resources must be harvested rapidly and it is easier to allow the sexual division to yield to the needs of the moment. Isolation also allows women to make extensive excursions into the bush and to accompany, if not assist in, hunting activities. Long walks that often become hunts are common, and men will help their wives pick berries for common consumption—something they will not let another man see them do.[14] A factor that affects this activity is weather. I do not think that women are allowed to leave the camp during the harsher parts of the winter unless the camp is moving. In any case, the main point is that the interdependency of the sexes derives not from sex-specific skills or physical attributes, or even from restricted knowledge, but from the fact that the interdependency itself is useful.

The best example of how male-female interdependency in the private sphere operates to shape the public sphere is the process of food sharing. Since food procurement is, publicly, a male activity, any borrowing that males do (if it goes outside the boundaries of the restricted cognatic descent group) weighs heavily upon their reputation for power/knowledge. This is reflected in the preemptive claim men have over foodstuffs and the tendency to give ostentatiously far more than they are asked for. No matter how skilled the hunter, there are times when there is not enough food. There are also other foodstuffs that are borrowed that are not obtained from the bush. In fact, borrowing is a continual necessity as people run short of meat, fish, bannock, particular cuts of meat, types of fish, and so on, or need condiments, sugar, or tea. Virtually all of this borrowing is done by women from women.

Borrowing, or rather the necessity to borrow, is in direct contravention of the symbolic values placed on males, since they are supposed to be competent and complete providers. By making this something women do, and hence not really of notice, the public system and the male's position can be preserved. It would be tempting, given the picture painted here, to view women as rational planners and men as irresponsible and unconcerned about daily life. If the Chipewyan planned as we do, particularly as regards meals, then the charge might have some validity, but the Chipewyan do not plan as we do. Meals are not served on any schedule, and it is not even usual for the members of a large family to eat together.

Ideally, food should always be available, and this is often the case in colder weather when a fire is always going and a pot of meat may be left on the stove. More often a meal is prepared only in response to a request or a woman's own hunger, and such a request may come at any time. In this situation there may be no food available, and the woman will go and borrow food. The point I wish to make is that meals are not budgeted or planned in a Western sense, so it does not make sense to think of the men as prodigal and the women as careful. Women borrow from each other on a normal basis, though some borrow more frequently than others, not only under unusual circumstances.

Borrowing serves as the mechanism for redistribution of food within a camp. Each person knows what has been killed or brought into camp, so there is little difficulty in knowing where to go. It is rather illuminating to watch this process when a carcass has been brought into the village during a meat shortage. The wife of the hunter receives a steady stream of visitors, each chatting for a while with the wife and other visitors, who await a piece of meat before starting home. If the pieces given are large they may be divided again at the woman's home and given to her female kin. Somehow the man who killed the animal seems to lurk, visibly but inconspicuously, in the background while the meat is shared. One of the problems of village life is the presence of so many kin and neighbors that even a moose carcass is gone in a short while. This problem has been solved in the past decade by adopting Western ideas and selling meat to distant kin or other persons who have little claim to a share.

In a sense the difference between male and female is the

difference between public and private, the general and the specific. Women, because of their ideological and social position, tend to be involved with specific cases, specific needs— their family, their food supply, their meals—while men tend to be involved with more general problems, or at least activities with less specific reference. Although men do hunt alone it is far more common for them to hunt in pairs, or at least in the same area as other men. Hunting seems to be directed to ends that often have little to do with their individual needs or family obligations.

Kinship and Sharing

Placing effective control of food and food lending in the hands of women is no insignificant feature of Chipewyan life. Control of routine borrowing and the distribution of dry meat may seem rather mundane, but it is a very significant aspect of social life.[15] In the postcontact system, as described elsewhere (Sharp 1977*a,b*, 1978), it is the conversion of caribou meat into dry meat, which is concentrated, storable, and transportable, that allowed the Chipewyan to cope with the uncertainty of caribou movements.

I suspect, but cannot demonstrate, that this acts as a partial foil to the patrilineal tendencies present in the Chipewyan system. The system is bilateral, but residence is preponderantly patrilocal. Since relatively few men are able to recruit their daughter's husbands into their restricted cognatic descent groups and the system is ideologically loaded toward males, the base of a patrilineal system is present. The kinship system stresses relationships between males as the principal structural links, yet the Chipewyan place a great deal of emphasis—in practice, not in ideology—upon affinal ties. In determining residence or participation in activities, the kin ties between women can become the deciding factor. This is especially the case since conflict between kin and affines is most frequently expressed in terms of stinginess, the unwillingness to engage in the normal sharing, which is largely controlled by women. I have little information about these things prior to my own fieldwork, but I am certain that the relations between the women in one's own group and the women of related groups were a deciding factor in determining where to relocate in times of social and economic stress.

Conclusion

The sexual division of labor in human society is so basic to all known cultures that it is difficult to imagine a system that does not possess a highly developed and complementary one. The case of the Caribou-Eater Chipewyan is interesting since it represents an unusual situation in which women have no role in the actual production of food. Even in these circumstances, which are not the result of environmental factors or of biological or behavioral differences between the sexes, we still find a highly structured division of labor. Of perhaps more interest is the structuring of the division of labor upon systematic symbolic oppositions between male or female in such a manner as to keep the social system in a balance between conflicting forces, and hence in a better position to respond to changes in the physical and social environment.

Acknowledgments

I wish to thank Dr. T. O. Beidelman and Dr. J. G. E. Smith for their comments on a previous draft of this chapter.

Notes

1. I have tried to make clear where the text refers to categories and where it refers to individuals within the categories.
2. I am using *game* to refer to large game animals and certain significant predators and birds. These ideas do not seem applicable to "small" creatures, although I am not positive of this and could not construct a complete typology of all species on this basis.
3. The consumption of certain parts of the carcass seems to have

been restricted to males, but my information is not adequate. There were special prohibitions on the consumption and/or disposal of the heads of game animals.

4. I am simplifying here. There are expectations for sharing and division of the yield of a hunt as well as certain social groups within which sharing is done without any statement of relative power/ knowledge being made. A discussion of these is beyond the scope of this chapter.

5. In a real sense the women are the camp. Wherever they stop becomes camp (culture) in opposition to the bush around them.

6. An example of this is the sending of meat, fresh or dried, to kin by aircraft. These gifts are public, and since aircraft arrive without warning, a man making a presentation may strip his camp of meat, completely disregarding his wife's objections. This would never be done for sharing within a camp.

7. Baking bannock, a now traditional bread, takes a fair amount of time, but even though this food is a staple it needs to be prepared only every few days, unless there is nothing else to eat—a not infrequent occurrence. Native cookery has degenerated. Western foods are too readily available, and the combination of wild ingredients too hard to come by, for anyone to take much interest in traditional dishes that require much work. This is particularly the case in the village, where virtually all ceremonial and special meals occur.

8. This is also a matter of taste. Many people's digestive systems are upset by smoked meat or fish.

9. Women can build drying racks, but this is regarded as a male task. I have seen meat and fish rot because the men were too busy procuring it to build a rack for the women to process it.

10. The techniques required to dry meat are far more complex than I am indicating here.

11. This general pattern holds for food obtained from the store, but since this food requires credit or cash to obtain, procurement is often done by women. Several types of government checks are payable to the woman of the family rather than the man—the Canadian government insists upon operating in terms of nuclear families— and purchasing food from the store is not really a male activity.

12. I am not trying to imply that men are lazy or that women always nag. It is rather the case that, under conditions of scarcity, the conflict between the sexes privately acts as a prod to keep the men active. As the key to hunting in times of scarcity is movement, the extra effort of the men is a factor in locating game.

13. As far as I know, women do not actively hunt in these circumstances but will kill small game, check fish nets, and the like. I do not doubt that they would also kill large game if it came close to camp, but I am unable to verify the use of a heavy-caliber rifle by women except women married to white trappers resident in the area.

14. Men pick berries for themselves, but picking for common consumption and processing does not happen as far as I know. Men do not say this; they simply do not do it.

15. One of the interesting aspects of the changes in bush life over the last decade is the increasing involvement of males in the sharing of dry meat as more and more men abandon bush life and come into the bush only for short hunting trips.

References

Burch, Ernest S., Jr. 1972. The caribou/wild reindeer as a human resource. *American Antiquity* 37:339–68.

Carter, R. M. 1974. Chipewyan semantics; form and meaning in the language and culture of an Athapaskan speaking people of Canada. Ph.D. dissertation, Duke University.

Curtis, Edward S. 1928. (Rpt. 1970.) *The North American Indian. Being a series of volumes picturing and describing the Indians of the United States and Alaska*, vol. 18. New York: Johnson Reprint Corporation.

Evans-Pritchard, E. E. 1956. *Nuer religion*. London: Oxford University Press.

Gillespie, B. C. 1975. Territorial expansion of the Chipewyan in the 18th century. *Proceedings/Northern Athapaskan Conference, 1971*, ed. Annette McFadyn Clark. 2 vols. Ottawa: National Museums of Canada.

Hearne, Samuel. 1971. *A journey from Prince of Wales Fort in Hudson's Bay to the northern ocean*. Edmonton: M. G. Hurting Ltd.

Helm, June, and David Damas. 1963. The contact-traditional all native community: the upper MacKenzie "bush" Athabascans and the Igluligmut. *Anthropologica* n.s. 5:9–22.

Lévi-Strauss, Claude. 1963. *Totemism*. Boston: Beacon Press.

Ortner, Sherry B. 1974. Is female to male as nature is to culture? In *Woman, culture and society*, ed. Michelle Z. Rosaldo and Louise Lamphere, pp. 67–87. Stanford, Calif.: Stanford University Press.

Seton, Ernest T. 1911. *The Arctic prairies. A canoe journey of 2,000 miles in search of the caribou: being the account of a voyage to the region north of Aylmer Lake*. New York: C. Scribner and Sons.

Sharp, Henry S. 1976. Man: wolf: woman: dog. *Arctic Anthropology* 13:25–43.

———. 1977a. The Chipewyan hunting unit. *American Ethnologist* 4:377–93.

———. 1977b. The Caribou-Eater Chipewyan: bilaterality, strategies of caribou hunting, and the fur trade. *Arctic Anthropology* 14:35–40.

———. 1978. Comparative ethnology of the wolf and the Chipewyan. In *Wolf and man: evolution in parallel,* ed. Roberta Hall and H. S. Sharp. New York: Academic Press.

———. 1979. *Chipewyan marriage.* Canadian Ethnology Service Paper No. 58. Ottawa: National Museum of Man Mercury Series.

———. n.d. The Chipewyan. Manuscript.

Smith, J. G. E. 1975. The ecological basis of Chipewyan socioterritorial organization. *Proceedings/Northern Athapaskan Conference, 1971,* ed. Annette McFadyn Clark. 2 vols. Ottawa: National Museums of Canada.

INDEX

CONTRIBUTORS

Catherine H. Berndt is a part-time lecturer in anthropology at the University of Western Australia. She received her Ph.D. from the London School of Economics and Political Science. Since 1941, she has been studying Aboriginal Australians in different geographic locations and of differing degrees of change, and she has also spent two years in New Guinea. Her publications include articles, books, and edited works written individually and with her husband, R. M. Berndt. Her specialties include women, religion, and mythology. In addition to her academic work, she has arranged and translated a book of Aboriginal children's stories and songs.

Frances Dahlberg is an associate professor of anthropology at Colorado Women's College in Denver. She received her Ph.D. from Cornell University. She has done field research in Uganda, Honduras, Australia, and Hawaii, and has written on these places.

Agnes Estioko-Griffin is an archaeologist for the Division of State Parks, Recreation and Historic Sites of the State of Hawaii, and is also a graduate student at the University of the Philippines-Diliman. As well as archaeology, her interests include the anthropology of small traditional societies in Southeast Asia. She is returning to the field in 1980–81 to continue her studies of Agta women hunters.

P. Bion Griffin is an associate professor of anthropology at the University of Hawaii at Manoa. He received his Ph.D. from the University of Arizona. Most of his published work is in archaeology, but he is also interested in the ethnology of hunters and gatherers of Southeast Asia, and he is returning to the field to continue his Agta studies.

W. C. McGrew is co-director of the Stirling African Primate Project at the Parc National du Niokolo-Koba, Senegal, and is at the department of psychology of the University of Stirling, Scotland. He was a Rhodes Scholar at Oxford and received his D.Phil. in psychology there for a study of the social behavior of preschool children. In addition to many papers on children, he writes extensively about chimpanzees.

Henry S. Sharp is an associate professor of anthropology at Simon Fraser University. He received his Ph.D. from Duke University. In addition to his work among the Chipewyan, which includes about two and a half years in the field and has resulted in many papers, he is interested in wolves and is co-editor of *Wolf and Man*.

Colin M. Turnbull teaches at George Washington University. He received his D.Phil. from Oxford University. He is the author of widely read books and articles on the Mbuti (*The Forest People*) and the Ik (*The Mountain People*).

Faith Williams received her Ph.D. in English from Columbia University and has taught English at universities in Colorado and Chicago. In addition to poems, she has written a children's book.

Adrienne L. Zihlman is professor of anthropology at the University of California, Santa Cruz. She received her Ph.D. from the University of California, Berkeley. She has studied and written on anatomy, locomotion, and the evolution of human behavior. In addition to work in museums and laboratories, she has done research on pygmy chimpanzees.